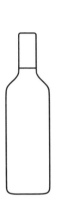

THE
ESSENTIAL
WINE
BOOK

A Modern Guide to
the Changing World of Wine

ZACHARY SUSSMAN

ILLUSTRATIONS BY ALEX GREEN

TEN SPEED PRESS
California | New York

PUNCH

CONTENTS

INTRODUCTION: WHAT DOES "ESSENTIAL" MEAN TODAY?

If you were to walk into the average upscale restaurant even just a couple of decades ago and order a bottle of wine, the available options would have likely conformed to a predictable set of references: namely, the usual roster of French classics (Burgundy, Champagne, Bordeaux) and, if you were lucky, perhaps a selection of Italy's greatest hits (Brunello, Barolo) and blue-chip offerings from California.

Enter that same restaurant today and you're sure to be bombarded by an astonishingly diverse range of bottles from across the globe, from Sicily and Croatia to Australia, the Canary Islands, the Republic of Georgia, and beyond. Never have we witnessed such an eclectic assortment of styles—Fizzy red Lambrusco? Skin-fermented orange wine? Nutty, oxidative whites aged for years under an active veil of yeast?—or such a dizzying spectrum of grapes. The cabernets and merlots our parents sipped have given way to a new influx of eclectic varieties: savagnin, assyrtiko, nerello mascalesé, hárslevelu—the list goes on.

It is both a blessing and a curse to be alive and of legal drinking age at this moment of unrivaled variety. If the "world of wine" once encompassed a narrowly defined set of borders with fixed pedigrees and hierarchies of taste, the collapse of that old system has given way to a contemporary era of endless possibilities—and, potentially, of endless confusion.

Not only is there more diversity in the marketplace than ever before—disrupting the conventional wisdom about where great wine is supposed to come from—but the way we value wine has transformed as well. Rather than care about ratings or scores, the latest generation of drinkers is deeply concerned with authenticity, wanting to be clued into wine's cultural and historical significance: who made it, where it comes from, what it has to say.

In the face of such rapid change, even the most dedicated enthusiasts and industry pros struggle to assimilate the constant stream of "next big things." How, then, is the average consumer—someone with, by definition, a limited amount of bandwidth to commit to wine knowledge—expected to make sense of it all?

That question provides the point of departure for this book. It also speaks to the intrinsic challenges involved in writing an "essential" wine guide to our twenty-first-century drinking culture. In place of one authoritative canon of important regions and growers, we now have several competing and overlapping ones. There are passionate advocates of natural wine and "classic" wine, cult wine and trophy wine, traditional wine and modern wine, Basque wine and Chilean wine, Balkan wine and Californian wine. So how does one decide what qualifies as "essential" wine?

After much deliberation, the criteria adopted here define "essential" in terms of those categories deemed the most relevant and attention-worthy today, which drinkers are actually liable to encounter "in the wild"—on restaurant lists, at wine bars, and stacked on wine shop shelves. Rather than an encyclopedic reference manual, these pages aspire to be a practical field guide to our current wine Zeitgeist, asking not only why a specific wine matters but also how it fits into the larger conversation. What emerges is a functional, user-oriented overview of the way we drink right now.

As a result, certain omissions might provoke objections. Consider this a survey course, Essential Wine 101. The intended scope requires affording some regions minimal attention. Others, sadly, make no appearance at all. But this shouldn't suggest they hold no interest. In fact, many of the great wines of the world have been excluded not because they're unimportant but rather because rare Burgundy and first-growth Bordeaux remain accessible to only the select few capable of affording them. Equally absent are several of the obscure oddities and fringe gems that often grace the Instagram feeds of Brooklyn and Portland sommeliers but hold little utilitarian value for the majority of everyday drinkers.

HOW TO USE THIS BOOK

In addition to outlining the basics of both making wine and tasting wine (see pages 5 and 16, respectively), we will begin by tackling fundamental questions about the many ways wine expresses a psychology of "place" (see page 23) and unpack the recent rise of "natural wine" (see page 29). The heart of the book, however, consists of a region-by-region break-down of the major areas that, together, define the new boundaries of the wine-world map.

Starting with the Old World European classics, then moving on to the emerging New World wines of the Americas, South Africa, Australia, and New Zealand, these overviews cover all you need to know about the area in question, including its history, its range of styles, a list of essential producers, and, most important, the cultural context necessary to understand its place within the changing world of wine. Each regional summary is prefaced by a short, bullet-pointed section called Just the Highlights, designed to provide a quick thirty-five-thousand-foot view of the place (basically, a user-friendly summary of basic talking points you might use at a restaurant or dinner party), and concludes with The Wine List, a tightly edited sampling of suggested bottles.

Bearing that in mind, these selections aren't intended to be exhaustive; instead, think of them as initial jumping-off points to fuel further exploration. Some will be textbook examples of their categories, while others deliberately run counter to expectations, highlighting how their regions have changed. Finally, applying to wine the same belief that once inspired journalist and notorious gourmand A. J. Liebling to remark that "in learning to eat, as in psychoanalysis, the customer, in order to profit, must be sensible of the cost," all selections were chosen with value to the consumer in mind. "Value," of course, is always relative, so for specific price points refer to the following chart.

$	**UNDER $25**
$ $	**$25–$50**
$ $ $	**$50–$80**
$ $ $ $	**$80 OR MORE**

Let this book be an excuse to venture forth and experiment. Order a bottle of blaufränkisch or frappato the next time you're dining out. Ask your local merchant about her selection of Loire Valley reds or "grower" Champagne. Compare a dry riesling from Germany's Mosel region to another from Rheingau. Now more than ever, your curiosity will be rewarded.

HOW WINE IS MADE

In the abstract, the winemaker's job seems straightforward. Grow some grapes, pick and crush said grapes, ferment the juice, and, before you know it, wine!

It's true that all wine follows the same basic steps on its journey from grape to glass. But the potential variations on that process have no end. Depending on the type of wine being made (red, white, sparkling, and so on) and the winemaker's own particular vision, each stage of production presents a complex set of technical choices, actions (or inactions, as the case may be), and interventions—some large, some small, but all impactful.

That said, you're not interested in quitting your job and becoming a winemaker. So why should you care about what took place behind the scenes at the winery when you could just be drinking some wine? Fair question. You don't need a PhD in art history to spend an afternoon at the Met, and you can polish off a bottle of Beaujolais without being able to cite chapter and verse on the finer points of carbonic maceration. But when it comes to understanding stylistic diversity—why certain wines taste different from others, aside from the obvious factors of climate, region, and grape—even a little technical knowledge is extremely empowering.

Imagine that you need to pick out a bottle of wine for a dinner party or some similar social occasion at which not embarrassing yourself is key. When you enter the shop, the salesperson on the floor asks what you're looking for, and, if you're anything like most Americans—through no fault of your own—the question throws you for a loop. Maybe the memory of an incredible pinot noir you once had at a restaurant lingers in your mind, but you can't remember the name of the winery or even the region where it was made. Of all the senses, taste and smell are the most fleeting and resistant to language. Faced with describing what the wine was like, the vocabulary escapes you: "Just a nice Pinot, I guess . . . something smooth but not *too* smooth."

That's why it helps to be familiar with such seemingly boring details as new versus neutral oak, residual sugar levels, lees stirring, or the differences between destemming the grapes and fermenting whole cluster. Instead of resorting to vague generalities, you're able to point to specific techniques with clear stylistic implications—all the better to define your own taste and ultimately end up drinking more of what you like.

Broken down by type, the following overview covers the key production methods for each major category, touching on the assorted tools and tricks of the trade that influence texture and taste. Still, disclaimers aside, if you truly prefer not to bother with all this shop talk, feel free to skip ahead.

WHITE WINE

White wine comes from white grapes, right? Well, not exactly. Regardless of skin pigment, the juice of almost all grapes runs clear. What makes a white wine "white" is removing the skins before fermentation (a white wine made from red-skinned grapes is known as a blanc de noir). From there, the yeast performs its magic, and if all goes according to plan, the juice is transformed into wine. At this phase, however, that wine is still young and untutored in the ways of the world. There's an apt French term for this formative period between fermentation and bottling: *élevage*, or "upbringing." Like finishing school, it's the stage where the wine is fine-tuned and molded into shape via several possible practices.

MALOLACTIC FERMENTATION

Commonly called "secondary fermentation," malolactic fermentation isn't really a form of fermentation at all, but rather a conversion that takes place when a wine's lactic bacteria consume its tart malic acid and transform it into rounder, creamier lactic acid—the same kind found in milk. Chemistry lessons aside, you'll probably recognize the effects from the creamy texture of certain chardonnays. For fresh, zippy thirst quenchers, like sauvignon blanc, on the other hand, intentionally blocking "malo" preserves the wine's snappy "Granny Smith apple" crunch.

LEES CONTACT

Postfermentation, it's common to remove the dead yeast cells, or lees, that have settled like so many fallen soldiers to the bottom of the tank. But let's say the wine could use a little extra oomph. In that case, it might be a good idea to keep that sediment right where it is. Prolonged contact with the lees fleshes out a wine and allows it to absorb all kinds of complex yeasty, brioche-like notes. Known as *sur lie* aging, the technique is standard operating procedure for the French growing area of Muscadet and a stylistic hallmark of white Burgundy, but it's practiced across the globe. The amount of rich leesy character a wine will acquire is determined by a process called *bâtonnage*, which involves stirring the sediment back into the liquid at regular intervals, kind of like a course of steroid injections.

OAK

The influence of oak on white wine can be subtle (or decidedly not), depending on the type, age, and size of the barrel and the amount of time the wine spends in it. Tighter grained and less dense than American oak, French oak tends to impart more elegant flavors and textures, whereas American is generally stronger and sweeter, with more intense vanilla and coconut notes. Brand-new barrels act like a form of seasoning—you'll notice a toasty vanilla spice right away—whereas older barrels primarily lend body and weight. The question of oak is also critical to oxygen management. The amount of oxygen to which a wine is exposed during vinification (a fancy word for turning grape juice into wine) has enormous stylistic consequences. Fermenting in stainless-steel tanks minimizes oxidation (aka reductive winemaking), preserving fruity freshness. But certain winemakers aim for an intentionally nutty "oxidative" style, allowing the wine to breathe slowly through the pores of old oak barrels.

RED WINE

The differences between red and white wine run only skin deep, but those skins count for a whole lot. That's because of a process called maceration, during which the juice ferments in contact with the grape skins, gradually extracting color and tannins. Like steeping tea, the longer the maceration time, the richer, darker, and more "extracted" the resulting wine will be. Other than this one aspect, the sequence of events for producing white and red wines is virtually the same. There are, however, a handful of variables specific to red wine production that profoundly impact style.

WHOLE CLUSTER FERMENTATION

Grapes arrive at the winery looking a lot like they do at the produce section of the supermarket: plump bunches of ripe berries attached at the stems. Separating those berries from the stems (aka destemming) has long been a standard feature of modern red-wine making. But advocates of whole cluster fermentation—the practice of fermenting intact bunches of grapes, stems and all—have recently sparked a debate that's at the very center of evolving public taste. Once viewed as outdated or rustic, stem inclusion is increasingly understood as a way to bring out a kind of classical European elegance, particularly with lighter-skinned grapes, like pinot noir and syrah, whose modern incarnations too often slip into the flashy fruit-bomb territory. Whole cluster fermentation, on the other hand, helps to dial back a wine's over-the-top fruit, introducing a whole new dimension of complexity: floral and spicy aromas coupled with a lighter color, "grippier" texture, and lifted sense of freshness. Stylistically, it's not an all-or-nothing decision: winemakers carefully select the percentage of whole cluster fruit to include.

CARBONIC MACERATION

It's easier to describe the effects of carbonic maceration than to explain what it is. You'll immediately recognize them if you've ever downed a super-fresh, juicy, low-alcohol bottle of Beaujolais, from the region with which the practice is most often associated. Lately, however, the style has been cropping up in all corners of the globe. As a result, we've seen the rise of a certain species of Beaujolais-like red—pale in color, low in tannin, and bursting with ripe cinnamon-and-strawberry fruit—that instantly screams carbonic. Meanwhile, it has also emerged as a stylistic calling card of the natural wine movement—but more on that later (see page 29). As a technique, carbonic maceration refers to a unique form of internal, or intracellular, fermentation that occurs when whole grape bunches are left to ferment in a sealed vessel that has been conveniently filled with carbon-dioxide gas. This oxygenless environment triggers a release of enzymes that stimulates fermentation inside the grape itself. Because of its low alcohol, lack of tannins, and exuberant fruit, this style is ideally suited to a quick chill in the ice bucket before serving.

OAK

The role of oak in red-wine making isn't all that different from its role in white, with one notable exception: how it affects a wine's tannic structure. The slow exchange of oxygen through the pores of the barrel softens the astringent tannins in rich red wines, resulting in a smoother, velvety mouthfeel. As with whites, the details of the type and age of the barrel, as well as the amount of time the wine spends within it, also offer a clue into winemaking philosophy. The tradition of many old-school European regions has been to age red wine in enormous neutral (in other words, used many times before) oak casks, which results in an austere but age-worthy style prized by traditionalists. The use of small French barrels (almost always new) signals a glossier modern approach—dominated by riper fruit, softer tannins, and lots of toasty vanilla—which came to fame in the 1990s and early 2000s.

ORANGE WINE

An ancient style recast as the industry's latest what's-old-is-new hipster obsession, orange wine is just a catchy contemporary name for skin-contact (or macerated) whites; that is, white wine that has been made as if it were red, fermented in contact with the grape skins. The result? Firmly structured, amber-tinted whites full of savory autumnal flavors, which, thanks to their *vin rouge*–like musculature, function a lot like reds at the table. How much time (days, weeks, or even months) the wine spends on the skins indicates how intensely orange it will be—a spectrum that ranges from just a faint hint of copper to brooding, tannic elixirs the hue of oversteeped tea.

ROSÉ

In almost all cases, rosé is created in one of two ways, but the fundamental idea is the same in both: to arrest a red wine's development prematurely before it's had time to soak up the pigment in the skins. The first method, known as *saignée,* is essentially a by-product of red wine production. To boost a red's concentration, midway through fermentation, winemakers sometimes siphon out, or "bleed off," some of the juice to create a darker, inkier red. Thanks to its brief stint on the skins, the discarded portion of juice will have acquired a vibrant pink hue, which can be repurposed into a deeper, plusher style of rosé.

The delicately pale, salmon-hued expression made famous by Provence, on the other hand, owes its elegance to the direct press method. More deliberate and precise, it involves gently pressing whole clusters of red grapes over several hours to release their juice slowly—just enough time for the skins to infuse the liquid with a touch of color. After being pressed, the juice is quickly pumped into a tank, fermented, and bottled, then shipped off to meet its adoring public. Of course, the most obvious way to make rosé is to blend red wine and white wine together, but that practice is frowned upon for higher-end wines.

SPARKLING

One of the happiest sounds on Earth is that miraculous "pop" of the cork of a bottle of bubbly as it shoots toward the ceiling of a crowded dining room (or let's be honest, your otherwise unoccupied one-bedroom apartment). But for such a popular and symbolically loaded style, sparkling wine is ironically one of the most misunderstood. If a certain region in northern France has become synonymous with all things fizzy, Champagne's celebrity status has obscured the incredible diversity of sparkling wines from across the globe. We're still perpetually cautioned to remember that *Champagne* isn't a generic style but a specific place. By the same token, to treat the world's rich and varied bubbly traditions as mere Champagne alternatives strips them of their own identities—which, just like any other category, vary according to region and raw material but also production method. There are several ways to put the sparkle into a bottle of sparkling wine, each impacting the size and shape of the bubbles (or "bead") and determining stylistic character.

TRADITIONAL OR "CLASSIC" METHOD

The traditional method is most famously used in Champagne, where, according to the longstanding French tradition of cultural superiority, it's known as the *méthode champenoise*. But it's also used in the production of Spain's Cava, Italy's Franciacorta, and the various regional French sparklers collectively grouped under the *crémant* umbrella (Crémant d'Alsace, de Jura, de Loire, and so on). The traditional method involves enacting a secondary fermentation within the bottle itself by injecting a solution of yeast, wine, and sugar, known as the *liqueur de tirage*. When yeast eats sugar, carbon dioxide is released, and when that gas gets trapped under pressure inside the bottle, you don't need an advanced degree in enology to imagine what comes next: bubbles. Is this process expensive and time-consuming? Absolutely. But the traditional method produces by far the most elegant results: a fine and delicate bead of bubbles that pirouettes across the palate. It also confers that wonderful yeasty, freshly baked biscuity quality associated with Champagne: a symptom of the lees generated by the secondary fermentation, which remain in contact with the wine until it's deemed ready for the market, often for years at a time. The process of removing the lees from the bottle prior to corking is called disgorgement.

CHARMAT METHOD

It's tempting to think of the Charmat (tank) method as the costume-jewelry equivalent of the four-carat-diamond traditional method, but rather than be derided as an ersatz knockoff, it deserves to be appreciated for what it is. If anything speaks to the style's easy-drinking mass appeal, it's the oceans of fizzy Prosecco that audiences from Milan to Macau ravenously guzzle each year. Far less costly, time-consuming, and labor-intensive than the traditional method, the Charmat approach is geared toward selling bubbly on an industrial scale. Rather than induce secondary fermentation in the bottle, it takes place inside gigantic pressurized tanks, where yeast and sugar are added to a base wine. Although the results lack the refinement and longevity of their traditional method counterparts, complexity isn't always what we crave. There's a high demand for drink-me-now wines that check off the boxes of *crisp* and *effervescent* and deliver immediate pleasure. In those cases, Charmat actually works best, preserving the fresh fruit character of aromatic grapes, such as Prosecco's glera, which would be overwhelmed by the *méthode champenoise*.

ANCESTRAL METHOD

As its name suggests, the ancestral method (aka *méthode ancestrale* or *metodo ancestrale*) predates Champagne by centuries as the oldest known method of sparkling wine production. Unlike the traditional and Charmat methods, both of which require a secondary fermentation, the ancestral method involves bottling and sealing the wine before the initial fermentation has finished. The released carbon dioxide gets caught in the bottle, imparting a soft froth of bubbles and often a faint kiss of sweetness thanks to the remaining traces of residual sugar that haven't been converted into alcohol. Although the practice has historical roots in areas of France and Italy (Gaillac, Limoux, Prosecco, and Emilia-Romagna, among others), where it has been practiced for centuries, it has lately skyrocketed to viral fame in the form of *pétillant naturel*. A playfully irreverent reincarnation of the ancestral approach, *pét-nat* (as insiders call it) emerged from the natural wine counterculture of the early aughts and has since taken the fringier factions of the wine scene by storm. Cloudy, funky, and sealed under a crown cap, the style deliberately plays up its lo-fi farmhouse appeal: one part preindustrial throwback, one part ultimate-hipster party wine.

SWEET

A legacy of the not-so-distant memory of saccharine bottom-shelf brands, like Lancers and Cold Duck (to say nothing of the white zinfandel craze of the 1980s), dryness has become a prerequisite of sophistication for most consumers. For the classic dessert wines of the fine wine canon, however, that spells an uncertain future. Rather than classified as dusty relics to be tacked onto the end of a formal tasting menu (cue the cigars), sweet wines deserve to be reclaimed as what they are: some of the most profound and historically pedigreed wines in existence. Far from monolithic, the finest examples encompass a glorious spectrum of "sticky" expressions.

LATE HARVEST

The logic behind late-harvest (aka *vendage tardive*) winemaking is simple. The longer that grapes hang on the vine, the riper they become—until they actually start to dehydrate, further intensifying sweetness. The only potential downside? As the grapes linger on the vine, their acidity slowly declines. Nobody likes a mouthful of maple syrup, which is why the late-harvest approach is best suited to cool-climate regions with varieties that retain naturally high acid levels: namely, riesling from

Alsace, Austria, and Germany, and Loire Valley chenin blanc. These all achieve a dazzling balance of candied apricot, lemon, and honey without any resulting loss of freshness.

ICE WINE

An extreme form of late-harvest winemaking, ice wine is exactly what its name would suggest: wine made from grapes that have been left to freeze on the vine, picked only in the middle of winter, when the mercury drops as low as 20°F. At such frigid temps, the water inside the grapes crystallizes, leaving behind a small amount of intensely sweet juice. If you're expecting a treacly, high-alcohol sugar grenade, however, think again. Despite its nectar-like concentration, the category is surprisingly delicate, with a distinct floral freshness and alcohol levels that rarely exceed 12 percent. Originally a Teutonic tradition (in Germany, it's called *Eiswein*), today it's a specialty of Canada (specifically British Columbia and Ontario), where it shares the company of Joni Mitchell and Drake as one of our northern neighbor's most beloved exports.

BOTRYTIS

Mold is something winegrowers usually battle with all their might. But in certain privileged parts of the globe, if the vintage cooperates and climatic conditions are just right, a little mold can be a good thing—at least when the mold in question is *Botrytis cinerea*, or "noble rot." Responsible for what experts deem the most singularly expressive sweet wines on the planet (such as Hungary's Tokaji Aszú and France's Sauternes), this gray fungus infects the grapes and dessicates them to the point of irresistible sweetness. At the same time, it imparts its own uniquely decadent set of flavors (honey, apricot, candied lemon peel) and textures (a sort of waxy golden unctuousness that's difficult to define but great fun to drink). Because each berry can only squeeze out a tiny drop or two of juice, you can expect to shell out a lot for these wines. Fortunately, they're worth it.

APPASSIMENTO

The warm-climate equivalent of ice wine production, the *appassimento* process involves drying out grapes on large straw mats to concentrate their sweetness. Among the oldest approaches to making sweet wine, it dates back to Greek and Roman antiquity, and continues to be practiced throughout Italy in the form of *passito*, the Italian word for any wine created through this specific technique of raisination. Lusciously sweet and figgy, with syrupy flavors of toffee and candied orange peel, examples such as Tuscan *vin santo* or Sicily's *passito di Pantelleria* function at the end of a meal as a form of liquid dessert—no cake or pastries required.

FORTIFICATION

First, a disclaimer: Not all fortified wine is sweet. If you don't believe it, just go out and order a crisp, briny glass of fino sherry. With that out of the way, let's look at how fortification—the addition of a distilled spirit (usually in the form of grape brandy) to the wine—is used to make historic "stickies," such as port and Madeira. Injected during the early stages of fermentation, that sudden dose of alcohol kills off the yeast, leaving the remaining sugar intact while also acting as a preservative. It's for this reason that fortified wines rose to fame as the first major exports of the global wine trade. Stronger and fuller bodied than their unfortified counterparts, they also enjoy a longer shelf life; it's not at all unusual to encounter bottles of Civil War–era Madeira, for example, that are still alive and kicking.

◆ ◆ ◆

Of course, none of this theoretical knowledge will be of any use until you put it into practice. So now that we've covered the basics of wine-making, we can finally get to the fun part: drinking it.

HOW TO TASTE WINE

The term *wine tasting* tends to conjure a self-consciously formal ritual that requires you to do things you would never do in real life, such as lifting your wine up to the light to inspect its "robe," or swishing it around like some kind of grape-flavored mouthwash before spitting into a strategically placed spittoon.

If there's any surefire way to drain all of the fun out of wine, the standard tasting protocol has to be it. But here's the good news: contrary to what you might have learned if you ever enrolled in a formal wine class, there's no right or wrong way to taste wine. Beyond the sniffing and the swirling, the fancy stemware and niche jargon, wine exists for one reason: to give pleasure. So feel free to chug straight from the bottle, if the spirit moves you. Certain wines practically call out to be consumed that way.

Still, occasions will inevitably arise when you'll want to take a step back and consciously reflect on what you're drinking. In these more contemplative moments, you might wonder: What are you actually looking for when you open a bottle of wine?

Ask that question to any wine professional and you'll probably receive the same one-word reply: balance. Like *finish* or *bouquet*, *balance* is one of those abstract but universally agreed upon terms that, for better or worse, everyone in the industry uses as a shorthand to describe wine. And when it comes to the actual experience of drinking the stuff, a sense of balance is always the first thing you're hoping to find.

WHAT IS BALANCE?

Balance refers to the interaction between the different components (think acidity, tannin, alcohol, and the like) that determine how any given wine will taste. When a wine is "balanced," no single element overpowers or dominates the rest. Instead, like the harmony among instruments in a jazz ensemble, each part is seamlessly integrated into the whole. You could consider balance as the minimum aesthetic requirement for a wine to be "drinkable." A balanced wine won't always blow your mind, but any great wine will exemplify it, and without it, there's not much to recommend a second sip.

Since it's a symptom of things working as they should, the absence of balance is often easier to diagnose than its presence. (Think about it: Have you ever visited the doctor to figure out why you're feeling so well?) In that same spirit, when a wine exhibits no obvious flaws, our first instinct isn't to scrutinize it carefully or pick it apart. On the other hand, everyone can remember a wine that somehow seemed a little disjointed or out of whack. Maybe it was cloyingly sweet or uncomfortably astringent or bitter, or maybe it was just dull and flabby, missing the vibrancy to make you want to keep drinking.

These are all examples of the myriad ways a wine can lack balance. And by the same token, there's no single formula for achieving it. Balance expresses itself through a seemingly infinite range of possibilities—as many, really, as there are types of wine to choose from.

THE ELEMENTS OF BALANCE

Here are the main elements to look for the next time you're evaluating a bottle of wine. As you taste, try to consider how the various parts are working together (or not) to form a cohesive impression. Do you sense a kind of synergy, where the wine feels like more than the sum of its parts, or does some aspect awkwardly stick out? It's important to remember that the "structural" or "textural" elements of a wine—how it physically feels in your mouth, whether light or heavy, viscous or crisp—are just as critical to balance as flavor.

ALCOHOL

Alcohol is the beautiful by-product that results from the yeasts that kick-start fermentation consuming the naturally occurring sugars in the "must," or grape juice. Aside from getting you buzzed, alcohol plays a decisive role in determining a wine's "body," or weight. As a general rule, the higher the ABV (alcohol by volume), the more unctuously rich the wine will feel in your mouth. When ABV starts to creep above a certain point, however, it risks throwing a wine out of balance: imagine the same unpleasant burning sensation (or "heat") that lingers on your tongue after a shot of vodka.

ACIDITY

A bunch of different types of acid are present in wine (tartaric, citric, malic, and so on). But all you really need to know is that acidity equals freshness. Whenever you hear adjectives such as "crisp," "lively," or "cleansing" applied to a wine, it's acidity that's being described. Too much comes across as tart or sour, but too little results in dull, heavy, or syrupy wine. Like adding a squeeze of lemon to brighten a dish, acidity also helps wine interact with food, dissolving fat and grease.

TANNINS

Organic compounds found in the skins, seeds, and stems of grapes, tannins produce that drying, puckering sensation (sometimes called "grip") that certain wines leave on your tongue and the sides of your mouth; you'll recognize it as that same astringency found in black tea and bitter dark chocolate. Primarily found in red wine, tannins provide the structural firmness, or "backbone," that allows it to age. They are not something you taste as much as you physically feel, and are what makes big, aggressive reds pair so amazingly with meat. Like acidity, they cut through rich fat and protein, which, in turn, diminish the perception of tannin, making the wine seem softer and easier to drink.

SWEETNESS

Most table wines are left to ferment to total dryness, meaning that all of their sugars have been magically transformed into alcohol during the winemaking process. But certain styles intentionally leave varying degrees of "residual sugar" behind. Don't roll your eyes; a hint (or more) of sweetness doesn't automatically make a wine cheap. In fact, it can add a thrilling dose of complexity, rounding out a wine's edges and offering a perfect foil for spicy cuisine. The amount of sweetness you actually perceive in a wine depends on several factors—most critically, acidity. Many of the world's greatest food wines—certain ethereally delicate German rieslings, for instance, or off-dry chenin blancs from the Loire—contain high amounts of residual sugar but still taste dry thanks to their tongue cleansing acidity.

FRUIT

The typical critical tasting note reads like the recipe for some sort of insane fruit salad. All those "hints of guava and pineapple" and "flavors of gooseberry, lingonberry, and white cherries" can start to feel meaningless after a while (seriously, when was the last time you tried a lingonberry?). But it's astonishing how fermented grape juice can display such a kaleidoscopic spectrum of flavors, ranging from citrus (lemon, lime) and orchard fruits (pear, apple) to tropical fruits (kiwi, mango), cherries, plums, raspberries, blackberries, and beyond. A reflection of both grape variety and growing region, fruit expression is usually the first thing you notice about a wine.

DECODING
VINTAGE WINE

To enjoy a properly aged bottle of wine that has spent years evolving in the cellar seemingly belongs to a bygone era of telegrams, livery uniforms, and Downton Abbey-esque country estates. The reality, though, is that there's never been a more opportune time to seek out mature bottles—whether via restaurant wine lists, merchants specializing in older wine, or the increasing number of direct-from-the-estate "library releases" that now frequently enter the market.

If you've never tasted a wine old enough to legally drink itself, you might wonder what all the fuss is about. A central part of wine's allure is its ability to evolve and even improve over time. When found in good condition, older bottles can offer some of the most memorable drinking experiences. That said, just as you probably don't entirely resemble the person you were twenty years ago, the changes that take place as a wine ages can be radical. If you don't know what to

anticipate—the good, the bad, and the ugly—you could easily be confused or misled.

The Good: Over time, white wines turn a deeper golden hue, acquiring a fuller, waxy texture with nutty, umami-like aromas (think truffle, honey, and, odd as it might sound, often a whiff of gasoline or kerosene), coupled with deeper flavors of baked apple and pear. Reds, on the other hand, grow lighter and more brick-colored with age, their muscular tannins softening into a subtler complexity. In place of "primary" fruit flavors, more sanguine and earthy "secondary" and "tertiary" tastes emerge, such as dried leaves, leather, mushroom, and herbs. It's a bit like the difference between eating a freshly butchered cut of steak and a sixty-day dry-aged rib eye: imagine more nuanced savoriness and intricate layers of flavor and texture.

The Bad and The Ugly: There's always an element of risk involved in the pursuit of older wine, so exercise caution. It's never a good idea to pick up that dusty bottle that's been lingering for god knows how long on the shelf of your local liquor store. Only purchase vintage wines from reputable sources who can vouch for their provenance. Restaurants with a knowledgeable team of sommeliers are typically the safest bet, as you can always send an "off" bottle back. When a wine has been cellared past its prime, or just poorly stored, there are plenty of telltale signs. While normal "bricking" is to be expected, any wine (white or red) that possesses a murky, brownish color is probably already past its prime; ditto if it smells of vinegar, nail polish, or a dank, musty basement. Additionally, be on guard for signs of heat damage. While stewed fruit flavors can be desirable in older wine, there should always be an element of freshness; if all you taste is syrupy prune or raisin (not in a good way), something's clearly amiss.

Like all matters of taste, however, the threshold for "too old" is entirely subjective. One drinker's "over the hill" is another's "aged to perfection," so the best advice is to experiment and discover first-hand where on the spectrum your own preferences fall.

OAK

Love it or hate it, if you've ever had a big, buttery chardonnay from California, you're already familiar with the effects of new oak barrels on a wine. When used judiciously, oak aging can bring out a wine's good qualities, filling out its body and imparting a creamy richness. On the flip side, it's easy to go overboard; if all you taste are the telltale notes of toast and vanilla and not so much the wine itself, you've crossed over to the dark side of the spectrum. The older the barrel, the less pronounced the oak influence will be. Wineries frequently avoid the use of new oak altogether, employing used (or "neutral") barrels to attain that round, voluptuous texture without all the distracting woody flavors and aromas.

MINERALITY

Want to pass as a card-carrying member of the wine world's progressive new guard? Just wax poetic over your wine's pronounced minerality. Usually reserved for elegant, cool-climate expressions defined by high acidity and more restrained fruit, minerality is the most fashionable industry buzzword that no one can fully explain. Still, anyone who has ever consumed a bottle of Muscadet or Chablis can attest that certain wines reveal a discernibly "mineral" profile reminiscent of crushed rock and wet gravel or the briny salinity of oyster shells. Fact or fancy, the term provides a useful descriptor for the savory, nonfruit qualities that are increasingly desirable to modern drinkers.

◆ ◆ ◆

It's critical to be able to pick apart the various components you're tasting whenever you drink a bottle of wine. But after a certain point, most lifelong wine lovers start looking for something deeper and more meaningful, which can't be boiled down to technical details or even aesthetic judgments such as balance. Namely, wine's mysterious ability to express the nuances of the specific place where it's made, known as terroir, is the quality that makes wine not just another beverage but an expression of culture, reflecting the story of the soil and the people who work it.

UNDERSTANDING TERROIR

....

The demands we make of most beverages generally stop at quenching our thirst and hopefully tasting halfway decent in the process. It would be hard, for instance, to imagine any sane individual sniffing and swirling her glass of morning OJ to detect the underlying character of the orange grove or determine what type of juice press might have been used at the processing plant.

Wine, on the other hand, tends to inspire an embarrassing level of geeky obsession. Many of us spend our entire lives, and even earn our livelihoods, poring over every last detail. It's a heavy set of expectations for one beverage to live up to. But beyond the price tags and point scores we attach to it, wine has always been more than a commodity. A staple of human existence since the dawn of civilization, from Homer's "wine-dark sea" to Biggie at "the back of the club, sippin' Moët," it has spoken to us across the ages.

Today, the growing awareness of wine as a cultural object represents one of the major paradigm shifts to transform our twenty-first-century drinking habits. If previous generations treated it like a status symbol or aspirational luxury, we've gradually embraced a different set of criteria—one that views wine, above all, as an expression of place, reflecting the traditions of the people who make it and the regions where it has been carefully crafted for centuries.

In the wider conversation about wine, this question of place keeps circling back to one all-important concept, which the French (who else?) take credit for coining. You've almost certainly heard it before, probably applied in a broad and confusing rage of contexts. That's because, no matter how quickly it has infiltrated the popular lexicon, the concept of terroir is notoriously slippery, impossible to translate into English, and nearly as hard to define.

That hasn't prevented *terroir* from becoming one of the industry's most frequently used buzzwords, however. Although the technical details fuel endless debate, in general, the term refers to the notion that, beyond just tasting delicious, wine is subject to another, more noble-minded responsibility: to tell us something about where the grapes were grown. Often described as a sense of "somewhere-ness," terroir is what makes specific wines taste as if they come from specific places, rather than just anywhere. From topography, grape variety, and soil composition to altitude, weather patterns, and even farming practices, it encompasses all the environmental, cultural, geological, and geographical factors that leave their unique stylistic imprint on a wine.

These days, more than pedigree or cost, terroir has emerged as the be-all and end-all for wine lovers—the magic currency that elevates wine above and beyond being merely a beverage. What modern drinkers value most in wine is identity, whether of an entire region, a village, a vineyard, or, in some cases, just a tiny parcel of vines. Generally, the smaller the scale, the better; our focus has become attuned to the minute, the particular, and the granular as a metric of authenticity.

By establishing place as the new benchmark for wine greatness, we've turned the page of a complicated new chapter in our evolution as consumers. Even just a few decades ago, we had a clear idea about what great wine was supposed to resemble. It meant big, bold Bordeaux, concentrated Napa cabernet, the unctuous richness of an oaked white Burgundy—wines that aimed to impress if not overload the palate. But lately, the question has grown more complicated. Since different wines from different places all convey their terroirs differently, there are no longer any official criteria to determine what qualifies as "serious" or "great."

This might leave you with the impression that the contemporary wine scene has spiraled into some kind of postmodern free-for-all, where quality is relative and all wines are created equal. But no one would dispute that some regions produce more complex or profound wines than others. It's just that our definitions of complexity and profundity have changed, encompassing a whole new set of possibilities.

Now that we've learned to celebrate wines from across the globe, produced in an enormous spectrum of styles, that old duality—fine wine versus table wine—no longer applies. As a result, a major market has developed for bottles that might not be conventionally "serious" but that we take just as seriously as any of the established classics. Greatness, then, assumes many guises. Yes, it's a powerful, age-worthy Barolo. But it's also a briny, bracingly mineral single-vineyard Muscadet from France's Loire Valley, or the ashy minerality of a bottle of listán negro from the Canary Islands. The only true sin is anonymity: wines that have sacrificed the underlying expression of place to fit a ready-made commercial mold.

This intricate interplay of soil, climate, grape, and human ingenuity is what we mean when we talk about terroir. To a new generation of drinkers, it's this miraculous ability to transmit the particularities of place that makes wine matter, and makes certain wines matter more than others. The wines that matter most are those that tell this story of their origins in the clearest possible terms, offering a lens through which to explore and better understand the areas they call home.

BUT WHAT DOES TERROIR ACTUALLY TASTE LIKE?

"Wait a second," you might be thinking. "I've never had a bottle of wine magically whisk me away to the rolling hillsides of Tuscany. If terroir is so important, how do we actually know it when it's there?"

It's true that to most of us—especially when we're first discovering it—wine tastes primarily like, well, wine, not any specific place. It also doesn't help that decades of oversimplified marketing efforts have indoctrinated American consumers into contextualizing wine in terms of grape variety instead of geography. How many times have you sidled up to the bar to order a glass of pinot noir without thinking twice about where that wine actually came from?

In Europe, the birthplace of terroir, things are done a bit differently. Over there, wines are mostly classified according to appellation, or geographical place-name. For this reason, you'll rarely encounter the word *chardonnay* or *pinot noir* on a French wine label. The underlying message is that grape variety can only tell you so much about what you're drinking. Take that hypothetical glass of pinot noir, for example. Cultivated from the Northern to the Southern Hemisphere, the variety does retain certain core characteristics no matter where it's grown. But the variations among regional expressions is so vast as to practically render "pinot noir" meaningless as a data point. The real question is this: Pinot noir from where? France? Oregon? California? A lighter coastal expression or a richer one from farther inland? Grown on granite or schist? From a high-elevation vineyard or one on the valley floor?

The wisdom of the European model's insistence on place becomes clear in view of one of the most basic aspects of terroir: climate. We usually talk about terroir on a much smaller scale, in terms of the distinct microclimates that differentiate one plot of vines from the next. But one of the most useful bits of information you can glean about a bottle, which reveals volumes about what to expect stylistically, is whether it hails from a warm- or cool-climate region.

This is a critical distinction. In broad strokes, grapes grown in hotter, southerly climes—the Mediterranean, for instance, or parts of California—ripen more fully, which means more sugar to be converted into alcohol. That's why richer, bigger-bodied wines typically come from warmer places. Cooler growing areas, on the other hand, where grapes struggle for ripeness—for instance, most of Germany, France's Loire Valley, or New York's Finger Lakes region—typically produce lighter, higher-acid wines with lower alcohol content and more restrained fruit flavors. Keeping that in mind, elevation also plays a critical role. The higher you climb, the cooler the average temperature gets, which explains why specific high-elevation areas in warmer countries still manage to deliver wines of elegance and finesse; the bright, nervy whites and reds from Spain's up-and-coming Sierra de Gredos region, just outside of Madrid, immediately spring to mind.

Soil type, the second major determinant of terroir, is far more problematic to account for. While there's no direct cause-and-effect relationship between a vineyard's geological makeup and the flavors found in its wine, it's undeniable that certain wines possess a distinct mineral character that seems to emanate from the dirt in which they're grown. And if you spend any amount of time talking to winemakers, you'll hear firsthand how the wines from one parcel of vines grown on limestone differ substantially from others grown on clay.

Whether minerality is more fiction than fact we may never know. There's no scientific evidence to suggest that the mineral content of the soil actually finds its way into the wine we drink. Still, the stony slate character of riesling from Germany's Mosel region has been revered by generations of wine lovers. Ditto the signature chalkiness of chardonnay grown in the limestone soils of Chablis and the gunflint aromas for which the region of Sancerre is famous, to cite just a few classic examples. But even growing regions that are much newer to the scene offer arresting illustrations of terroir, especially the various areas composed of volcanic soils that have lately received critical attention. The rugged, ashy reds grown on the slopes of Sicily's Mount Etna, for instance, and the powerfully smoky whites from the island of Santorini have emerged as beloved sommelier darlings for their ability to evoke such an uncanny sense of place.

Ultimately, though, there's an abiding sense of mystery at the heart of terroir. It's one of those intuitive things that, frankly, we wouldn't want to break down into scientific formulas even if we could. Yes, terroir is the pH level of the soils and the exposition of the vineyard and the diurnal temperature shifts that create the fog that comes over the hills in the evenings to keep the grapes cool and retain freshness in the wine. But it's also the experience of drinking a glass of Bandol, a heady red wine from Provence, and getting a nostalgic whiff of what the locals call *garrigue*, the scrubby bunches of lavender and thyme that grow wild there by the side of the road—a sense memory that catapults you back to driving down some tiny country road twenty miles outside of Aix with the windows cracked and everything in blossom.

How did those flavors get in there? It's impossible to say for sure. But whatever the reason, it's why we keep coming back to wine and why we discover something new in it each time.

Still, just because most wine lovers agree on the importance of place in wine, that doesn't mean there's unanimous agreement concerning how to express it. Sure, it's commonly accepted that a bottle of wine shouldn't be too heavily marked by the winemaker's hand, allowing terroir to shine unimpeded, but just how hands-off should that approach be? Is a little bit of stabilizing sulfur okay to add before bottling? If so, how much? You'd be surprised at how much infighting questions like these tend to inspire. In fact, the subject probes to the heart of one of the wine world's most polarizing topics: the rise of natural wine.

WHAT'S UP WITH NATURAL WINE?

Grapes come from the earth, and wine comes from grapes. So, doesn't that make all wine *natural*? If only it were that easy. For such an innocent-sounding term, natural wine has been thrust into the center of a debate that has roiled the wine world for almost two decades.

To loyalists, the phenomenon is an unequivocal force for good, arriving on the scene to deliver wine from the existential threat of corporate homogeneity and restore it to its original state of pastoral grace. The movement's equally impassioned detractors, on the other hand, tend to view it, at best, as a well-intentioned but misguided cult of authenticity, whose members unfairly denigrate all other wines as the enological equivalent of Budweiser. At worst, they side with wine critic Robert Parker, who once described natural wine as "one of the major scams being foisted on wine consumers," railing against the latest rash of flawed, microbial wines that, in their estimation, put ideology above actual enjoyment.

Whether it signals wine's spiritual salvation or just a clever marketing ploy, one thing is for sure: natural wine isn't going anywhere. What began as a loose affiliation of fringe growers in France—first in its birthplace of Beaujolais but quickly spreading to the Loire, the movement's current cultural capital—has since evolved into a global sensation. Today, there's a thriving scene in just about every country where grapes are grown.

Amid all the controversy, natural wine has remained a force to be reckoned with, giving voice to an alternative narrative about wine that speaks to the values of the current generation of consumers and industry professionals. Now that the movement is entering the mainstream, it has codified its own canon of classic producers and wines, which are swiftly finding their way into the press and top restaurant beverage programs. Some conservative drinkers might balk at these unconventional upstarts. But once you set aside the dogma and judge natural wines on their own merits—in other words, as wines like any other—all the punditry and semantic hand-wringing start to sound silly.

THE ART OF DOING NOTHING

The basic idea behind natural wine is extremely simple. What that first wave of French naturalists was rebelling against—giant factory cooperatives churning out oceans of mass-produced supermarket wine, or score-hunting consulting enologists who stylistically air-brushed so many wines beyond recognition—was the sense that the modern wine industry had lost its soul. Disgusted by the multibillion-dollar agribusiness model they saw swallowing up the identities of their regions, early pioneers such as the late Marcel Lapierre of Beaujolais and Loire icon Thierry Puzelat embraced a radical back-to-the-basics approach that has since formed the foundation of the movement's "minimal intervention" creed.

That gospel is built on a singular premise: the most authentic wine is that which has had the least "done" to it in the way of chemical or technical manipulation. In addition to mandating organic or biodynamic farming (no pesticides, no chemical sprays), that translates to an equally hands-off stance in the cellar. Fermentation occurs "spontaneously," relying only on the ambient yeasts already present in the environment as opposed to the lab-created commercial strains used in conventional winemaking. It also means no chemical additives, no artificial tinkering with acidity levels, no fining agents, no colorants, no oak chips, and no high-tech high jinks or other gimmickry of any kind.

According to the popular mantra, the naturalist ideal is to "let the wine make itself" so it reveals the slightest trace of the winemaker's hand—and by extension, the most direct transmission of the vineyard's underlying terroir. Out of this belief system an entire subculture was born that has forever left its mark on the zeitgeist. But theory is one thing; to the drinker, it's the practical results that matter. So, what's the real deal with natural wine? Between the harsh condemnations coming from one side of the divide and the rhapsodic praise emanating from the other, what are we actually supposed to make of it?

Short answer, that depends. At their best, natural wines possess a stunning purity of expression: a vibrant sense of aliveness that elevates them into some of the most compelling wines in the market today. That's equally true of those that consciously identify as natural as it is of those that abide by naturalist principles without directly labeling themselves as such; either way, they're perfectly transparent expressions of their terroirs whose sheer deliciousness transcends ideology.

On the other hand, just because a wine purports to be natural doesn't make it good. There's always a risk involved in relinquishing control and intentionally doing without the various technical advantages that the past thirty years of progress have made possible. Paradoxically, a great deal of knowledge and rigor is required to just let the wine make itself—especially if the winemaker is adamant about bottling without the addition of sulfur as a stabilizing agent to protect against spoilage and oxidation.

One result of this lo-fi orientation is that there's generally a higher incidence of "bottle variation" (the same wine tasting differently from one bottle to the next) among natural wines. Insiders consider this more of a feature than a bug, chalking it up to a kind of *wabi-sabi*-like celebration of imperfection that, in their view, only enhances the experience. But at a time when it's all too easy for novice winemakers to jump on the philosophical bandwagon without the necessary skills and experience, the market has seen a rash of murky, unhygienic natural wines that exhibit no discernible sense of place. Worst of all, these dubious ambassadors give unfair fodder to critics eager to dismiss the movement as a whole.

CARBONIC MACERATION AND TASTE

Further complicating the terms of the debate, certain natural wines (even those from totally different places) often taste quite similar to one another—an ironic development for what began as a backlash against cookie-cutter sameness. The culprit (at least, in part) is carbonic maceration, a fermentation technique traditionally used in Beaujolais, where early visionaries such as enologist Jules Chauvet first experimented with abandoning sulfur. As a method, "carbonic," as insiders call it, is particularly well suited to sulfur-free winemaking. This explains why it has spread like wildfire throughout the natural community in France and beyond. But as critics have pointed out, it also tends to leave its own distinct stamp on a wine: a sort of fresh, juicy, hyper-gulpable expression that has developed into something of a trademark natural aesthetic. The movement's lexicon even has a word to describe it: glou-glou, a rough approximation of the glugging sound supposedly made while guzzling it down.

Don't get the wrong idea. This glou-glou subgenre can be tons of fun. It ecstatically embodies the French ideal of the *vin de soif*, or "wine of thirst"—the sort of effortlessly easy-drinking quaffer you can knock back with reckless abandon. To that end, it serves as the perfect antidote to the hegemony of heavy, extracted oak bombs against which the movement initially revolted. But as author and natural wine advocate Alice Feiring explains in her 2011 book *Naked Wine*, the carbonic style is just that: a style that in many cases tastes more of process than place. "Many people, including me," she writes, "have confused the flavors of carbonic maceration with the true taste of natural wine, instead of just a winemaking choice among many."

Not every natural wine employs carbonic maceration. And many that do, including some of the most celebrated wines of Beaujolais, achieve profound results with it. There, it enjoys both a long history and a rich heritage, offering a vehicle to highlight aspects of the region's granitic soils. When adopted as a default stylistic fallback by winemakers in regions as disparate as Sicily and Sonoma, on the other hand, it risks becoming just another beverage.

◆ ◆ ◆

The bottom line is that "natural" is a big umbrella. A category as diverse as the world of wine itself, it resists simple generalizations. So, it's about time that we ditched the divisive "natural or not" binary and acknowledged that naturalness exists along a continuum. For every bottle that announces its "nattiness" in an obvious way (the proudly cloudy and funky, the goes-down-easy glou-glou), there are countless classically structured wines that ring true to their places of origin and others that fall somewhere in between.

All considered, it's probably easiest to frame the issue like this: virtually all great wine is made on an intimate scale by dedicated growers who believe in healthy farming and a less intrusive touch in the cellar. A wine doesn't have to present itself as natural to meet this set of criteria, but the movement's values inherently overlap with them. So, while there are plenty of mediocre (and let's be honest, even downright unpleasant) natural wines out there, it's not a coincidence that many of the wines recommended in these pages lay claim to some sort of natural street cred.

Rather than ideology, the conversation ultimately comes down to the particular practices of individual producers and how they inform specific wines. The winemakers worthy of attention today never embrace a mentality of natural for natural's sake. Instead, they make conscious choices at each step of the process with one goal in mind: to express the underlying character of the vineyard.

Natural or not, that's simply the definition of good winemaking. And it's this key commitment to the principle of place that will guide us through the "essential" wines and wine regions that follow.

PART ONE
THE OLD WORLD

The vast world of wine is commonly divided into two main spheres: the Old World (that is, Europe) and the New World (pretty much everywhere else). This distinction is crucial. In cultural terms, it amounts to the difference between inheriting a centuries-old set of traditions and—by trial and error—inventing them from scratch. Compared to the track records of France and Italy, which extend back millennia, even the most firmly established New World areas, like California's Napa Valley, have barely emerged from infancy.

If you're making wine in the Loire or Tuscany, for instance, you already know which grapes grow best in your climate (the ones that have been there for thousands of years). You also know the top places to plant them, and the range of styles that best capture the identity of your soils. Sure, there's always room to experiment, but when you do, you're pushing up against generations of history.

In the New World, faced with making wine in a terra incognita of sorts, producers have been forced to improvise. It's a daunting prospect, for sure. But on the other hand, there's a certain freedom in operating without the burden of history. Want to plant some odd Italian grapes, like aglianico or vermentino? Go for it. What's to stop you?

The conventional wisdom has always insisted on a stylistic divide between these two poles as well. Old World wines, the standard argument goes, tend to be lighter, more restrained, and earthy in style, with greater acidity and freshness. The wines of North America and the Southern Hemisphere, by contrast, have been characterized by a more modern or international style, highlighting riper fruit and higher alcohol.

Lately, however, as winemakers in places such as California, Chile, and Australia, among many others, increasingly strive for an Old World sense of balance, that timeworn dichotomy is quickly starting to break down. What are we to make, for instance, of a gamay-based wine from Oregon's cool-climate Eola-Amity Hills that clocks in at 12 percent alcohol and takes its inspiration from the minimalist aesthetic of France's natural wine counterculture? Or what about a skin-fermented orange wine sourced from a vineyard of biodynamically farmed sauvignon blanc in Australia's Adelaide Hills?

Still, in order to rewrite the rules, it helps to understand them. In that spirit, we'll begin at the beginning, by introducing the standard canon European classics that provide the foundation upon which today's multifaceted wine world was first built.

FRANCE

By pretty much unanimous consensus, France is the most significant wine-producing nation on the planet. Home to more essential regions (Burgundy, Bordeaux, Champagne—the list goes on) than any other, it has always defined the meaning of wine for the rest of the world. At the same time, however, as the birthplace of the natural wine movement, the country has experienced a radical rethinking of its centuries-old traditions and how they relate to the complex world of wine we're living in today. In true Gallic spirit, this constant tug-of-war between classicism and rebellion has pumped fresh energy into the country's wine industry, ensuring that it will continue to hold its preeminent position for generations to come.

BURGUNDY

·······················

JUST THE HIGHLIGHTS

◆ **Burgundy is the birthplace of terroir.** The region's site-based classification system puts the emphasis on the soil itself—hence, the region's reputation as the world's most sophisticated case study in the nuances of terroir.

◆ **Burgundy has emerged as the benchmark for wine greatness.** Home to the original examples of pinot noir and chardonnay, the region invented a formula for identity in wine (that is, single variety, single site) that has come to define our notion of what wine should be.

◆ **Yes, it is definitely expensive.** Now a cult obsession, Burgundy has officially upstaged Bordeaux as the wine world's most important region, fueling rabid demand among trophy-hunting collectors and making it a dangerously pricy habit to acquire.

◆ **But you can still drink it without breaking the bank.** The key is to explore the region's lesser-known villages, whose lack of name recognition works in favor of your wallet.

Everyone remembers their first time, as the saying goes. And it's true: wine nerds can always recall their earliest encounters with Burgundy. By now, its status as the most important wine region on Earth is almost universally acknowledged. The question is why. Out of the thousands of places where grape juice is fermented into alcohol, what makes this tiny stretch of land, extending roughly from Dijon in the north to Lyon in the south, so uniquely special?

On one level, that's easy. Burgundy makes *really* good wine. The ancestral home of the world's most complex pinot noirs and chardonnays, it embodies the platonic ideal for those two massively popular grapes. Although they're grown in just about every corner of the globe, the majesty these varieties achieve in their native soil can't be replicated elsewhere, no matter how hard some vintners might try. Silky, elegant reds defined by a signature earthiness, and rich yet powerfully mineral-driven whites often rounded out with a slight touch of oak, they're what every pinot noir or chardonnay grape secretly aspires to be.

But the explanation necessarily runs deeper. Plenty of places make excellent wine, but few, if any, enjoy Burgundy's prestige. Historically, the region's renown can be traced all the way back to the year 1336, when the Cistercian monks in residence established Burgundy's largest walled vineyard, the celebrated Clos de Vougeot. As enterprising as they were pious, the Cistercians were the first to make a massively influential discovery: that different plots of vines regularly yielded wines of perceptibly different characteristics and quality levels.

Over the coming centuries, efforts to delineate and rank Burgundy's finest vineyard sites would lay the foundation for the famous pyramid-like classification system that regulates its production today. This hierarchy of specific geographic designations—from the broadest regional and village-named bottlings to the tiniest single-vineyard premier and, rarest of all, grand crus—codifies into law what Burgundy has taught us all along: that soil matters most of all.

Although those pioneering monks wouldn't have recognized the word, they established Burgundy's reputation as the birthplace of terroir. Today, this Burgundian paradigm for wine—that of an individual site articulated through a single grape—exists as the archetype for greatness against which all other regions are judged.

For this reason, we think of Burgundy as a region of small, dirt-under-the-fingernails farmers who have worked the land of their ancestors for centuries. It exists in the collective imagination as a triumph of the artisanal over the industrial, the heirloom and homespun over the mass-produced and commercial. To pledge allegiance to Burgundy, then, is to align with a specific set of values that conform to our idea of what we want wine to be. And that's exactly why it has become the ne plus ultra of current-day wine cool.

BURGUNDY IS WORTH IT

Today's Burgundy market operates pretty much as you'd expect from a minuscule area capable of producing only limited supplies of the world's most coveted wines. That's another way of saying that the stuff generally doesn't come cheap. When you see a hyper-rare bottle of 1945 Romanée-Conti—the holiest of holy grails for Burgundy collectors—fetch a record-breaking half a million dollars at a 2018 Sotheby's auction, it's easy to dismiss the entire category as the exclusive amusement of heiresses and hedge-fund bros.

This luxury aura is increasingly at odds with the region's longstanding agrarian image. But even if the Burgundy bubble shows no signs of bursting anytime soon, the area's winemakers tend to cringe at the ransom-like sums their bottles command in the secondary market. Preferring to think of themselves as stewards of the land rather than investment brokers for the 1 percent, they're the first to insist that Burgundy has more to offer than the scarcest bottles from a small number of blue-chip estates.

WHERE TO LOOK FOR VALUE

When wine lovers bemoan the state of the Burgundy market, they're referring to a specific cluster of world-renowned villages that make up the region's prime real estate. Generally considered Burgundy proper, the vineyards of the Côte d'Or (Golden Slope) unfurl across a narrow twenty-five-mile-long limestone escarpment that extends from just south of Dijon roughly down to the town of Santenay. Further divided into the Côte de Nuits in the north (where pinot reigns supreme) and the Côte de Beaune in the south (prime chardonnay territory, but both white and red are made), this tiny strip contains a concentration of liquid assets unrivaled the world over. If you drive down the D974, or Route des Grand Crus, the white-lettered townships emblazoned on the passing road signs read like a roll call of wine world royalty: Vosne-Romanée, Chambolle-Musigny, Gevrey-Chambertin, Puligny-Montrachet, Meursault.

The best examples of these legendary villages are universally revered touchstones of the fine wine canon, as storied and significant as wine gets. But they're hardly the most practical points of entry to gain a sense of what Burgundy is all about. As a rule, value in wine is discovered off the beaten path—in the peripheries and margins, the unnoticed and underappreciated outer boroughs. And even in a region as famous as Burgundy, there are still plenty of neglected nooks and crannies left to explore. The key is knowing where to look. Here are a few areas that, while not quite as fashionable as some of their neighbors, give a taste of real Burgundian character at a fraction of the cost.

CHABLIS

Isolated at the northernmost tip of Burgundy, Chablis stands apart both geographically and culturally from the rest of the region. A direct expression of the area's stark climate and famous Kimmeridgian soils—made up of the fossilized oyster shells left over from the shallow seabeds of the Jurassic period—Chablis drinks like chardonnay raw and "uncut," stripped of the usual fancy production values. Flinty, briny, and extremely brisk, even the humblest village-level wines can be incredibly energetic and long-lived, thanks to their signature spine of acidity.

The scarcest bottles made by the area's two living legends, François Raveneau and Vincent Dauvissat, have followed the inevitable path to cult status (with price tags to match). But Chablis has lately experienced a fresh injection of energy from an expanding group of producers who are bringing an alternative spirit to this traditionally conservative region. Intrinsically calibrated to present-day taste, these wines are rapidly making waves on US shores—and for the moment, at least, remain highly affordable. Pro tip: Keep an eye out for well-priced premier crus, many of which can be had below the $50 mark.

Essential Producers: Patrick Piuze, Domaine Pattes Loup, Moreau-Naudet, Corinne et Jean-Pierre Grossot, Alice et Olivier de Moor, Gérard Duplessis, Domaine Oudin, Gilbert Picq, Vincent Mothe

THE CÔTE DE NUITS

Given the global lust for red Burgundy these days, there aren't many bastions of affordability left within the Côte de Nuits—with two notable exceptions located at the area's northernmost border.

Marsannay and Fixin

If Gevrey-Chambertin and Chambolle-Musigny are the Beverly Hills and Hollywood of this part of Burgundy, then Marsannay and Fixin would find their counterparts somewhere around Burbank. But a late-twentieth-century renaissance of quality has helped them shed their pedestrian stereotypes. And in the mad rush to stash away as much of the fancy stuff as possible, cult Burgundy collectors have largely overlooked these two villages, partially insulating them from some of the more extreme price inflation that has permeated the region.

Priced between $30 and $50 per bottle (cheap by Burgundian standards), they're the rare sort of Burgundies you can feel good about throwing back on a Tuesday night. Site-specific examples from top estates—Domaine Sylvain Pataille's earthy "Clos du Roy," for instance, or Domaine Berthaut-Gerbet's surprisingly silky "Les Crais" sourced from a tiny parcel of old vines in Fixin—manage to walk the razor's edge between country rusticity and classic Burgundian finesse.

Essential Producers: Domaine Trapet Père et Fils, Domaine Jean Fournier, Domaine Bart, Domaine Sylvain Pataille, Domaine Berthaut-Gerbet, Domaine Régis Bouvier, Domaine Bruno Clair

THE CÔTE DE BEAUNE

Boasting as many famous names as its northern neighbor, the Côte de Beaune is also home to several off-the-radar (read: value-oriented) villages that deserve far more respect than they're given. It's here, even more than in Côte d'Or's posher areas, that a dedicated producer makes all the difference. The most talented regularly manage to produce wines that rival the region's best.

Savigny-lès-Beaunes, Pernand-Vergelesses, Santenay

At the head of the Côte de Beaune looms the grand cru of Corton, which lends its name to the regal whites of Corton-Charlemagne and the powerful reds of Le Corton (such as Corton-Renardes and Corton Les Maréchaudes). Sadly, you'll need pockets as deep as Charlemagne's to drink these with any regularity. But in less aristocratic villages, like Savigny-lès-Beaunes and Pernand-Vergelesses, you'll find spicy, earthy pinot noir and steely chardonnay in the mode of Corton-lite.

Down at the very bottom of the Côte de Beaune, the primarily red-producing village of Santenay is perhaps better known among locals for its thermal springs and gaudy casino (think "Burgundy meets Atlantic City") than its wine. But year in and year out, the smattering of premier crus clustered at the top of the village—Les Gravières, Clos de Tavannes, and Grand Clos Rousseau—offer some of Burgundy's best bang for the buck.

Essential Producers: Jean-Marc & Hugues Pavelot, Chandon de Briailles, Simon Bize, Jean-Marc Vincent, Domaine Rollin, Marc Colin, David Moreau

Saint-Aubin, Auxey-Duresses, Saint-Romain

The Côte de Beaune is first and foremost chardonnay country. Burgundy lovers speak in hushed, almost religious tones of classics such as Meursault and the famous Montrachets (Puligny and Chassagne). Thankfully, places still exist where you can catch a glimpse of that greatness without burning a hole in your wallet.

Although early signs of luxury creep have infiltrated the village of Saint-Aubin—due, in large part, to the buzz surrounding star winemaker Pierre-Yves Colin-Morey (or PYCM to the progressive sommelier set)—the area has emerged as a go-to destination for authentic whites that overdeliver on quality. Sandwiched between the grand cru of Chevalier-Montrachet and the top vineyards of Chassagne-Montrachet and Puligny-Montrachet, Saint-Aubin is practically surrounded by greatness. Think of it as Burgundy's George Harrison, overshadowed by two larger luminaries but possessed with a genius of its own.

Overlooked but not to be forgotten, the towns of Auxey-Duresses and Saint-Romain consistently pull off convincing impersonations of neighboring Meursault, if in a leaner, lighter fame. The old-school Domaine Jean & Gilles Lafouge reliably churns out supple, tightly structured single-vineyard Auxeys that punch well above their weight class; ditto the ambitious Saint-Romains of winemaker Alain Gras, which have brought fresh attention to that habitually overlooked village.

Essential Producers: Domaine Henri Prudhon, Hubert Lamy, Pierre-Yves Colin-Morey, Domaine Sylvain Langoureau, Domaine Jean & Gilles Lafouge, Alain Gras

OTHER BURGUNDY: CÔTE CHALONNAISE AND MÂCON

The Côte d'Or is widely considered the true Burgundy, but beyond its sanctified borders there's still plenty of proper Burgundy to be had.

Due south, the villages of the Côte Chalonnaise can boast of no grand crus but overdeliver on delicious, ready-to-drink Burgundy. Mercurey, the region's most visible and highly respected village, is known for rustic yet richly concentrated pinot noir. Next door, Givry and Rully offer much of the same, whereas in neighboring Montagny, sophisticated, classically styled chardonnay is the only game in town.

The wines of the Mâconnais, known mostly for its whites, range from the crisp, zippy, and unoaked to fleshier village-designated examples (such as Mâcon-Cruzille and Mâcon-Vergisson) that usually warrant the extra few bucks. A bit pricier but a step up in quality, Pouilly-Fuissé and Viré-Clessé yield a more unctuous style of chardonnay that bridges the aesthetic divide for fans of California's lusher interpretations of the grape.

Essential Producers: Bret Brothers, Domaine Michel Juillot, Les Héritiers du Comte Lafon, Domaine Joblot, Les Champs de l'Abbaye, Domaine A. & P. de Villaine, Domaine Dureuil-Janthial, Julien Guillot (Clos des vignes du Maynes), Domaine Guillot-Broux, Domaine Jean-Claude Thévenet

THE WINE LIST

◆ Domaine Pattes Loup Chablis "Vent d'Ange" ($): Founded in 2005 in the village of Courgis, winemaker Thomas Pico's Domaine Pattes Loup has established itself as one of the most exciting young estates in the classic region of Chablis. Organically farmed, like all of Pico's wines, and sourced from vines averaging fifty-five years old, this entry-level bottling is always a textbook rendition of the area's fossilized limestone soils.

- **Julien Guillot (Clos des vignes du Maynes) Macon Cruzille "Aragonite" ($$):** Julien Guillot's family has been biodynamically farming their seven-hectare estate in Cruzille, in the northern Mâconnais, for three generations. One of the region's most compelling wines, his Aragonite shows off the lush yet energetic profile that chardonnay is capable of attaining in this area when yields are kept low and meticulous care is practiced in the cellar.

- **Domaine Henri Prudhon Saint-Aubin 1er cru "Sur Gamay" ($$):** Henri Prudhon's Saint-Aubins remain among the best-kept secrets in the world of affordable, traditional Burgundy. Sourced from the Sur Gamay vineyard, a stone's throw from the storied grand cru Le Montrachet, this is your go-to introduction to white Burgundy.

- **Domaine Sylvain Pataille Marsannay "Clos du Roy" ($$):** An early leader of Marsannay's quality renaissance, Sylvain Pataille separately vinifies several different parcels under their own names. Considered the equal of the grand crus of Gevrey-Chambertin in the sixteenth and seventeenth centuries, the excellent "Clos du Roy" epitomizes the brambly, red-berried concentration and iron-rich mineral edge that run through all his wines.

- **Alain Hudelot-Noëllat Bourgogne Rouge ($$):** The fact that you can buy a bottle of pinot noir as silky, spicy, and expressive as this from a producer as celebrated as Hudelot-Noëllat for a sticker price of $30 should forever silence all complaints of Burgundy's unapproachability. Always one of the region's top wines to buy, and even stash away for a while, if you can.

- **Domaine Jean-Marc Morey Santenay 1er cru "Grand Clos Rousseau" ($$$):** Santenay has always been the kind of place that allows you to drink premier cru wines for the cost of other areas' village-level wine, and this classic expression from one of the region's top producers is no exception: earthy yet bright, with an aromatic wash of herbs, rust, and juicy red-berry fruit. All that, plus it has the staying power to age.

A WORD ON BOURGOGNE ROUGE (AND PASSETOUTGRAINS)

An enormously broad designation, the Bourgogne label indicates that a wine's grapes were sourced from anywhere within the entire region of Burgundy. For an area that prizes geographical specificity, that's not the surest guarantee of quality. What's more, with a sea of mass-produced examples on the market, navigating the category can be tricky. When in doubt, the best strategy is to rely on the reputation of the producer. Any self-respecting winemaker will apply the same level of attention to her simplest bottles as her rarest grand crus. In fact, an entry-level Bourgogne has an important role to play in the Burgundian chain of command, functioning a bit like a producer's stylistic calling card. For many of Burgundy's elite estates, whose top bottles cost hundreds or thousands of dollars, entering through the basement at least allows you to get a foot in the door. (Among the best are Domaine Hudelot-Noëllat, Benoit Ente, Domaine Bachelet, Camille Giroud, Olivier Merlin, Simone Bize, and Bachelet-Monnot.)

That maxim perfectly encapsulates the hyper-niche category of Bourgogne Passetoutgrains, which is finally developing a cult following stateside. Thanks go to such visionary importers as Neal Rosenthal, Becky Wasserman, and Kermit Lynch, who have championed many of the best examples. A juicy, chuggable blend of pinot noir and gamay, Passetoutgrains is a throwback to the bygone era when the two varieties were commonly planted side by side in Burgundy. The gold standard comes courtesy of two iconic producers: Volnay's Domaine Lafarge and Robert Chevillon in Nuits-Saint-Georges. But keep an eye out for bottlings from Fanny Sabre, Stéphane Magnien, and Hubert Lignier, all produced on a microscopic scale and full of everyday Burgundian character.

BORDEAUX

· ·

JUST THE HIGHLIGHTS

◆ **Bordeaux is the world's original trophy wine.** The region's aristocratic châteaus (famous names such as Latour, Mouton, and Lafite) are still the wine world's most recognizable status symbols.

◆ **Bordeaux offers the archetypal expression of cabernet sauvignon and merlot.** This classic Bordeaux blend has been copied all over the world, but few compare to the elegance and complexity of the original.

◆ **What Bordeaux isn't, however, is hip.** Lately, younger drinkers have turned away from Bordeaux, viewing it as stodgy, old-fashioned, and, most of all, too expensive. But that flashy facade accounts for just one side of the region.

◆ **It's the smaller producers from off-the-grid subregions that are making Bordeaux great again.** Many of the most interesting wines coming out of Bordeaux today are from less heralded parts of the region, where independent growers are making authentic, affordable wines of place.

Rumors of Bordeaux's highly anticipated comeback have been circulating for a while now—so long, in fact, that the speculation has started to feel like the one constant in an industry that never stops cycling between hot takes.

Before weighing in on that hot-button issue, however, let's back up a bit. As you probably know, Bordeaux is the most famous wine region in France (and, arguably, the world). Across the generations, its storied châteaus have been synonymous with luxury and prestige, embodying the idea of wine as an object of cultural and social aspiration.

Why then, you might be wondering, would a benchmark such as Bordeaux ever require a comeback?

On the business front, there's no cause for concern. Bordeaux remains France's top-selling wine region (by value rather than volume), a statistic that's unlikely to change anytime soon. Rather than stagnant sales or diminishing market share, the region's current woes run deeper. Ultimately, it's a crisis of relevance.

In our brave new wine world, all of the old beliefs about status and prestige no longer apply. Less is the new more, artisanality is the new luxury, and authenticity is the most valuable form of currency. So, while serious connoisseurs and collectors increasingly worship at the altar of Burgundy, that great Mecca of terroir, and younger drinkers thrill-seek with all sorts of trendy esoterica (Savoyard gringet, Jura poulsard), stuffy, mainstream Bordeaux finds itself on the losing side of wine's culture wars.

For their part, the Bordelais tend to write this off as mere jealousy, dismissing the rise of Bordeaux bashing as so much fake news. The ramifications, however, are tangible. While extensive vertical flights of its top back vintages remain a necessary staple of leather-bound fine-dining wine lists, in today's most influential, cutting-edge beverage programs, the region has increasingly become a persona non grata.

One can't help but feel a little badly for Bordeaux. Despite all the reasons why it's no longer cool, no matter how deeply it has alienated the current generation of tastemakers, there's no justification for blindly dismissing it. There's a reason, after all, why Bordeaux became a classic in the first place, and why it remains one today.

Aside from its historic significance, which can't easily be ignored, Bordeaux is capable of great beauty and intrigue. An intrinsic sense of harmony arises in Bordeaux's signature blend of cabernet sauvignon and merlot, the region's principal players, augmented with occasional support from cabernet franc, malbec, and petit verdot.

This basic varietal template has been replicated all over the world, from Napa and the coast of Tuscany to, well, pretty much everywhere grapes are grown. Nowhere else, however, has it approached the depths it reaches in the alluvial soils of Bordeaux: earthy, herbal, dark fruited (think blackberry, currant, plum), and often possessing a graphite minerality not unlike that of freshly sharpened no. 2 pencils. When traditionally made, avoiding the luxury trappings of overextraction and indulgent new oak, the combination belongs to that rare order of humanity's most perfect creations.

THE ALTERNATIVE BORDEAUX

It would be natural to assume that it's necessary to shell out a small fortune for a taste of such greatness. But that's the tragic irony about Bordeaux's image these days. All those flashy stereotypes—the high price tags and fancy labels and absentee château owners in slick Armani suits—really only apply to a handful of blue-chip estates that have come to define the area as a whole.

It all goes back to the famous 1855 classification that ranked Bordeaux's top properties, a hierarchy that remarkably still holds sway over the market today. The so-called classified estates at the top of the pyramid (aka the exclusive "first" and "second" growths) easily fetch hundreds, if not thousands, of dollars. If you're lucky enough to experience them on someone else's dime, count your blessings. If not, no worries. No matter what you've heard, Bordeaux isn't the exclusive plaything of blue bloods and the jet set.

In fact, these elite properties (ranked in order of prestige from the first to fifth growths) account for just 3 percent of Bordeaux's annual production. That leaves a whole other Bordeaux to explore. Far removed from the usual upper-crust associations, this alternative Bordeaux is populated by the countless small, independent family estates that dot the banks of the Garonne and Dordogne Rivers; an increasing number of them farm organically or biodynamically (on the rise, but still a rarity). Typically hailing from the area's less fashionable postal codes, they specialize in honest, everyday wines made with a gentle touch that respects the identity of their homegrown terroirs.

THE LAY OF THE LAND

To seek out these earthy, authentic wines of Bordeaux—the ones crafted on a human scale, which mortals can actually afford—it helps to know a thing or two about the lay of the land. Lucky for us, compared to the cartographic confusion that is Burgundy, the basics of Bordeaux geography are pretty straightforward. Aside from a few minor footnotes, it's really as simple as knowing your right from your left.

Formed by the intersection of the Dordogne and Garonne Rivers, which merge just beyond the city of Bordeaux, the Gironde estuary runs like an artery through the center of the region, dividing it into two main banks: the Left Bank and the Right Bank. The wineries located in the rockier, gravelly soils of the Left Bank feature a higher percentage of cabernet sauvignon (offering darker, more structured wines), whereas the softer, plusher wines of the Right Bank, grown in clay, predominantly feature merlot.

Aside from these stylistic, terroir-based differences, the two areas tend to be divided along cultural lines as well. With its lavish castles overseeing perfectly manicured rows of vines, the rarified Left Bank is home to most of Bordeaux's most collectible châteaus—specifically, the highly coveted classified growths that crown a small cluster of villages (Margaux, Pauillac, Saint-Julien, and Saint-Estèphe) in the elite Médoc subregion.

Not that the Right Bank lacks its fair share of famous names. The villages of Saint-Émilion and Pomerol, for instance, boast Château Cheval Blanc and Château Pétrus, two of Bordeaux's costliest wines. On the whole, though, the attitude is a bit more rustic and laid-back, playing the role of country gentleman to the Left Bank's landed gentry.

Unsurprisingly, it's here—in the outskirts, or satellite, districts of the Right Bank, where the area's original farming culture remains relatively intact—that the region's resistance movement has gathered the greatest momentum. Outer-borough areas, like the Côtes de Castillon, Fronsac, Lussac-Saint-Émilion, the Côtes de Bourg, and the Côtes de Blaye, feel a world away from Bordeaux's snobby status quo while often offering plenty of classic Bordeaux charm.

Even the exclusive "gated community" of the Left Bank still delivers plenty of options. For one, the biodynamically farmed Clos du Jaugueyron, located in Margaux (home to the fabled first-growth Château Margaux) produces several excellent, albeit slightly pricey, bottles under the village name. But their entry-level Haut-Médoc, an incredibly drinkable case study in the region's rich fruit, firm minerality, and tobacco-leaf complexity, offers the best introduction to the house style. Then there are the lesser-known wines of Moulis and Listrac, both worthy of attention, and farther south in the Graves area, you find not only excellent reds but also dense, mouthwatering whites based on sémillon and sauvignon blanc. Château Auney l'Hermitage, for instance, is a consistent favorite.

Essential Producers: Clos du Jaugueyron, Château le Puy, Château Moulin de Tricot, Maison Blanche, Planquette, Château Tire Pé, Château du Champ des Treilles, Château de Grandchamp, Château Peybonhomme-les-Tours, Château Belregard-Figeac

THE WINE LIST

- **Château Peybonhomme-les-Tours Côtes de Bourg "Quintessence" ($):** Jean-Luc Humbert of the Côtes de Bourg's biodynamically farmed Château Peybonhomme-les-Tours epitomizes Bordeaux's soulful side. A merlot-dominant blend from some of his family's oldest vines, his flagship "Quintessence" bottling demonstrates why the satellite regions of Bordeaux's Right Bank have become ground zero for bargain hunters.

- **Château Tire Pé "Diem" Bordeaux ($):** Winemakers Hélène and David Barrault specialize in an easy-drinking Tuesday-night style of Bordeaux. Based entirely on young-vines merlot, their "Diem" bottling highlights the grape's juicy, brambly side. Drink it with burgers or just about anything.

- **Château du Champ des Treilles "Le Petit Champ" Bordeaux Rouge ($):** Winemakers Jean-Michel and Corinne Comme bought a small plot of sixty-year-old vines in the unheralded area of Sainte-Foy in 1998. Naturally fermented and aged in steel tanks, this merlot and cab franc blend is bright, firm, and floral (and best served with a slight chill).

- **Château Moulin de Tricot Haut-Médoc ($$):** From his family holdings in the village of Arsac, winemaker Bruno Rey produces just two different wines—a stellar Margaux, meant for aging, and this invitingly humble Haut-Médoc. All black fruit and graphite minerality, it's a perfect—and perfectly affordable—intro to the firm-edged classicism of Left Bank cabernet.

- **Château Belregard-Figeac Saint-Émilion Grand Cru ($$):** Mostly merlot and cab franc, with a touch of cabernet sauvignon, this organically farmed wine from the Pueyo family sees very little new oak, choosing a savory earthiness over the polish that defines many of the fancier efforts of the village. A taste of textbook Saint-Émilion.

CHAMPAGNE

·······················

JUST THE HIGHLIGHTS

- Champagne is produced exclusively in the celebrated, cool-climate vineyards outside of the city of Reims. If it comes from anywhere else, it might be bubbly, but it's not Champagne.

- Champagne's brand-conscious image is quickly changing. Long associated with the *grandes marques,* or "big houses" (like Veuve Clicquot and Moët & Chandon), that assembled their wines into a consistent house style, the region is currently in the midst of a massive cultural reorganization.

- The region's small independent farmers, or "growers," are responsible for that change. Sourced from a single village or individual parcel of vines, these homegrown, terroir-focused Champagnes have injected an alternative paradigm into the region.

- Among the industry's tastemakers, Champagne is now embraced as a wine of place, rather than a luxury good or celebratory totem. That means no longer reserving Champagne for special occasions and reclaiming its identity as one of the world's most versatile food wines.

More than a beverage, Champagne is a symbol. That festive cork pop has forever been synonymous with the good life—a kind of liquid bling.

That didn't happen by accident. Ever since the late eighteenth century, when Champagne merchants deliberately advertised the wine's royal pedigree to cater to France's growing middle-class market, Champagne's identity has been inseparable from this aspirational narrative. Fast-forward to the present and it's easy to draw a straight line between this early history and Jay-Z acquiring Champagne Armand de Brignac, better known as Ace of Spades, for an undisclosed sum in 2014.

This genius for self-promotion has preserved Champagne's status as the world's most famous sparkling wine, widely imitated yet utterly inimitable: no other region can quite achieve its signature cool-climate combo of high acidity, chalky minerality, and saliva-inducing savoriness. Ironically, however, Champagne is famous in the same way that Rolex or Gucci is famous: as a high-end brand. The quintessential special-occasion wine, ceremoniously brought out for weddings and anniversaries, it exists in the popular imagination as more of a celebratory totem than a wine of place.

But as happens to any symbol over time, the meaning of Champagne has started to change—radically, in fact. Within the last two decades, a revolution has come to this traditionally commercial region, upending its longstanding balance of power and raising serious questions about the way its wines are produced, distributed, served, and enjoyed.

Rarely does a place as historic (or for that matter, as historically conservative) as Champagne undergo such a major cultural overhaul. But the transformation that continues to redefine Champagne in the wake of the region's small-scale grower uprising has ushered in a new golden age of Champagne consumption. Never before have we been able to enjoy such a wide range of styles and expressions, nor has quality ever been higher.

THE GROWER CHAMPAGNE REVOLUTION

If drinkers tend to treat Champagne as a luxury good, that's probably because the region has always done the same. For centuries, Champagne has been dominated by the brand-name *grandes marques* such as Moët & Chandon, Tattinger, and Veuve Clicquot. They have built a multibillion-dollar industry on their ability to deliver a consistent product to a vast audience of drinkers across the globe.

Typically, this process involves purchasing vast quantities of grapes from thousands of growers scattered across the region, and blending together mulitple wines from vintages past and present to arrive at a signature house style. In this way, for much of the region's history, the art of Champagne production took place in the cellar, rather than in the vineyard: the cellar master, or *chef de cave*, literally assembles the finished product from the available materials at hand.

This explains why, come rain or shine, that ubiquitous bottle of yellow-label Veuve Clicquot tastes almost exactly the same. While useful from a branding perspective, this mass-market formula lacks the qualities we normally look for in the great wines of the world: namely, the unique stamp of vintage and vineyard.

Starting in the 1990s, a handful of small growers rallied around a game-changing question: What if, rather than selling off their grapes to the corporate Champagne houses, they made their own estate-grown and bottled wines? What would Champagne look like if it were reimagined as a wine of terroir, crafted on a human scale by real people with the goal of reflecting the identity of a specific village, or even a single parcel of vines?

At first, very few of these so-called grower Champagnes trickled into the US market. But thanks to the work of importers such as Kermit Lynch and Terry Theise, who brought some of the first examples to US shores, the category has since exploded.

Although the movement's impact might not come across on paper (the large Champagne firms still account for more than 70 percent of production, making the grower movement feel niche by comparison), on a symbolic level it has unequivocally triumphed. Now a necessary fixture on restaurant wine lists with even the slightest alternative bent, these site-specific and generally vintage-dated, organically farmed, and naturally fermented bottles of "farmer fizz" have taught a new generation of drinkers to recognize Champagne as an actual wine—one that just happens to contain bubbles.

To be fair, this shouldn't imply a false dichotomy. The large Champagne houses—especially those such as Champagne Louis Roederer that have adopted more of a grower mentality, bringing the focus back into the vineyards—produce truly exquisite wines. (No self-respecting wine lover would ever turn up her nose at a glass of Bollinger or Krug.) The point is that the grower insurgence has introduced a whole new perspective on Champagne, shifting the emphasis from product to place.

Not only have we started discussing Champagne in the language of wine, evaluating it in terms of criteria such as soil type, farming practices, and vintage variation, but the way we're interacting with it has evolved as well. If you order Champagne in a restaurant today, chances are it will be served to you in a white-wine glass as opposed to the once customary flute—all the better, the thinking goes, to taste what's actually in the glass.

Similarly, a natural part of reclaiming Champagne as a table wine is rediscovering its incredible compatibility with food: not just the usual oysters and caviar, but everyday comfort cuisines, like pizza and fried chicken, for which the wine's inherent acidity and refreshing effervescence act as a natural foil. (If you harbor any doubts, just try it: a crisp bottle of Champagne and a bucket of fried wings is a match made in heaven.)

A QUICK GUIDE TO THE SUBREGIONS

If the main legacy of the grower movement has been to insert place back into the conversation about Champagne, it follows that, like any other area, Champagne is increasingly being understood in the context of its five specific subregions. Each of these roughly corresponds to its own set of styles and blends of the region's three main grapes: chardonnay, pinot noir, and pinot meunier.

MONTAGNE DE REIMS

Curling northward just above the village of Épernay, the Montagne de Reims (to be honest, it's really more of a hill than a mountain) is a celebrated source of pinot noir, giving richer, spicier wines in the classic blanc de noir style (that is, a white wine produced by fermenting red grapes off the skins).

CÔTE DES BLANCS

Just south of Épernay, the Côte des Blancs is aptly named, as it is planted almost exclusively with chardonnay, which reaches a maximum of elegance, racy acidity, and mineral tension in the area's chalky limestone soils. It's here that many of the region's greatest all-chardonnay blanc des blancs bottlings call home, such as Krug's famous single-vineyard Clos du Mesnil.

VALLÉE DE LA MARNE

Traditionally used as a workhorse grape to fatten up blends, pinot meunier was once rarely encountered as a single-variety wine. Recently, however, the early-ripening, frost-resistant variety has acquired a kind of cult status among wine geeks thanks to a handful of grower-producers in the Vallée de la Marne, where it represents a local specialty (keep an eye out for Jérôme Prévost, Christophe Mignon, and Laherte Frères, among others). On its own, the grape gives robust, savory, extremely food-friendly wines with fleshy fruit and big personalities. Even so, plenty of chardonnay and pinot noir are planted here as well, and blends remain far more common.

CÔTE DE SÉZANNE

Not nearly as renowned as the regions mentioned above, the Côte de Sézanne, located due south of the Côte des Blancs, is often viewed as a mini version of the latter given its preponderance of chardonnay vines. Thanks to the higher percentage of clay in its soils, its wines tend to be riper and slightly lower in acidity than the filigreed expression of the grape found farther north. Still, in the right hands, the area is capable of magic: for example, its top producer, Ulysse Collin, regularly channels a penchant for ripeness into wines of stunning depth and complexity.

THE AUBE

Also known as the Côte des Bar, the Aube has historically been treated like an afterthought by the rest of the region. That's due, in part, to its remoteness—on the map, the area lies around an hour southwest of Épernay, closer to Chablis than to the heart of Champagne country. Formerly considered a source of cheap blending grapes for the big houses, the Aube is now staking its claim as the new capital of Champagne's naturalist avant-garde. Thanks are due to the vision of pioneering producers, like Cédric Bouchard, Jacques Lassaigne, and Vouette et Sorbée, who first injected a terroir-centric Burgundian sensibility into the area. Pinot noir has a long history here, but the proximity to Chablis translates to some racy, mineral expressions of chardonnay as well.

BRUT NATURE CHAMPAGNE

As you begin to explore the alternate universe of grower Champagne, you'll eventually begin to notice a pattern: namely, a spate of bottles labeled brut nature (the official term) or brut zéro. These interchangeable terms designate an increasingly popular style of Champagne to which extremely little (if any) sugar, or *dosage*, has been added before bottling.

Although *dosage* has traditionally been viewed as a critical measure to help balance Champagne's sharp acidity, today, many growers view the practice with skepticism. For one, thanks to rising ripeness levels (courtesy of global warming), it's simply not as necessary as it was in the past. But on a deeper level, given Champagne's general shift toward site expression and specificity of place, the general consensus is that too much *dosage* obscures a wine's underlying expression of the soil.

For this reason, the brut nature/brut zéro category has become highly fashionable among the latest generation of Champagne purists. Powerfully mineral and savory, this new crop of bracingly dry expressions has helped to push Champagne one step closer to being treated like any other serious wine.

Essential Producers: Cédric Bouchard, Jacques Lassaigne, Vouette et Sorbée, Jérôme Prévost, Christophe Mignon, Laherte Frères, Champagne Aubry, R. Pouillon & Fils, Champagne Savart, Val Frison, Pierre Gerbais, J. Vignier, A. Margaine, Pierre Paillard, Flavien Nowack, Agrapart et Fils, André Beaufort, Bérêche et Fils, Emmanuel Brochet, Larmandier-Bernier, Marguet

THE WINE LIST

◆ **Champagne Aubry Premier Cru Brut ($$):** Always one of Champagne's top bargains, this crunchy, pear-scented crowd-pleaser from the Montagne de Reims' Aubry brothers offers up far more complexity—thanks, in part, to the high percentage of older reserve wine used in the blend—than its modest price tag would suggest.

◆ **R. Pouillon & Fils Réserve Brut ($$$):** Based in the town of Mareuil-sur-Aÿ, Fabrice Pouillon is making some of the most impressive terroir-focused, biodynamic wines in the Vallée de la Marne. Here, the red-skinned grapes (pinot noir and pinot meunier) set the tone structurally: firm and big-boned, it cleans up nicely with a wash of ginger-root spice.

◆ **Champagne Savart "L'Ouverture" Premier Cru Brut ($$):** Grower Frédéric Savart's entry-level (but by no means basic) "L'Ouverture" cuvée, made entirely from pinot noir from the village of Ecueil, combines that grape's textural density with delicate rose-petal aromatics and a refreshing bite of Japanese pear.

◆ **Val Frison "Lalore" Blanc de Blancs Brut Nature ($$$):** Better known for her knack with pinot noir, the Côte des Bar's Valérie Frison's skill with chardonnay comes across in this textbook take on the blanc de blancs style, sourced from two organic parcels planted in the limestone soils of Les Colannes.

◆ **Vouette et Sorbée "Fidèle" Extra Brut ($$$):** Bertrand Gautherot of the cult Vouette et Sorbée estate produces this stellar blanc de noir with pinot noir from the experimental hotbed of the Aube. Lees aged for twenty months, it wears its extra brut (that is, no *dosage*) designation proudly, with a lean chalkiness and chiseled acidity.

BEAUJOLAIS

JUST THE HIGHLIGHTS

◆ There's more to Beaujolais than lowbrow *nouveau*. The cheap, mass-produced *nouveau* category defined Beaujolais for a generation of drinkers, but the region also produces some of France's most beloved table wines.

◆ The top wines come from ten specific village-designated crus. Although they won't say Beaujolais on the label, the wines of villages such as Morgon and Fleurie show Beaujolais at its best, and have lately become sommelier darlings.

◆ Beaujolais is leading the charge for lighter, fresher, low-alcohol reds. The region's native gamay grape is synonymous with the new fashion for drinkable reds that choose elegance over extraction.

◆ Beaujolais is where natural wine began. In the 1970s, groundbreaking winemakers, like Marcel Lapierre and Jean Foillard, incited a rebellion against industrial winemaking that lives on in the next generation of winemakers who are following in their footsteps.

Long considered little more than a pleasant country pit stop between the holy land of Burgundy and the great syrah strongholds of the northern Rhône, Beaujolais has been fighting an uphill battle for respectability since 1395. That was the year Philip the Bold, Duke of Burgundy, banned the classic Beaujolais grape, gamay noir, from the Côte d'Or, exiling the "very bad and disloyal" variety to its current outpost just south of Lyon.

If only our royal friend Phil could see what gamay—specifically gamay from the lowly backwater of Beaujolais—has turned into today.

No longer living in the shadows of its illustrious neighbors, Beaujolais is now required drinking, an essential pillar of the canon of regions that have shifted pereceptions about what wine should be. The story of its late reclamation—one that just happens to overlap with the origin myth of France's natural wine movement—offers as emblematic an account as any of how our relationship to wine has changed.

Whenever that story is told, the central conceit always involves defending real Beaujolais—made by small, conscientious growers and, ideally, sourced from the region's ten village-designated crus (the specific villages that are allowed to bottle under their own township names)—against that ersatz impostor, Beaujolais *nouveau*. If you're familiar with the insipid, bubble-gum-meets-Hawaiian-punch profile associated with the style, you can easily understand why.

Like so many famous storybook villains, however, *nouveau* wasn't born evil. Initially, the style was conceived as a festive, juicy harvest wine, bottled shortly after the last grapes had been picked off the vine, and consumed in celebration of the new vintage. It only developed its sinister side in the 1970s and 1980s, when corporate *négociant* Georges Duboeuf masterminded the annual ritual of airlifting thousands of crates of garishly labeled, mass-market *nouveau* to destinations as far-flung as New York, London, and Tokyo.

As a sales gimmick, the *nouveau* fad brought Duboeuf instant fame and fortune, but it ended up inflicting almost irreparable damage to the region's reputation. Not only did it violate the original spirit of *nouveau*, turning a distinctly local tradition into a global marketing frenzy, but, worst of all, it also branded the entire Beaujolais region with a stigma it wouldn't shake off for decades.

In fairness, there are plenty of excellent examples of artisanal *nouveau* produced in small quantities by some of the region's top growers. But if, like many Americans, your formative experiences with Beaujolais have been limited to the usual high-volume swill, you're in for a pleasant surprise.

The "real" Beaujolais is dangerously addictive. No other region more successfully combines the playful with the profound. Whether in the form of its basic regional bottlings, simply labeled Beaujolais or Beaujolais-Villages, or the deeper, more concentrated crus, it offers as much pure drinking pleasure as any wine in existence, while still offering the sommelier in-crowd ample fodder for geeky contemplation and debate.

THE GANG OF FOUR AND THE BIRTH OF NATURAL WINE

It's impossible to trace the region's path from industrial plonk to hipster-approved darling without mentioning the Gang of Four, the band of visionary winemakers who are widely credited with making Beaujolais great again.

Rejecting the industrialization that had come to dominate the region, poisoning its soils with chemicals and reducing its wines to cheap facsimiles of what they once were, Guy Breton, Jean Foillard, Jean-Paul Thévenet, and the late Marcel Lapierre—along with a handful of others, according to which account you're reading—planted the seeds of an insurrection that still reverberates to this day. Under the guidance of their mentor, famed enologist Jules Chauvet, they advocated for a return to traditional practices (organic farming, no chemical sprays or additives, natural yeast fermentations, no fining or filtration, and minimal use of sulfur at bottling), convinced that such old-school measures would pave the way to salvation.

Now revered as founding fathers of the natural wine movement, they inaugurated a new era for Beaujolais. Over the years, examples such as Lapierre's crystalline, cherry-scented Morgon (now produced by his son, Mathieu) and Foillard's monumental "Côte du Py," sourced from one of the village's most famous individual terroirs, have come to represent hallowed classics—not just for Beaujolais but also for the wider world of natural wine.

Their example has inspired a wave of disciples to follow in their foot-steps. This younger generation has since established its own crop of luminaries (such as Julien Sunier, Rémi Dufaitre, Jean-Louis Dutraive, and Jean-Claude Lapalu), who are busy making many of the region's—and, to be honest, the country's—most exciting and irresistibly alluring wines.

WHY YOU SHOULD BE DRINKING THE CRUS

That early "natty" street cred, combined with rampant price inflation in neighboring Burgundy (one New York sommelier famously called cru Beaujolais "methadone for Burgundy junkies," given its rising popularity as an affordable alternative) and the wider stylistic preference for lighter, fresher wines created the perfect storm for Beaujolais's reconsideration as a serious wine, if not an industry obsession.

The category's elevation also goes to show that seriousness no lon-ger means what it once did. We don't approach Beaujolais with the same hushed reverence we reserve for mature Bordeaux or top-shelf Burgundy. To the contrary, Beaujolais has always been a wine of visceral pleasure, not meant to be sipped so much as ecstatically slurped.

Traditional notions of seriousness do come into play, however, in refram-ing the Beaujolais narrative around the particularities of place—namely, the brilliant diversity of the ten individual crus. For modern Beaujolais lovers, it's here, at the elevated cru level, that the region becomes more than a source of simple quaffers, showcasing the lip-smacking succu-lence and mineral brilliance that is the hallmark of gamay planted in the granite-rich slopes of these celebrated terroirs.

- **Domaine de la Grand'Cour Fleurie "Clos de la Grand'Cour" ($$):** Through his range of stunning site-specific, organically farmed parcels in the crus of Fleurie and Brouilly, Jean-Louis Dutraive has earned a reputation as one of Beaujolais's indisputed masters. This bottling, sourced from the walled vineyard surrounding his fourth-generation family domaine, exemplifies the purity of his terroir-driven style, possessing the high-toned delicacy that is particular to the wines of Fleurie.

- **Julien Sunier Régnié ($):** Régnié isn't exactly the best known of Beaujolais's ten village-designated crus, but the results that rising star Julien Sunier gets out of his small plot of fifty-year-old vines can compete with any of Morgon's most coveted darlings. Organically farmed and (true to his low-impact philosophy) fermented with ambient yeasts, it weaves flavors of wild raspberry and sour cherry over granite.

- **Château Thivin Côte de Brouilly ($$):** Despite the estate's reputation as a standard bearer for Côte de Brouilly, Thivin's efforts tend to get overlooked in favor of some of Beaujolais's cultier producers. Revealing a bit of the extra flesh and tannic grip that distinguishes wines from the hillside vineyards of Côte de Brouilly from those of neighboring Brouilly, it makes a convincing case for Beaujolais's ability to age.

THE GREAT
CARBONIC DEBATE

Much has been made of Beaujolais's carefree spirit. But that inherent Beaujolais sexiness—the juicy freshness that makes it easy to wash down—isn't strictly the by-product of soil and grape.

Indeed, a great deal of this signature style can be ascribed to the widespread adoption of a specific winemaking technique called carbonic maceration (see page 9). Responsible for producing bright, snappy wines that are light red, low in alcohol and tannins, and bursting with fruit flavors, it has become synonymous with the region of Beaujolais.

Lately, however, as the region evolves toward a more sophisticated (read: site-specific) understanding of itself, as evidenced by a proliferation of vineyard-designated bottlings, certain producers have started to wonder whether "carbonic," as they call it, might not be the best way to telegraph the subtle nuances of place.

To that end, many would argue that wines made according to the method actually taste more of process than place. Therefore, in order to better capture their terroirs, they're embracing a traditional Burgundian approach designed to substitute that telltale carbonic crunch with greater concentration, tannic structure, and depth.

Rather than pit one style against the other, it's possible to take a bigger-picture view. There are now two different paradigms for interpreting what Beaujolais means as a region. If we're taking its wines seriously, that means expanding the possibilities for what those wines can be; this can only be a good thing for those of us who want to see Beaujolais reach its full potential. For examples of this noncarbonic (or low-carbonic) style, seek out top practitioners, like Jean-Paul Brun's Domaine des Terres Dorées, Château de Moulin-à-Vent, and Anne Sophie Dubois.

THE RHÔNE VALLEY

JUST THE HIGHLIGHTS

◆ **There's not one Rhône Valley, but two.** The region is traditionally split into the northern Rhône and the southern Rhône. More than geographical, the differences between them fall along stylistic and philosophical lines.

◆ **The northern Rhône is the spiritual home of syrah.** Cool climate in style and produced in limited quantities, the syrah-based wines from the villages of Hermitage, Côté-Rôtie, and Cornas (plus a couple of others) possess an elegance and purity not found in any other expression of the grape.

◆ **The southern Rhône is where the South of France officially begins.** Riper, richer, and full of Mediterranean warmth, southern Rhône reds—like the famously robust wines of Châteauneuf-du-Pape—consist primarily of the classic regional blend of grenache, syrah, and mourvèdre.

◆ **Côtes du Rhône spans north and south.** This ubiquitous regional designation applies to bottles that come from anywhere in the entire Rhône Valley, so it helps to know the producer's location. Although many are mediocre, in the right winemaker's hands, they offer excellent value.

Waverley Root, legendary food writer, famously divided France into three general regions, or domains, based on their cooking fat of choice: the domain of butter (occupying most of the country's north), the domain of oil (the friendly, olive-producing south), and, finally, the domain of lard (essentially Alsace and the Périgord, where you wouldn't want to be reincarnated as a pig or a goose). Beyond geographical distinctions, these boundaries demarcate social and cultural borders, accounting for major differences in customs, attitude, lifestyle, and, of course, approach to wine.

This symbolic framework offers a useful way to understand the fundamental division at the heart of France's Rhône Valley, which is traditionally split between the northern and southern Rhône: think of it as encompassing the final frontier between the domain of butter and that of oil. The drive between Tain l'Hermitage, the northern Rhône's spiritual capital (just below Lyon), and Avignon, the capital of the south, takes just over an hour, but they might as well be a universe apart. At some point in the journey, as you follow the region's namesake river from one to the other, the realization suddenly dawns on you: you've left behind the chilly, buttoned-up formality of the *nord* and entered the sun-dappled, cypress-studded *sud* of the romantic imagination.

Neither area claims a monopoly on great wine; each supplies some of France's most evocative and historically significant expressions. Both in mentality and style, however, the opposition between them couldn't be starker.

With its continental climate and culture of small independent growers, the northern Rhône is more closely aligned with the monastic rigor of Burgundy than the carefree charms of Provence. As in Burgundy, the area's reds focus on a lone variety as a prism for interpreting the nuances of a single vineyard or village. That grape, of course, is syrah. And in the terraced slopes of just a handful of villages tightly clustered along the banks of the river, syrah achieves its platonic ideal: dark fruited, savory, and elegant, with shadings of white pepper, violets, and grilled meat.

The ripe, sunny wines of the southern Rhône, by contrast, immediately reveal their Mediterranean warmth, assuming the wild, scrubby flavors known as *garrigue* (think rosemary, sage, and thyme, plus any other local herb you might use to marinate a leg of lamb). Compared to the narrow strip of terraced hillside vineyards that form its northern counterpart, everything about the southern half of the region feels vaster and more expansive: the luminous skies, the scale of production, the surface area of the vineyards, and even the permitted number of grapes. It was here that the classic southern Rhône blend of grenache, syrah, and mourvèdre (often with a smattering of others) first originated, as epitomized by the area's most prestigious example: the big reds of Châteauneuf-du-Pape.

Beyond these differences in style, geography, and grape variety, as the two areas came to occupy different identities in the marketplace, an ideological division arose between them as well.

On a philosophical level, the northern Rhône's appeal closely echoes Burgundy's, predicated on a similar set of small-scale, artisanal values. Responsible for just 5 percent of the entire Rhône Valley's annual production, the area's image is increasingly that of a handful of highly revered family firms and small independent growers whose limited output checks off all the right boxes of a younger generation raised to worship at the holy altar of terroir.

The southern Rhône, on the other hand, followed a different path— one that some would argue led to the dark side of the 1990s and early aughts, when the emergence of a fashionable, modern style of red (over-ripe, over-oaked, overly alcoholic) held the region captive. Ground zero for this arms race of ripeness, Châteauneuf was the guiltiest culprit, positioning itself as a magnet for the same trophy-hunting collectors who lusted after cult Napa cab and Bordeaux.

That more or less sums up perceptions of the regions today. The hallowed villages of the north tend to enjoy a greater share of wine-geek street cred, whereas the south, while not exactly uncool, generally lacks the same star power that drives today's sommelier in-crowd to snap bottle shots. In fairness, however, this simplistic view quickly breaks down when the region is examined more closely.

Each area has its advantages and drawbacks. The northern Rhône, for one, is increasingly commanding Burgundy-like prices, as top bottles from revered producers, like Thierry Allemand and Jean-Louis Chave, approach ever-greater levels of rarity and exclusivity. And having emerged from some of the worst excesses of its recent past, the southern Rhône abounds in joyously drinkable, everyday country wines that offer sensational value and typically hail from its assortment of lesser-known villages (or are simply bottled as generic Côtes du Rhône, but more on that in a bit). Even flashy Châteauneuf-du-Pape, for that matter, never lacked its share of legendary old-school holdouts; classic estates such as Vieux Télégraphe and Château de Beaucastel always resisted the worst impulses of modernity, taking an important stand for traditional winemaking when doing so was anything but fashionable.

Ultimately, these dueling identities give the Rhône Valley its incredible dynamism and captivating complexity. Navigating such a multifaceted region, however, is no simple task. Here's a rough guide to the essential villages, producers, and individual bottlings that tell the story of the Rhône in all of its multifaceted glory.

But first, a brief disclaimer: Although both parts of the Rhône make rich yet chiseled whites from an eclectic group of native grapes—in the north, marsanne, roussanne, and viognier; in the south, all of the above, plus others such as clairette and grenache blanc—red wine has always been the Rhône's main attraction, so that's where we'll be focusing.

NORTHERN RHÔNE

By the numbers, the northern Rhône is by far the simplest to assimilate. Unlike the south's complex patchwork of winemaking villages and hodgepodge of grapes, there are just five main red-producing northern

Rhône districts to keep in mind. According to longstanding wisdom, three areas stand apart at the top of the quality pyramid. Of these, the vine-studded hill of Hermitage enjoys the greatest historical prestige and still commands the most modern-day esteem. Crowned with its famous stone chapel, its granitic, south-facing vineyards give birth to what many consider syrah's most sublime incarnation, capable of aging for decades. A taste of such greatness will cost you, though.

The wines of Côte-Rôtie (or "roasted slope")—the most immediately hedonistic of the northern Rhône reds with their brambly fruit, smoked meat, and spice—have also steadily crept up in price. And Cornas, once considered rustic, is now home to some of the region's most highly coveted cult wines, thanks to the hype surrounding producers such as Auguste Clape and Thierry Allemand.

Still, all of the above are culturally essential and worth seeking out—plus, if you know where to look, there are still relative values lurking about, particularly if you manage to steer clear of the most buzzed-about producers.

For the money, however, the true sweet spot for northern Rhône syrah can be found in the humbler villages of Saint-Joseph and (to a slightly lesser extent) Crozes-Hermitage. They might lack some of the fireworks of their more prestigious neighbors, but they can't be beat as affordable introductions to the sappy, gamy, floral goodness that is the region's hallmark.

Essential Producers: Bernard Levet, Jamet, Vincent Paris, Franck Balthazar, Lionel Faury, Yves Cuilleron, Alain Graillot, Domaine Lionnet, Thierry Allemand, Jean-Michel Stephan, Guillaume Gilles, Domaine des Miquettes, La Ferme des Sept Lunes, Hervé Souhaut

SOUTHERN RHÔNE

Châteauneuf-du-Pape enjoys hall-of-fame status for a reason. When fashioned in a classic style, it provides all you could ever want from a luscious southern French red. While it also doesn't come cheap, with the exception of just a handful of top producers (for example, Château Rayas, Château de Beaucastel, and Vieux Télégraphe), prices rarely rival the tariffs imposed up north, keeping it within the realm of affordable splurge.

Here's the catch: there's a whole lot of iffy Châteauneuf in the market. Given the wide swings in quality, it's critical to know a thing or two about a producer's individual style. Look for forward-thinking traditionalists, like Domaine de la Mordorée, Vieille Julienne, and Vieux Télégraphe (its young-vines "Télégramme" bottling is a steal for under $50).

Or better yet, set your sites on the many lesser-known villages of the southern Rhône, where you'll find the same roll call of native grapes, a similar terroir, and all of the region's wild, herbaceous, and gamy flavors—with none of the luxury pretenses. Just outside of Châteauneuf, the villages of Gigondas and Vacqueyras do a great job of approximating the former's grandeur (pegged as "baby" versions, many of them outshine the original). But also take a look at Rasteau, Cairanne, and Beaumes deVenise, among others, which typically sell for a song compared with the area's more fashionable wines.

Essential Producers: Sang des Cailloux, Domaine Gramenon, Vieux Télégraphe, Château de Beaucastel, Domaine Charvin, Château Rayas, Domaine Les Pallières, Anne Pichon, Domaine Marcel Richaud, Les Vignerons d'Estézargues, Château Redortier, Bois de Boursan, Vieux Donjon

THE WINE LIST

◆ **Lionel Faury Saint-Joseph ($$):** Lionel Faury's Saint-Joseph--sourced from hillside vineyards outside the tiny village of Chavanay—bundles all of the classic notes (cracked pepper, bacon fat, dried lavender, olives) found in the northern Rhône's priciest bottlings into a fresher, more approachable package.

- **J. L. Chave "Offerus" Saint-Joseph ($$):** A royal figure of the northern Rhône, Jean-Louis Chave produces the most renowned and highly sought-after expression of Hermitage. While those flagship bottles cost hundreds of dollars, his "Offerus" bottling— blended from younger vines—provides a glimpse of the master's style at literally a tenth of the price.

- **Domaine Romaneaux-Destezet (Hervé Souhaut) Syrah, IGP Ardèche ($$):** Hervé Souhaut's minimalist reds employ semi-carbonic maceration to achieve a pure-fruited, drink-me-now freshness that has made them the darlings of the natural wine bars of Paris (and the rest of the world). This shows syrah's chuggable side, but there's a savory seriousness to it as well.

- **Bernard Levet Côte-Rôtie "Les Journaries" ($$$):** Northern Rhône syrah doesn't get any more old-school than the wild, untamed versions of Côte-Rôtie that master traditionalist Bernard Levet ekes out of his tiny holdings above the village of Ampuis. A blend of different parcels, his "Les Journaries" bottling is technically his basic, earliest-drinking wine, but it's still loaded with dark-fruited intensity and a gamy, sanguine complexity.

- **Domaine Marcel Richaud Cairanne ($$):** For decades, Marcel Richaud—the godfather of natural winemaking in the remote southern Rhône village of Cairanne—has been quietly making some of the region's most compelling reds. His signature blend of grenache, syrah, and mourvèdre (with a touch of carignan) wields its robust Mediterannean flavors with an unusual elegance.

- **Domaine Gramenon Côtes du Rhône "Poignée de Raisins" ($):** This young-vines grenache from the incomparable Gramenon estate checks off all the right boxes to earn its natural street cred (biodynamic farming, native yeast fermentations, the absence of new oak), but none of that would matter if it weren't such a joy to drink. It's the kind of juicy, thirst-quenching Côtes du Rhône that calls for a quick dunk in the ice bucket.

A BRIEF WORD ON CÔTES DU RHÔNE

The vast majority of Rhône wine comes not from the region's name-designated villages but instead under the lowly Côtes du Rhône label.

In France (well, really, in all of Europe), geographical specificity usually correlates to increasingly higher quality. As you can imagine, this broad regional designation indicates that the grapes could have been sourced from anywhere across the vast swathe of the Rhône Valley—which isn't exactly the most reassuring guarantee.

While it can't be denied that the market overflows with bland, insipid Côtes du Rhône, in theory it can be one of wine's great low-maintenance pleasures: the sort of slurpable, unfussy Tuesday-night wine you can pair with pretty much anything. The key is to stick with the right producers: most winemakers in the region's prime postal codes still bottle a fresh, zippy Côtes du Rhône, usually sourced from younger vines and ready to drink right now.

Essential Producers: Domaine Les Aphillanthes, Domaine La Manarine, Domaine de la Mordorée, Clos du Mont-Olivet, Domaine Gramenon, Domaine de Montvac, Les Vins de Vienne, Roger Perrin, Domaine Monpertuis, Château Redortier

LOIRE VALLEY

······························

JUST THE HIGHLIGHTS

◆ **The Loire is a region of astonishing diversity.** Red, white, rosé, sparkling, off-dry, sweet—the large, sprawling region excels at all of them and even produces multiple styles of each.

◆ **The Loire is a historic supplier of France's iconic everyday drinking wines.** Its array of time-honored bistro classics include such benchmarks as Chinon, Sancerre, Vouvray, and Muscadet—all testaments to the national belief in wine as a staple of daily life.

◆ **The region is on the front lines of the natural wine revolution.** If the movement began in Beaujolais, it reached critical mass in the Loire; today, it's home to many of natural wine's most influential practitioners.

◆ **The Loire is embracing its fringe.** Formerly unsung Loire grapes, like grolleau, pineau d'Aunis, côt, and menu pineau, among others, are now being made into fun (and often natural) table wines that are popping up across the United States.

It took a while before the United States learned to appreciate what the Loire was all about. In part, the barrier was stylistic: at a time when the public thirst for big, showstopping wines had reached a climax, the Loire's particular charms—freshness, acidity, minerality—ran counter to trend. Status-conscious collectors rarely gave it a thought, favoring flashier wines, and the general public remained indifferent. (Of course, the one big exception is the viral popularity of Sancerre, but that excitement never trickled down to the rest of the Loire, and let's face it, most consumers know Sancerre not as a wine of place but as a brand unto itself.)

But if the Loire was never meant to be France's fanciest region, it has always been its most diverse. Of course, that's to be expected of an area that straddles such an enormous distance. Incredibly, its vineyards follow the banks of the Loire River (the nation's longest) from the district of Pouilly-Fumé, smack in the center of France, all the way west to the outskirts of Nantes, beyond which it empties into the Atlantic. Over the course of this three-hundred-mile journey, the river zigs and zags through some of France's most gorgeous wine country, encompassing a tapestry of terroirs that are collectively capable of producing just about every style of wine: dry to sweet, still to sparkling, red, white, rosé, and everything in between.

What connects these varied expressions (besides the river) is the way they exemplify the core French belief in wine as a staple of daily life. No other region has more faithfully championed this ideal across the years. What it lacked in sought-after trophy wines, the Loire always made up for with its roll call of reliable classics, supplying a steady stream of excellent everyday bottles to the thirsty citizens of France. Touchstones of the great Gallic table-wine tradition, wines such as Chinon, Vouvray, Muscadet, and (yes, of course) Sancerre have provided liquid sustenance to generations upon generations of drinkers.

This historic importance, however, only begins to account for the enormous influence the Loire wields within today's universe of wine. To its latest admirers, the region signals something far more radical than a source of nostalgic bistro standards to be consumed by the carafe while humming along to "La vie en rose."

If its image these days leans more punk rock than Piaf, that's because the Loire has emerged as the headquarters of France's natural wine counterculture; the movement might have been born in Beaujolais, but it was in the Loire that it first went global, inspiring an international revolution, and the area continues to lead the natural conversation today. Home to so many of its folkloric heroes—figures such as René Mosse, Christian Chaussard, Thierry Puzelat, Olivier Cousin, and Nicolas Joly, among countless others—the Loire emerged as an early battleground for a culture war that has since transformed it into France's greatest hotbed of experimentation.

Universally worshipped by sommeliers who came of age alongside natural wine's rise, the Loire remains at the cutting edge of the drinking culture, its fresh range of styles kept in constant rotation in progressive wine bars and restaurants across the United States.

But even with its newfound alternative appeal—and despite a handful of elite producers having since reached unattainable cult status (above all, Clos Rougeard, the famed estate in the area of Samur)—the Loire has never turned its back on the democratic values that originally defined it. As in the past, it continues to overdeliver on deliciousness, drinkability, and bang for the buck. For these reasons, the Loire might just be France's most essential region of all.

THE REGIONS AND STYLES OF THE LOIRE

It's impossible to do justice to a wine region as vast as the Loire in the space of just a few pages. For the sake of brevity, we'll limit our scope to the main expressions for which it is best known. Helpfully, it can be divided into three major areas—the Upper, Middle, and Lower Loire—which break down relatively neatly according to style and grape variety. There are four main players: sauvignon blanc, chenin blanc, cabernet franc, and melon de Bourgogne.

THE UPPER LOIRE: THE LAND OF SAUVIGNON BLANC

What's commonly called the Upper Loire is actually the easternmost tranche of the region, about a two-hour drive south of Paris. Here, in the vineyards surrounding the villages of Pouilly-sur-Loire and Sancerre, one grape reigns supreme: sauvignon blanc.

We've already touched on the great public obsession with Sancerre. By far the most famous wine produced in the region, it represents the definitive version of a grape that, with good reason, has been promiscuously planted across the globe. To that end, Sancerre offers all the things that people love about sauvignon blanc. The default by-the-glass crowd-pleaser, it exists as a familiar reference point that consistently offers what consumers have come to expect from it: namely, a crisp, citrusy white.

Those same expectations, however, can also be met elsewhere in the region—and far less expensively at that. The names of Sancerre's neighboring districts don't roll off the tongue quite as easily. But the dry, flinty wines of Reuilly, Quincy, Menetou-Salon, and Pouilly-Fumé, produced just a little farther up- or downstream, offer classic regional riffs on Savignon blanc minus the usual name-brand premium.

Meanwhile, while the scourge of commercial Sancerre has transformed the region into a household name, there are still plenty of exemplary versions to be found. Rather than trade on the easy, breezy charms of sauvignon blanc, the type of Sancerre that's worthy of its name channels the grape as a window into the region's limestone-rich soils. For the record, that's the same ridge of Kimmeridgian limestone responsible for imparting the famous minerality of Chablis and Champagne, and as luck would have it, the area boasts a handful of producers who are committed to channeling it with the same precision and meticulous attention to detail.

Take, for instance, winemakers such as François Cotat or Edmond Vatan—the cultiest of Sancerre's cult producers—whose revered single-vineyard expressions exemplify this more rigorous paradigm. Unfortunately, benchmark bottles, like Cotat's "Les Monts Damnés," sourced from the steep north-facing slopes of what is arguably Sancerre's most famous crus, have acquired a cult following with prices to match. That said, at least you're getting what you pay for, unlike so much of what passes for Sancerre these days. Besides, they're not the only ones in Sancerre you'll find working in this elevated vein.

Essential Producers: Gérard Boulay, Thomas-Labaille, Vincent Gaudry, Marc Deschamps, Lucien Crochet, François Cotat, Domaine Vacheron

THE MIDDLE LOIRE: THE LAND OF CHENIN BLANC AND CABERNET FRANC

The great winemaking villages of the Middle Loire are many (and quite difficult to keep track of), so here's the easy part: the only grapes you really need to know are chenin blanc (for whites) and cabernet franc (for reds). What's more, they're certainly worth knowing, both having triumphantly come back into fashion in the wake of a wider recalibration of taste.

The most versatile grape of France's most diverse region, chenin blanc's adaptability runs the aesthetic gamut, rivaled only by riesling in its multiplicity of guises. Nowhere is that extreme dexterity more prominently displayed than in the villages of Vouvray and Montlouis-sur-Loire, located on opposite sides of the river just ten miles east of Tours.

Of the two, Vouvray is the most famous and historically prestigious. It also lays claim to the region's most celebrated estates, Domaine Huet and Domaine Foreau. But despite its humbler pedigree, Montlouis is arguably the more exciting today, having transformed into a cutting-edge incubator for fresh (and generally natural-leaning) talent, thanks in no small part to the example set by its two luminaries, François Chidaine and Jacky Blot.

Both villages are capable of coaxing chenin into every possible register of the stylistic continuum, from bone-dry sec bottlings to the off-dry demi-sec versions and sweet dessert wines, plus some of France's most exceptional (and affordable) fizzy *crémants*. (That said, as a general rule, you'll find fewer sweetish to fully sweet versions of Montlouis.)

Across all of these permutations, what shines through is chenin's riveting balancing act between a textual richness, or roundness, often described as a "waxy" or "woolly" lanolin quality, and an electric jolt of acidity, buffered by the chalky minerality of the area's classic *tuffeau* (limestone) soil.

But the Vouvray-Montlouis nexus is just one of several areas where chenin shows off its virtuosity. There's the broad region of Anjou to the west, closer to the city of Angers, where a growing cohort of naturally minded producers are crafting gorgeously mineral, vibrant chenins under the general Anjou designation (including the incredible versions by Richard Leroy and René Mosse, for starters). Then there's the village of Savennières, where chenin assumes its most powerful, almost aggressively dry form, capable of aging for years, to say nothing of the famous dessert wines of Coteaux du Layon and Quarts de Chaume.

It would be possible to sing chenin's praises indefinitely, but that would leave little room for the glories of cabernet franc, the Loire's great red. Unlike in Bordeaux, where the grape functions as one part of a blend (alongside that far more famous member of the cabernet family, cabernet sauvignon), in the Loire, cab franc is the star of the show, even if it hasn't always enjoyed star power.

If it's easy to love a grape such as cabernet sauvignon, with its suave structure and rich blackberry flavors, then cabernet franc is more of an acquired taste. Lacking its sibling's penchant for ripeness, it typically veers toward the leaner and earthier side of the spectrum, displaying a signature herbaceousness (think tarragon and green bell pepper) that drinkers reared on riper reds might find austere. But as audiences continue to favor fresher, lighter reds, and drinkers learn to embrace more complex and savory flavors—the very same qualities that originally made it a bistro staple—Loire cabernet franc is finally having its big moment.

Accordingly, the spotlight has been trained on the three famous villages that constitute the grape's historical heart of production: Chinon, Bourgueil, and Saumur.

While all three have long excelled at making bright, juicy reds that practically beg for a dunk in the ice bucket (and a heaping platter of *steak-frites*), that's hardly the full extent of their powers. No other category more seamlessly bridges the gap between thirst-quenching *vin de soif* and cellar-worthy *vin de garde.* This balance between casual drinkability and legit profundity is the abiding hallmark of great Loire cab franc.

Of the grape's three mainstays, Chinon has always enjoyed the greatest recognition, and die-hard Loire fans have long been clued into the area's ambitious side. If there was ever any doubt, the track record of stalwart producers such as Olga Raffault (her "Les Picasses" bottling, in particular, has been known to age gracefully for decades), Charles Joguet, and Bernard Baudry speaks for itself. Over the years, these local legends have consistently proved just how elegant and long-lived the village's wine can be.

The conventional wisdom has always maintained Chinon's superiority to its next-door neighbor Bourgueil, but that view is increasingly difficult to stand behind. These days, Bourgueil has been stepping up its game, proving itself capable of earthy, structured reds that can rival any of Chinon's. (Frankly, at this point, it can be difficult to tell them apart). The wines of Catherine and Pierre Breton, natural wine legends in their own right, number among the best.

Even more surprising is the mini-renaissance of minimal-intervention winemaking that has arrived in the traditionally unassuming area of

Saumur, which has drawn inspiration from the revered Clos Rougeard estate. For decades a lone pioneer in the region, Rougeard proved to the world that it was possible to endow Saumur reds (and whites, too) with the same majesty as grand cru Burgundy. That legacy has lured a small entourage of disciples to the area—including Romain Guiberteau of Domaine Guiberteau, Thierry Germain of Domaine des Roches Neuves, and Arnaud Lambert, winemaker at Château de Brézé—who are following a similar naturalist playbook to world-class results (even if they're also charging Burgundy-adjacent prices).

Essential Producers: François Chidaine, Jacky Blot, Domaine Huet, Domaine du Clos Naudin, Domaine Vincent Carême, François Pinon, Frantz Saumon, Château de Brézé, La Grange Tiphaine, Lise et Bertrand Jousset, Richard Leroy, Domaine du Closel, Eric Morgat, Olivier Cousin, Domaine Guiberteau, Bernard Baudry, Olga Raffault, Catherine et Pierre Breton, Domaine des Roches Neuves, Domaine de la Chanteleuserie

THE LOWER LOIRE: THE LAND OF MELON DE BOURGOGNE

Before it drains into the Atlantic, the Loire makes one last important detour in the hillsides just outside Nantes. This final stretch of the region is known as the Lower Loire or, more commonly, the Pays Nantais. To the initiated, however, it will always be Muscadet country, in honor of its famously crisp white based on the melon de Bourgogne grape.

Like many of its Loire counterparts, Muscadet has long endured a familiar set of simplistic bistro stereotypes, regarded as little more than a serviceable (if ultimately forgettable) *apéro*-styled white meant for washing down oysters. (For the record, the whole oyster thing shouldn't be discarded; there's still no better pairing.)

Out of pure self-interest, Muscadet's die-hard crop of admirers would be all too happy for the situation to stay that way. That's because they've discovered that the current class of Muscadet—the kind that's farmed organically and produced on a microscale by small independent growers—bears zero resemblance to the overcropped, hastily made wines of the past. In fact, it wouldn't be a stretch to call Muscadet the most underrated wine in the market today; the bang-to-buck ratio is off the charts.

This is particularly true of the bottles that, after recent legislation, are now permitted to carry the names of the region's ten individual crus, or subzones, such as Gorges, Clisson, and Le Pallet, founded on their own particular soil types. True to local tradition, they're also aged extensively on their lees (see page 7), a process that imparts extra richness and depth. (The best Muscadets always spent a certain period aging *sur lie*, but many of these new crus age for several years before bottling.)

Wines such as Domaine de la Pépière's "Clisson" and its single-vineyard "Clos des Briords" or Domaine Luneau-Papin's "Excelsior," among many others, represent a profound and incredibly age-worthy style of Muscadet capable of standing toe-to-toe with plenty of premier cru Chablis in terms of concentration, depth, and mineral intensity. These are the wines you need to drink if you're still a bit confused by the notion of minerality in wine. One sip will remove all uncertainty: there's no mistaking that signature blast of crushed rock and salinity.

Essential Producers: Domaine de la Pépière, Domane Luneau-Papin, Domaine de l'Ecu, Domaine Michel Brégeon, Vincent Caillé (Domaine le Fay d'Homme), Jo Landron (Domaine de la Louvetrie)

THE WINE LIST

◆ **François Chidaine Montlouis "Clos du Breuil" ($$):** The spiritual leader of a younger wave of Montlouis winemakers who have turned the area—long eclipsed by Vouvray's shadow—into one of the Loire's brightest spots of innovation, François Chidaine's genius with the chenin blanc grape is manifest across his entire range of wines. His "Clos du Breuil" is the definitive dry Loire chenin, balancing its textural depth with racy acidity and a mouthful of chalky minerality.

THE OTHER LOIRE

Beyond the region's established touchstones, it's worth mentioning the other side of the Loire that is home to an eclectic grab bag of fringe and previously unsung grapes (from grolleau and pineau d'Aunis to côt, menu pineau, romorantin, and gros plant) that are increasingly appearing as fun table wines on wine lists in Paris, New York, San Francisco, Tokyo and beyond.

In a sense, these crushable, effortlessly uncomplicated whites and reds are the Loire's next generation of easygoing bistro wines updated for the twenty-first century courtesy of natural wine's irreverent glou-glou aesthetic. Typically bottled as *vin de France* and bearing playful puns and cartoons on the label, they come in all shapes and sizes: funky carbonic reds, hazy unfiltered whites, fizzy *pét-nats*, juicy rosés; and even the occasional orange outlier.

This ever-expanding genre is hard to pin down (there are countless examples), but more often than not, they represent a winemaker's friendly, entry-level wine, sourced from younger vines and meant to supplement the more ambitious offerings in his or her lineup.

Essential Producers: Honestly, it's too hard to choose. Many of the Loire's top natural winemakers (including several of those mentioned previously) also offer fun table wines made from unusual grapes in addition to their main focus. In no particular order, some additional favorites include Domaines des Sablonettes, La Lunotte, Thierry Puzelat's Clos du Tue-Boeuf, Philippe Tessier, Domaine de l'Ange Vin (Jean-Pierre Robinot), Patrick Corbineau, Domaine La Bohème, Claude and Etienne Courtois, and Emeline and Sebastien Bobinet, among countless others.

◆ **Domaine de la Pépière Muscadet sur lie "Clos des Briords" ($):** The fact that this piercingly pure, age-worthy, single-vineyard bottling from Muscadet legend Marc Olivier costs less than $20 is borderline criminal. Here is proof that top Muscadet is among the world's most absurdly undervalued wines.

◆ **Olga Raffault Chinon "Les Picasses" ($$):** Yet another mind-bending value from the Loire, Olga Raffault's "Les Picasses" bottling—arguably Chinon's most famous site—is far more than a simple bistro wine. This is cabernet franc at its most structured and age-worthy, but you can still enjoy it in its youthful firmness.

◆ **Marc Deschamps Pouilly-Fumé "Vinealis" ($):** An old-vine cuvée only made in exceptional years, organic grower Marc Deschamps's "Vinealis" bottling is sourced from the oldest vines in the Champs de Cri vineyard, revealing a richness and density that is a far cry from (and an eye-opening alternative to) the usual run-of-the-mill Sancerre.

◆ **Pascal Janvier Coteaux du Loir Rouge ($):** Based in the chenin stronghold of Jasnières, Pascal Janvier makes a range of elegant whites, but his pale, peppery take on the quirky pineau d'Aunis grape has acquired a small but passionate cult following. This red is featherweight, floral, and rainwater fresh, epitomizing the kind of delightfully offbeat offerings that have become the Loire's specialty.

◆ **Les Capriades "Piège à Filles" ($$):** Les Capriades—the brainchild of natural wine icon/hero Pascal Potaire—elevates the typically easygoing *pétillant naturel* category to an art form. A rosé version of the fizzy style (blended from côt, cabernet franc, and pineau d'Aunis), it's always bottled with a delicate hint of sweetness (more fresh summer strawberries than strawberry jolly ranchers) and a whiff of earthy funk.

THE JURA

....

JUST THE HIGHLIGHTS

- **The Jura is every wine geek's dream come true.** Little known to the outside world until recently, the region exploded to viral fame based on the mystique of its idiosyncratic, ultratraditional wines.

- **Jura whites come in two different styles.** The first, known as *ouillé*, is produced in essentially the same way as you'd expect in any other region. It was the Jura's deliberately oxidative *sous-voile* whites, however—aged, like sherry, under a veil of live yeast—that first hooked adventurous US audiences.

- **Jura reds have also gained traction.** While its pinot noirs often resemble those of neighboring Burgundy, the region's indigenous reds—the extremely pale, delicate poulsard and rustic yet racy trousseau—hold the greatest interest for today's drinkers.

- **We're living in a golden age for Jura wine.** As ever-greater numbers of boutique importers jump on the Jura bandwagon, we've never been presented with a richer mosaic of producers and styles—a situation that would have been unthinkable even a decade earlier.

Fifteen years ago, to call the Jura *niche* would have been a generous overstatement. Overlooked as a rural backwater in Burgundy's backyard, the region barely registered on the industry radar. Then, all of a sudden, at some point in the mid-aughts, the Jura went viral.

It's difficult to pinpoint exactly what triggered it, but in retrospect, the region's rapid turnaround signaled a pivotal moment in the development of public taste. At the height of the wider pushback against generic international winemaking, the narrative that grew up around the Jura described a last bastion of untouched, unadulterated winemaking, the perfect antidote to the encroaching march of modernity.

It wouldn't be long before the media latched on to the trend, anointing the region as the latest sommelier "secret handshake." Within the span of a decade, a windfall of small-production Jura wines entered the market, imported by boutique companies specializing in natural and organic bottlings, and the rest is history.

Fast-forward to the present and the Jura remains at the industry's cutting edge. But if all of this sounds a bit too weird or obscure, don't worry. It's not necessary to "Columbus" the Jura in order to appreciate it.

Despite the fashionable spotlight that remains fixed on it, the Jura has always been a modest and traditionally minded farming culture. The wines that continue to attract attention today are essentially the same as those produced long before Jura began popping up in wine bars in Brooklyn and Portland. It's this timeless quality, rather than any kind of flash-in-the-pan trendiness, that has given the Jura true staying power.

A DEEPER DIVE INTO THE STYLES AND GRAPES

The Jura's catalog of idiosyncrasies runs deep, but high up on that list is the fact that its reds are typically lighter and fresher than its whites. Over the course of a meal, it's common practice to start off with red and gradually progress toward the region's richer, more structured whites, so we'll proceed accordingly here.

The palest, most delicate of the Jura's reds is poulsard (also known locally as ploussard), a thin-skinned variety that typically drinks more like a darker-hued rosé than any typical *vin rouge*. Fittingly, the grape has acquired a cult following in nerdy sommelier circles, prescribed as a corrective to the standard glut of heavy, overextracted reds. Be sure to drink it with a slight chill to highlight its essence of tart cranberry and mineral freshness.

With its proximity to Burgundy and its similar mix of marl and limestone soils, the region fares exceptionally well with pinot noir. The best Jura pinot possess the same classic combo of sappy fruit and earth that charms the hell out of Burgundy lovers, but the greater interest lies in the Jura's second native red, trousseau. High-toned, perfumed, and floral, it gives a bit more heft and earthiness, as well as an irresistible pine-needle herbaceous quality.

As distinctive as Jura reds may be, there's no denying that its complex, profoundly savory whites are the main attraction. To do them justice, however, let's back up a bit, as the Jura's white-wine-making traditions exist in their own anomalous bubble.

On the indigenous side, the area's star is the hearty savagnin grape. Like chenin blanc, it's one of those rich, texturally dense varieties that somehow manages to retain an electric spine of acidity even at high levels of ripeness. This ability serves it extremely well when it comes to the Jura's traditionally oxidative style of winemaking, in which the wine is matured, like sherry, under a thin *voile* (veil) of yeast.

Although applied (with varying degrees of intensity) to a wide range of Jura whites, the most extreme example of the practice is the area's celebrated *vin jaune*, or "yellow wine," which spends a minimum of six years in barrel. During that time, the wine soaks up a piercingly pungent, umami-rich complexity (think walnuts, lemon curd, sea salt, and freshly baked bread).

These hyper-rustic *sous-voile* whites aren't for the faint of heart. In fact, they're about as unusual as wine gets. But with the right foods (hard cheeses, for example, like the local Comté, or roast pork or poultry), they can be sublime, a world apart from most anything you've tried before.

This fringe factor is what first inducted the Jura into the wine-geek hall of fame. Considerably less attention, however, has been paid to the region's more recent push toward more conventional, nonoxidative whites.

Do they lack the obvious cool factor of their oxidative counterparts? Maybe. But these *ouillé*, or "topped up," wines (referred to as such because the wine gets filled to the top of the barrel, leaving less room for oxygen) compensate with vibrancy, tension, and, according to many, greater sensitivity to terroir.

That's particularly true of the results the style gets with chardonnay. In place of the usual tangy, briny imprint of the old-school *sous-voile* approach, more of the grape's underlying fruit flavors (crunchy green apple, pear skin, citrus) are noticeable, and, as in Burgundy, you can pick apart the subtleties of the Jura's diverse mix of clay and limestone soils. At their best, *ouillé* Jura chardonnays attain the same heights of elegance and mineral purity as the famous examples made by their neighbors to the west.

Rather than compete with each other, these two white wine paradigms represent different but complementary lenses for understanding the Jura. Many of the region's top producers make both, and with good reason: no matter the style, they're among the most intriguing whites to be found in the market today.

Essential Producers: Bénédicte et Stéphane Tissot, Jean-François Ganevat, Domaine de Montbourgeau, Philippe Bornard, Domaine de la Tournelle, Michel Gahier, Domaine de La Pinte, Domaine des Marnes Blanches, Ratapoil (Raphaël Monnier), Domaine du Pélican, Julien Labet, Caves Jean Bourdy

THE WINE LIST

- **Domaine des Marnes Blanches Savagnin "Empreinte" ($$):** Displaying the nutty, saline tang that is the hallmark of *sous-voile* savagnin, this is a great place for Jura novices to develop a taste for the style. Drink this with roast chicken, cheese, or risotto.

- **Bénédicte et Stéphane Tissot Arbois "Les Bruyères" ($$):** All of Tissot's site-specific *ouillé* chardonnays transmit the underlying identity of their soils. His "Les Bruyères" is often the most focused of the bunch, balancing layers of orchard fruit and roasted hazelnut with a citric twist and a streak of chalky limestone.

- **Domaine de la Tournelle "Ploussard de Monteiller" ($$):** Pale crimson in the glass with bright acidity and a twang of red currant, Domaine de la Tournelle's textbook poulsard (or ploussard, as it is referred to on the label) offers an object lesson in evolving taste. Delicate reds such as this would have once raised eyebrows; now they're all the rage.

- **Michel Gahier Trousseau "Grands Vergers" ($$):** Michel Gahier's top trousseau, from a parcel of eighty-year-old organically farmed vines in the village of Montigny-lès-Arsures, highlights the grape's resinous aspect (imagine pine sap, but in a good way), with a redfruited depth that is the hallmark of his style.

- **Domaine de Montbourgeau L'Étoile Vin Jaune ($$$):** Domaine de Montbourgeau's full range of Jura wines consistently overperforms, but its talent for the *sous-voile* style reaches an apotheosis with its powerfully pungent, nutty *vin jaune*. Made from late-harvest savagnin, its version is defined by its unusual elegance (relative to other examples, that is), but it has the structure to age indefinitely.

SAVOIE

·················

JUST THE HIGHLIGHTS

◆ **Savoie is France's "mountain wine" region.** Tucked away in the shadows of Mont Blanc, the area's slopes have historically been better known for skiing than for wine. But the brilliant bottles coming out of Savoie today are nothing like the simple quaffing wines of days gone by.

◆ **The region is finally stepping into the spotlight.** After existing for decades as an afterthought, viewed as little more than an alpine extension of the neighboring Jura, Savoie is now fine-tuning its identity and demanding to be taken on its own terms.

◆ **The deeply flavored yet bracing whites of Savoie are perfect emblems of contemporary taste.** Whether made from the floral jacquère grape, the nutty altesse, or the increasingly cult gringet, the area's wines walk a tightrope between textural depth and piercing freshness.

◆ **Savoie reds display the same high-elevation purity.** Nervy, floral, and often a little bit smoky, the region's leading red grape, mondeuse, reveals its genetic kinship with syrah, but with an added sense of alpine weightlessness.

It has only been since the mid-2010s that anyone considered the snow-capped peaks of Savoie a place for compelling wine. Before then, no one really thought about the wines of Savoie at all, unless they happened to encounter them in their native environment, the ski chalets of the French Alps, where mediocre specimens of the local whites traditionally lubricated the throats of thirsty tourists after a long day on the slopes.

Even today, when discussed in wine books and reference guides, Savoie tends to get lumped in with the neighboring Jura to form the hyphen-ated Jura-Savoie, an ill-fitting hybrid designation (like Languedoc and Roussillon; see page 108) that only highlights Savoie's footnote status. Given the modern rise of the Jura to beloved sommelier sensation, you'd think Savoie might have benefited from some of that reflected glory. But on just about every level—cultural, climatic, stylistic—the regions have almost nothing in common, and if anything, the industry spotlight on the Jura has, rather than rub off on Savoie, only exaggerated the inequities between them.

As the Jura went on to colonize wine lists across the United States, boosted by a surge of interest from boutique importers, Savoie contin-ued to be represented stateside by standard-issue inexpensive whites that offered little more than simple refreshment. In fact, it's safe to assume that Savoie would have faded entirely into the background if it weren't for a handful of daring Savoyard producers who made it their mission to reveal the region for what it truly is: France's singular con-tribution to the greater "mountain wine" family.

For such a small region, Savoie makes an impressively diverse range of expressions, from crisp, aromatic whites and fuller, nuttier examples to top-notch sparklers and even a smattering of highly intriguing reds. The through line tying them together is the same crystalline purity that unites all of Europe's alpine growing areas. As it turns out, that clarity is exactly what people want from their wine these days.

THE GRAPES AND STYLES OF SAVOIE

Although it shares a common grape or two with Switzerland (notably chasselas), and others with the nearby northern Rhône (marsanne and roussanne also call Savoie home), the area's trove of odd indigenous varieties has generated the widest interest. For whites, there's the fresh and vibrant jacquère and the fleshier, nuttier altesse (aka roussette), whereas the area's major red is mondeuse, a light-bodied yet grippy red that is related to syrah. It reveals a lot about our contemporary drinking habits, however, that the grape that has attracted the greatest share of industry admiration is also Savoie's rarest and most obscure: the utterly niche gringet.

The improbable wave of fanfare that now surrounds this formerly unknown grape is the result of a single producer, Dominique Belluard of Domaine Belluard in the tiny town of Ayse, who has obsessively dedicated himself to revealing the potential of gringet for world-class whites.

All of his efforts with the variety achieve an almost impossible balance between richness, ripe orchard fruit (often with a suggestion of gingery spice), and electrifying acidity. These include his sparkling "Mont Blanc Brut Zéro," which first won him viral acclaim, and two still versions of the grape, the floral yet textured "Les Alpes," grown on yellow marl at elevations of nearly fifteen hundred feet, and his highly coveted single-vineyard "Le Feu," an ode to the complexity of his oldest vines.

Belluard now enjoys the kind of cult status reserved for a handful of anointed producers, making his wines increasingly difficult to track down in the wild. But he's just one of several winemakers who are reinterpreting Savoie through a more expansive paradigm.

The jacquère grape, for example, is generally known for pleasantly crisp, aperitif-styled whites that don't require a whole lot of contemplation. In the hands of serious growers, like Gilles Berlioz, Jean-François Quénard, or Denis and Didier Berthollier, all located in the village of Chignin (just south of Chambéry, where the most famous vermouths of France are made), the humble grape is transformed into something far more conse-quential. The best—for instance, Quénard's "Anne de la Biguerne" from a single parcel of sixty-five-year-old jacquère vines—possess a mineral depth and cut reminiscent of top lees-aged Muscadet.

If jacquère brings to mind mountain Muscadet, the late-ripening altesse grape—richer, structured, and sometimes lightly honeyed—is closer to chenin blanc. Rising star Maxime Dancoine of Domaine de l'Aitonnement makes one of the most riveting versions. Called "Solar," it's harvested slightly earlier than normal to avoid the flabbiness that occasionally afflicts other examples of the variety, delivering a bright jolt of acidity to balance its honeyed depth.

Finally, Savoie's reds, which boast an undeniable rustic charm, hold plenty of interest as well. In particular, mondeuse has gained a foothold on wine lists as a sort of high-elevation analogue to syrah, exhibiting a similar savory, floral character in a leaner, high-acid frame. You'll also find grapes such as persan, a finicky native that yields structured, deeply colored reds, and gamay, which in Savoie acquires a distinctly alpine clarity of focus.

Essential Producers: Domaine des Ardoisières, Domaine Belluard, Domaine des 13 Lunes, Domaine Louis Magnin, Domaine Dupasquier, Jacques Maillet, Domaine de l'Aitonnement, Domaine Labbé, Denis et Didier Berthollier, Jean-Yves Péron, Franck Peillot, Charles Gonnet

THE WINE LIST

◆ **Domaine Dupasquier Vin de Savoie Jacquère ($):** As old-school as they come, David Dupasquier's "Marastel," based off of old-vine, late-harvest altesse, is widely viewed as the estate's showstopper, but his basic jacquère can't be beat for an intro to Savoie's more serious side. This goes down easy, with its pale-straw color, lemony tang, and glacial freshness, but there's plenty of nonfruit complexity (wet stones, white almond, meadow flowers) and a yeasty savoriness that elevates it above the status quo.

- **Domaine Belluard Vin de Savoie "Les Alpes" ($$):** Few wines manage to pull off the balancing act between mouth-coating viscosity and chiseled precision that Dominique Belluard achieves here. His "Les Alpes"—the more affordable and widely available of his two gringets–is a tour de force of mountain air, chalky minerals, and quince and yellow plum, with that telltale ginger spice that defines his interpretation of the grape.

- **Domaine de l'Aitonnement "Solar" ($$):** This isn't the most representative take on the altesse grape (for more traditional, slightly fuller-bodied versions look for Domaine Dupasquier or Franck Peillot), but Maxime Dancoine's "Solar"—all white flowers and chalky acidity—is without question one of Savoie's most original wines. To be sure, there's ample richness (the product of those old vines), but also that same Belluard-like sense of weightless intensity that is the hallmark of Savoie's new class.

- **Domaine des Ardoisières "Argile" Rouge ($$):** Brice Omont, the talent behind Ardoisières' stunning range of Savoie wines, bottles his entry-level wines under the "Argile" label. The white version—a blend of jacquère, chardonnay, and the rare mondeuse blanche from incredibly steep slopes—is equally compelling, but the rouge displays the crunchy red fruits and shimmering purity that have brought renewed attention to Savoie reds.

- **Franck Peillot Bugey Mondeuse ($):** Other, "cultier" mondeuse bottlings might turn more sommelier heads, but year in, year out, Franck Peillot, located in the village of Bugey, supplies one of the most reliable and representative versions of the grape. Always peppery, savory, and pleasantly rustic, this is archetypal mondeuse, the sort of approachable, everyday red that still gives you plenty to think about.

ALSACE

· · · · · · · · · · · · · · · ·

JUST THE HIGHLIGHTS

◆ **Alsace is France's misunderstood classic.** Once a global benchmark for white wine greatness, the region's rich, opulent *vins blancs* tend to be overlooked by modern drinkers who are accustomed to leaner, brighter styles.

◆ **The area's wines owe as much to Germany as to France.** Traded back and forth between two nations for much of its history, Alsace's wine culture borrows from both traditions. For instance, its main grapes include riesling and gewürztraminer, and it's the only French region to adopt the German custom of labeling its wines by variety.

◆ **Alsatian wines aren't (at least, not usually) sweet.** These days, Alsace typically drinks dry unless specifically advertised to the contrary. Sugary, late-harvest wines can be identified with the labels *vendanges tardives* or *sélection de grains nobles*.

◆ **Alsatian wines are the quintessential "winter" whites.** In their native land, they're paired with cream sauces and rich, hearty pork and poultry dishes and foie gras; this is the context in which Alsatian whites truly shine.

Oh, Alsace. Poor, puzzling Alsace. Of all the classic French wine regions (and if anything, Alsace is a true classic), it's the perennial underdog.

But that wasn't always the case. Throughout history, the region's fleshy, aromatic whites have represented a rare standard bearer of greatness, beloved by drinkers the world over for their complexity and ability to age.

Today, Alsace seems to check off the right boxes for carrying that acclaim into the twenty-first century. With its treasure trove of different soil types and microclimates, the region is a terroir junkie's dream come true. It also boasts France's highest percentage of organic and biodynamic wineries, and an enviable arsenal of winemaking talent, including established family firms, like Trimbach and Hugel, as well as a thriving minimal-intervention crowd.

Yet even with all of this working in its favor, Alsace is often out of mind for most consumers these days. That's a major opportunity missed—and not just out of a sense of duty to the region's important place in wine history. In addition to being culturally central, the wines of Alsace also happen to be extremely delicious. So, what gives?

THE ALSACE IMAGE PROBLEM

Some have called it an image problem, and others, an identity crisis. But no matter the nomenclature, the fact remains: Alsace refuses to fit into any of the neat little boxes we use to classify wine.

Most obviously, there's the region's bicultural heritage. Nestled between the Vosges Mountains and the winding Rhine, which marks the German border, Alsace's wine culture owes as much to Germany as it does to France, having spent much of its history tugged back and forth between the two.

The area's Teutonic influence manifests on a number of fronts, including a devotion (unique among French regions) to producing single-varietal wines (that is, labeled by grape name, in typical German fashion) as well as those varieties themselves. Here, French examples such as pinot gris and pinot blanc share turf with typically German grapes, like riesling, gewürztraminer, and sylvaner.

Like Germany, Alsace has also struggled with the stigma of sugar. Although most back labels now feature a "sweetness index" to clear up any uncertainty, for years it was anyone's guess whether a bottle of Alsace would yield a bone-dry wine or one with a hint (or more) of residual sugar; not the best policy for building a clear, consumer-friendly identity.

These challenges, however, only partially account for the region's issues. The biggest problem it faces today is one of shifting taste. Once rivaled only by Burgundy and Germany for white wine preeminence, Alsace now faces increasingly stiff competition. Alongside the latest crop of crisp, mineral, Zeitgeisty whites (from Galicia, Sicily, or Santorini, to name just a few), Alsace's signature opulence risks reading a bit fusty or outdated—as if belonging to an earlier age.

And yet this refusal to fall in line with changing fashion is precisely why Alsace will always have its loyal defenders. After all, the classics are classic for a reason—even neglected classics, like Alsace.

ALSACE IS THE IDEAL COLD-WEATHER WHITE

The arguments for loving Alsace are many. But given the usual roster of wines that make up our standard playbook today, they might not always be obvious. Think about it: We all know our way around a bottle of easygoing pinot grigio. But the honeyed depth of a lush, full-bodied pinot gris? That's far less familiar territory.

This lack of context makes it easy to ignore just how useful Alsace's dense, aromatic whites can be. Not only is there a place for wines like that, but they're also able to perform in ways that few others could ever pull off. Specifically, with its palate-coating complexity and aromatic intensity, Alsace is the quintessential cold-weather white.

Not that its appeal is strictly seasonal; the region can do fresh and zippy, too. But when the air gets crisp and we start to crave butter and fat and all the usual autumnal tastes and smells (root vegetables, cream sauces, roast poultry and pork), Alsace is truly in its element. Just consider the staples of the region's notoriously caloric cuisine. This is the land of foie gras and Munster cheese, of choucroute garnie (essentially, a heaping plate of sauerkraut laden with pork and sausage) and creamy, bacon-y *Flàmmeküeche* (or, to the rest of France, *tarte flambée*). For hearty dishes like these, you need an equally substantial white, one that can hold up to all those rich, robust flavors. All of a sudden, that sumptuous pinot gris or spicy gewürztraminer doesn't sound so bad.

THE STYLES OF ALSACE WINE

Because Alsace is the only French region to label its wines primarily by grape name rather than grape-growing region, the clearest entry into its spectrum of styles is through the prism of variety.

The region has always distinguished between the so-called noble grapes—riesling, pinot gris, gewürztraminer, and muscat—and the "common" varieties, like sylvaner, chasselas, and pinot blanc. Following this logic, only wines produced from the former qualify to bear the names of Alsace's fifty-one grand cru vineyards (that said, many producers choose to ignore the area's highly controversial classification system, which was only introduced a few decades ago).

In Alsace, it's customary for wineries to produce several different versions of each grape. Typically, that breaks down to a fresh, drinkable entry-level wine, followed by any number of higher-end reserve bottlings (labeled with a specific vineyard site, if applicable), and finally, the decadently sweet *vendanges tardives*, or late-harvest expressions.

RIESLING

The noblest of Alsace's noble grapes, riesling is responsible for many of its greatest wines. If you're expecting the crystalline transparency of the German versions, however, think again. Broader, riper, and more muscular than its counterparts across the Rhine, Alsatian riesling represents another classic paradigm for the grape. Bone-dry, tightly coiled, and loaded with steely minerality, the top examples can age for decades.

PINOT GRIS

Although technically the same grape, that's where the similarities between mass-market pinot grigio and Alsatian pinot gris end. One is typically cheap, watery, and made in bulk (the wine equivalent of Top 40 radio), while the other is structured, multifaceted, and profound (let's go with something like Mahler's Fifth). Gold in color, with flavors of baked apple and pear and often a smoky, mushroomy earthiness, pinot gris is what Alsatians traditionally serve with savory meat dishes in lieu of red wine. While you can expect most examples to drink dry (or at least dryish), it's not uncommon for pinot gris to reveal a touch of sweetness. When in doubt, consult your sommelier or friendly neighborhood wine merchant.

GEWÜRZTRAMINER

Is there a wine more polarizing than Alsatian gewürztraminer? At its best, it tastes more like some kind of ambrosial nectar than anything you could ever hope to squeeze out of a grape. This is white wine at its most aromatically extroverted, all rose petals and cardamom and clove (*Gewürz* means "spice," and you'll quickly smell why), with a veritable luau's worth of tropical flavors (think lychee, grapefruit, pineapple, and more lychee). The standard line of advice is to pair gewürztraminer with spicy Asian fare, but cheese (the stinkier and runnier, the better) is definitely the way to go.

MUSCAT

The region's quirkiest grape, muscat from Alsace is almost always produced in a dry style that emphasizes freshness and drinkability. Fragrant, grapey, and floral, it makes for a killer aperitif but rarely delivers the gravitas of its fellow noble varieties. Still, there are exceptions, such as Zind-Humbrecht's racy muscat from the grand cru "Goldert."

THE OTHERS

The noble grapes occupy the region's prime real estate and factor into its best wines, but don't neglect the common folk. Dry, herbal sylvaner, in particular, offers excellent value; so, too, does pinot blanc, the quintessential crowd-pleaser, which is unmatched in its versatility at the table. These are the honest, everyday wines that Alsatians have been drinking for centuries. Try them on their own, or keep an eye out for Edelzwicker, the traditional Alsatian blend that is currently experiencing a mini-renaissance.

CRÉMANT D'ALSACE

Some of the best bargains to be found in the world of sparkling wine come from Alsace. Produced in the traditional method of secondary fermentation in bottle (that is, the same technique used in Champagne), Crémant d'Alsace delivers a whole lot of fizz for a fraction of the price (most can be had for $20 or so).

Essential Producers: Domaine Bechtold, Domaine Christian Binner, Domaine Barmès-Beucher, Albert Mann, Dirler-Cadé, Meyer-Fonné, Albert Boxler, Domaine Pfister, Domaine Ostertag, Valentin Zusslin, Domaine Marcel Deiss, Josmeyer, Hugel, Trimbach, Kuentz-Bas, Laurent Barth, Schofitt, Zind-Humbrecht, Domaine Weinbach

THE WINE LIST

- ◆ **Valentin Zusslin Crémant d'Alsace Brut Zéro ($$):** The brother-and-sister team of Jean-Paul and Marie Zusslin have made waves for their range of wines, but their no-*dosage* biodynamic sparkler has been singled out for its leanness and raw sense of purity. Bottled without sulfur, its yellow apple fruit gives way to a cleansing froth of acidity.

- **Albert Boxler Edelzwicker Reserve ($$):** Edelzwicker, the traditional Alsatian field blend of native grapes, has lately been making a comeback. If you're familiar with his excellent higher-end wines, it's no surprise that Boxler's is among the very best. The varieties change from vintage to vintage but the wine is always lively and floral, with a surprising weight.

- **Laurent Barth Alsace Pinot Gris ($):** Although technically slightly off dry, Barth's pinot gris epitomizes the kind of balance that only Alsatian whites can manage. It doesn't taste sweet so much as ripe, reminiscent of orange skins and baked pear, with mouthwatering acidity that calls out for rich or even spicy cuisine.

- **Domaine Bechtold Gewürztraminer "Silberberg" ($):** Gewürztraminer is the definitive love it or hate it grape, but even the variety's most ardent haters will find something to love in this example from the Silberberg vineyard, near the village of Dahlenheim. You get the usual tropical fruit (lychee, guava, lime), but with an elegance and precision rarely found in conventional versions.

- **Domaine Ostertag Riesling "Fronholz" ($$):** Ever since the 1990s, André Ostertag has been quietly making some of Alsace's purest and most transparent wines. That unadorned vibrancy comes across most clearly in his rieslings, which carefully avoid the stylistic excesses to which that grape is sometimes subjected in the region. From thirty-year-old biodynamically farmed vines near the village of Epfig, his "Fronholz" is all about honeysuckle, white peach, and a stony minerality.

LANGUEDOC AND ROUSSILLON

························

JUST THE HIGHLIGHTS

◆ Once the country's main bulk supplier, the Languedoc and Roussillon region are only now discovering their potential for quality. This has made them something of a magnet for younger winemakers attracted to cheap land, old vines, and the freedom to experiment.

◆ The Languedoc and Roussillon are places for value. Compared to more established regions, like the Rhône, their wild, brambly reds (made from many of the same classic southern French grapes) rank among the country's best bargains.

◆ The Roussillon area, located just over the border with Spain, is becoming a hotbed of experimentation. Historically lumped together with the Languedoc, the area's wines are acquiring an identity of their own, particularly the whites. Made from southerly grapes, like grenache blanc, macabeo (macabeu in the Catalan dialect), and rolle (French for vermentino), they're salty, vivid, and vibrantly mineral.

Every country has its version of the workhorse wine region. It may not be glamorous, but it isn't supposed to be. What it's supposed to do is crank out as much wine as possible as quickly as possible and then launch it into the market.

In France, that duty has always fallen upon the vast, southerly regions of the Languedoc and Roussillon. Historically lumped together (although that's starting to change), the two areas collectively encompass a vast tract of vines that unfurls across the country's Mediterranean coast from the eastern edge of Provence to the Spanish border.

Until 2016, the Languedoc and Roussillon were linked by a hyphen to form the administrative region of Languedoc-Roussillon, which is what most drinkers still call it. Its official name is now Occitanie, but don't call it that unless you're looking to utterly confuse your sommelier.

However you refer to it, the area is France's largest wine region in both size and volume, responsible for roughly a quarter of the country's annual output. If you've ever found yourself in the wine section of a French supermarket staring down bottle after bottle of €4 *vin rouge*, you're already familiar with the fate of much of this wine. But not of all of it. Long branded as the great southern French "wine lake," the area has morphed from a bulk wine wasteland into—well, to be honest, it's still in the process of figuring that out.

This is the part of the story where we arrive at the radical shift from quantity to quality (to adopt a popular refrain) that has disrupted the Languedoc's high-volume status quo. If that plotline sounds familiar— "industrial-scale region undergoes artisanal renaissance, now makes awesome under-the-radar wine"—we largely have the Languedoc to thank for that.

Today, the region has reimagined itself as something like France's Wild West, a final frontier whose full potential hasn't yet been discovered. It's no coincidence that in so many of these resurrection stories (the Languedoc's included), the big turnaround coincides with the early stirrings of a natural wine revolution. The promise of cheap vineyard land has lured a new generation of producers to the area, many of them well versed in the low-maintenance school of winemaking, who are busy converting its scattered, ancient plots of vines to organics after decades of industrial neglect.

At the same time, they've been joined by a fair share of famous names from Burgundy and Bordeaux (Vosne-Romanée's iconic Anne Gros, for example, arrived in the village of Minervois in 2008), who see in it a fresh horizon to explore without feeling as encumbered by the weight of tradition. Along with a handful of old stalwarts (such as Mas de Daumas Gassac, a longtime beacon of quality), these producers have taken it upon themselves to discover what the area's native grapes and diverse terroirs are capable of beyond the usual bottom-shelf stereotypes.

So far, the results are among the most exciting and (more to the point) value driven that France has to offer: vivid, earthy, unabashedly Mediterranean reds (and whites and rosés too) that embody the image of France's new south.

THE VILLAGES OF THE LANGUEDOC AND ROUSSILLON

Most of the wine produced in the region in the past was simply labeled as *vin de France*, the lowliest designation in the French classification system. But a handful of specific villages always enjoyed a local reputation for superior quality: Corbières, Minervois, Saint-Chinian, and Faugères. Because these areas remain relatively under the radar, they offer a treasure trove of bargains. The common theme running through them all is a focus on rustic, earthy blends of the classic southern French varieties, which wear their bold Mediterranean flavors with pride.

For reds, which dominate production, that means grenache, syrah, mourvèdre, cinsault, and particularly old-vine carignan, a local specialty. As a whole, they deliver all the vivid fruit, mineral savoriness, and herbal underbrushy flavors (thyme, rosemary, oregano) we associate with the

Rhône and Provence at a fraction of the price. The whites, made from any number of local grapes, such as roussanne, marsanne, rolle, clairette blanche, and grenache blanc, can be equally compelling but generally more challenging to find.

As the entire region matures, the Roussillon—lying just across the border with Spain and still bearing a strong Catalan influence—is quickly establishing its own identity separate from the Languedoc. That process has centered, in part, upon the area of Banyuls, historically famous for its sweet fortified *vin doux naturel*. As interest in the style has dimmed over recent years, the area's producers have been turning to the production of dry, mineral wines of undeniable power yet disarming freshness.

Bottled under the place-name of Collioure, or often just the generic Côtes Catalanes designation, the reds feel even wilder and somehow more quintessentially *southern* than their Languedoc cousins. But it's the Roussillon's piercingly vibrant whites that arguably show the greatest promise, sharing some of the same grapes (like macabeo) that have been turning heads on the Spanish side of Catalonia.

Essential Producers: Domaine Rimbert, Maxime Magnon, Domaine Leon Barral, Mas Jullien, Mas Cal Demoura, Mas de Daumas Gassac, Domaine des Amiel, Domaine Gauby, Clos Fantine, Domaine des 2 Ânes, Cyril Fhal (Clos du Rouge Gorge), Domaine Matassa, Domaine des Enfants, Domaine de Majas, Domaine de l'Horizon, La Cave des Nomades

THE WINE LIST

◆ **Domaine Leon Barral Faugères ($$):** A standard bearer not just for his native area of Faugères but for the Languedoc as a whole, Didier Barral has emerged as one of the region's living legends through the careful stewardship of his land and his unobtrusive work in the cellar. In his surprisingly fresh entry-level red, he highlights the untamed earthiness of old-vine carignan, which comprises half of the blend.

- Maxime Magnon Corbières "La Démarrante" ($$): Magnon's apprenticeship under Beaujolais icon Jean Foillard comes across in his approach to the various plots of scraggly vines he farms across the area of Corbières. As with his full range of wines, his "La Démarrante"—a wild, juicy blend of carignan, grenache, and syrah—bears the telltale signs of carbonic maceration (see page 9), but never to the point that the technique overtakes its powerfully southern sense of place.

- Domaine Rimbert Saint-Chinian "Le Mas au Schiste" ($): One of the region's most gifted winemakers and an avid advocate of old-vine carignan, Jean-Marie Rimbert deserves more attention for his linear, mineral-driven interpretations of Saint-Chinian dirt. A play on words, the name of his flagship blend references the *schiste* (schist) soils of his steepest parcels while acknowledging the punishing (that is, masochistic) task of farming them.

- Domaine Gauby "Vieilles Vignes" Vin de Pays Côtes Catalanes Blanc ($$): You'd think it would be impossible to achieve this level of high-acid tension out of grapes planted in such a southerly clime, but Gérard Gauby practically invented the mouthwateringly mineral style that defines the new wave of Roussillon whites. The "Vieilles Vignes" in question refer to a mix of mostly macabeo and two types of grenache (blanc and gris) farmed organically in the village of Calce.

- Domaine de Majas Vin de Pays Côtes Catalanes Blanc ($): A case study in the Roussillon's modern evolution, Domaine de Majas's Alain Carrère went from bulk selling of his wines to a major supermarket chain to farming organically, ditching commercial yeasts, and crafting some of the region's standout expressions. A blend of equal parts macabeo and rolle with 10 percent carignan blanc, his basic white delivers a whole lot of Roussillon freshness at a mercifully low price point.

PROVENCE

JUST THE HIGHLIGHTS

◆ **Provence is the rosé capital of France.** The delicate, pale salmon–hued style of pink wine it developed has become the global benchmark, fueling what is now a multimillion-dollar industry.

◆ **Not all Provençal rosé is created equal.** The recent rosé boom has led to a scourge of cheap, watery versions that exist only to capitalize on the trend, making the good ones harder and harder to track down.

◆ **"Real" rosé de Provence has a historic home base.** The seaside village of Bandol is just one time-honored source of serious, terroir-driven pink wine, and still produces many of the best examples. It's also where you'll find the greatest Provence reds, based off the rustic mourvèdre grape.

◆ **Provence isn't all about rosé.** In fact, some the region's most interesting wines aren't rosé at all, though they've been overshadowed amid the pink wine hysteria.

Unless you've been living in a monastery or recently woke up from a coma, you will have noticed that rosé is having a moment. More than just a moment, really—sales have skyrocketed for multiple years in a row, with no end in sight. So it's hard to believe that, not so long ago, rosé was synonymous with sweet, low-budget blush wine. For decades, no amount of convincing from the press or the trade could persuade skeptical drinkers to give the category a chance.

Somewhere along the way, however, rosé didn't just shed that lowbrow stigma; it became oddly, improbably hip. By now, it has practically grown into its own aspirational lifestyle brand. From May to September, our Instagram feeds are awash in pink, resulting in any number of trendy hashtags (#yeswayrosé, #roséallday, and so on). Brad Pitt and Angelina Jolie have their own French rosé brand, Château Miraval. Jon Bon Jovi has one too.

At the center of the current rosé craze is the style's most emblematic expression: *rosé de Provence*. Of all the world's diverse rosé traditions, the textbook Provençal version—with its pale onion-skin hue, rainwater freshness, and zippy flavors of grapefruit and white peach—represents the platonic ideal, indelibly linked to summer in the South of France. It's no wonder we've been downing so much of the stuff. One of the wine world's original simple pleasures; it's versatile with all kinds of food, Mediterranean or otherwise, and represents a staple of the area's highly mythologized local cuisine.

But the category's triumphant success story is not without its dark underbelly. To us, rosé might conjure the glamor of "spending the season" in Cap d'Antibes or Saint-Tropez. In Provence, however, rosé means big business, and the frenzied rush to churn out as much of it as quickly as possible has generated some less-than-desirable results.

For one, a rash of generic, mass-produced rosé has infected the market that banks on it being drunk so cold that nobody can tell the difference. But what's more, rosé has historically been just one of many wines that call Provence home. The style's meteoric rise, however, has all but obscured the full spectrum of wines the region has to offer, its rich, spicy reds and elegant whites drowned out in an endless sea of pink.

None of this, for the record, has diminished the many reasons to love Provençal wine (and yes, that includes its popular rosés). To the contrary, the situation has only made it all the more necessary to champion the real Provence—which, thankfully, still survives despite the ongoing pink wine hysteria.

THE OTHER PROVENCE: A DRINKER'S GUIDE

Where there's rosé, there is always red wine. So it's no coincidence that Provence's rosé wine capital, the picturesque coastal town of Bandol, also produces many of its most compelling reds; the two go hand in hand.

Showcasing the wild, herbal intensity of the mourvèdre grape, Bandol's reds are notoriously rugged and long-lived, their ripe, sunny fruit tempered by a brooding earthiness and brambly spice. Once the area's main attraction, they're just the sort of rustic yet elegant country wines that deserve a second look. Home to a trio of iconic producers—Château Pradeaux, Château de Pibarnon, and, most famous of all, Domaine Tempier—Bandol also specializes in an equally complex and age-worthy (yes, you read that correctly) style of rosé, designed to complement food.

Over the years, these three most prestigious examples have steadily crept up in price—none more so than Tempier's rosé, which, at $50 per bottle, is now an allocated sommelier trophy. Ditto the revered rosé from Château Simone, a small cult property in the tiny area of Palette that makes what many consider to be the region's greatest rosé (plus a wonderfully complex white and one of Provence's classic reds). On the other hand, compared to the latest parade of mindless luxury rosés packaged in sleek, curvy bottles (to distract, no doubt, from the mediocrity within), these classics represent money well spent. Besides, they're not the only ones demonstrating rosé's serious side.

Across Provence, producers are making distinctive pink wines with a legit sense of place. That includes lesser-known Bandol estates, like Domaine de la Tour du Bon, Domaine de Terrebrune, and Domaine du Gros' Noré, as well as outliers such as Clos Cibonne in the village of Le Pradet. There, the current generation follows the same rosé regimen put into place more than a century ago, naturally fermenting and aging its savory, structured rosés in large, old casks. While you could easily drink any of these wines by the pool (after all, serious doesn't mean stuffy, especially when it comes to Provence), they're truly meant for the dinner table—preferably alfresco on a warm evening surrounded by friends.

But that raises another important topical issue. If the best *rosé de Provence* transcends the typical "summer water" stereotype, it follows that the style can (and *should*) be enjoyed year-round. The category's supposed Labor Day expiration date makes even less sense when you consider that many top expressions benefit from a little time in bottle, truly hitting their stride around Thanksgiving. (To that end, cue the turkey, because rosé's incredible versatility hits all the flavors on the holiday spectrum, including the elusive cranberry sauce pairing.)

Essential Producers: Clos Cibonne, Château Simone, Domaine Tempier, Clos Sainte-Magdeleine, Domaine de Terrebrune, Domaine de la Tour du Bon, Domaine du Gros' Noré, Domaine de Triennes, Sulauze, Domaine Hauvette, Château Pradeaux, Château de Pibarnon

THE WINE LIST

- **Domaine Tempier Bandol Rosé ($$$):** No single bottle is more emblematic of authentic Provence than Tempier's legendary Bandol rosé. Over the years, it has evolved into a fairly allocated cult wine (and has accordingly climbed in price), but it remains the archetypal expression of its kind and a reference point for pink wine's serious side.

- **Domaine de Triennes IGP Méditerranée Rosé ($):** Proof that it's possible to make quality rosé even at larger volumes, the Triennes project is a collaboration between Jeremy Seysses of Domaine Dujac and Aubert de Villaine of Domaine de la Romanée-Conti, two of Burgundy's most prestigious estates. Based on cinsault, their rosé is everything pink wine should be, with more depth than most at this price point.

- **Clos Sainte-Magdeleine Cassis Blanc ($$):** The sleepy little fishing village of Cassis exists as a refreshing oasis of nervy, floral whites within the wider sprawl of Provence's rosé boom. Here's the text-book version, an herbal, textured blend of the local marsanne, ugni blanc, clairette blanche, and bourboulenc grapes that proves Provence can be more than pretty in pink.

- **Château Pradeaux Bandol Rouge ($$):** The four-hundred-year-old Château Pradeaux estate remains a staunch defender of age-worthy, old-fashioned Provençal reds that showcase the raw, brooding power of the rustic mourvèdre grape. That tradition lives on in its flagship Bandol rouge, with its formidable tannic grip and its concentrated core of blackberry, crushed rock, and Provençal herbs.

ITALY

Defined, until recently, by just a few major regions (most notably Tuscany and Piedmont), Italy's centuries-old local wine traditions are now flourishing. Unlike in France, wine in Italy is produced in all corners of the country, and the astonishing renaissance of local winemaking that has spread across the nation has ushered new areas and signature grapes into the spotlight. Critically, Italian winemakers have finally seemed to grasp that the key to the future lies in mining the rich array of indigenous expressions and native styles that have existed for generations. If wine lovers of a certain ideological bent feared that globalization would stamp out these unique regional wines, then Italy's embrace and celebration of them shows that the way forward is a reexamination of the past.

PIEDMONT

JUST THE HIGHLIGHTS

- Piedmont is home to two of the world's greatest red wines. In terms of complexity, sophistication, and the capacity to age, Barolo and Barbaresco represent an apex of greatness seldom seen anywhere else on the planet.

- The key to Piedmont's prestige is the noble nebbiolo grape. When planted in the region's rolling hillside vineyards, nebbiolo attains a cool-climate purity and site sensitivity rivaled only by the greatest Burgundian pinot noirs.

- Barolo and Barbaresco are as age-worthy as red wines get. Capable of maturing in the cellar for decades, many of the region's top wines will outlive any of the competition, making vintage bottles a particular obsession among collectors.

- Piedmont also has its everyday side. Nobody can drink Barolo and Barbaresco all the time. Luckily, the area also specializes in an incredible array of humbler table wines made from indigenous grapes, like barbera, dolcetto, grignolino, and freisa.

It's difficult to describe the spiritual levels of devotion that the Piedmont region—or Piemonte, to sound like one of the initiated—inspires in the hearts and minds of Italian wine lovers the world over.

Tucked away in the fog-shrouded foothills of the Alps just a few hours' drive from France and Switzerland, this land of gastronomical bounty is every sybarite's dream come true. The realm of roasted hazelnuts and white truffles, of pungent robiola cheese, plump agnolotti, and some of the best beef money can buy (traditionally served *tagliata*-style, grilled and carved into thin, blood-rare slices), Piedmont also happens to be the birthplace of Barolo and Barbaresco, Italy's crowning achievements in the world of wine. Although it also produces a generous helping of delicious wines designed for everyday drinking, Piedmont's reputation indisputably rests on the legend of its two big Bs, located just fifteen miles from each other in the subregion of the Langhe. To call these wines essential would be a massive understatement; it's impossible to overstate how profoundly Barolo and Barbaresco figure into the current conversation about wine—not just as it relates to Italy but to the global scene as a whole.

To find their equal in cultural significance, you'd have to exit Italy altogether and cross the Alps into the sacred slopes of Burgundy, to which Piedmont is often compared. That's not by coincidence. Not only do the two areas share a common history—between the late eighteenth century and Italy's unification in 1861, both fell under the rule of the House of Savoy—they enjoy a philosophical kinship as well. Composed mostly of small artisanal producers who craft their wines on an intimate, site-sensitive scale, Piedmont has built its identity around a narrative that intrinsically mirrors our evolving notions of authenticity. If we define a wine's greatness not only in terms of "typicity" (that is, tasting correct, or "typical" of its category) but also according to the Burgundian model, as the singular expression of a single grape from a single plot of soil, then Barolo and Barbaresco fit that paradigm to a T.

NEBBIOLO: PIEDMONT'S SUPERSTAR GRAPE

In Piedmont's case, the noble variety in question is the thin-skinned, notoriously finicky nebbiolo. As a medium for expressing the nuances of site and place—including the identities of the area's celebrated single-vineyard crus—nebbiolo does the job every bit as well as pinot noir from Burgundy.

In fact, you could argue that nebbiolo is even more distinctive. Unlike pinot—a grape that crops up everywhere from California to New Zealand—nebbiolo struggles to thrive outside the narrow borders of its ancestral home. So while Burgundy has inspired a sea of imitators—many of which will do in a pinch—the fact remains that there's no viable alternative for scratching that specific nebbiolo itch.

It's this inimitable quality that ultimately puts Piedmont in a league of its own. When you're fortunate enough to be served a glass of perfumed, ruby-hued Barolo or Barbaresco, you can't mistake it for anything else: that deceptively pale color; those classic aromas of leather, tar, and rose petals; that pleasant bite of bitterness (think licorice, burnt orange peel, sour cherry) and the earthiness of wild mushrooms; that firm, mouth-puckering tannic grip that gives way to a paradoxical sense of weightless intensity—all of these attributes conjure only one majestic place.

Not that you should be keeping score, but another point in Piedmont's favor is its unrivaled capacity to age. Given their assertive (and at times, even aggressive) tannins and brisk acidity, Barolo and Barbaresco rank among the most cellar-worthy wines in existence. Bottles from the 1950s and 1960s have emerged as a special fetish among Italian wine collectors, fueling an obsessive niche market for vintage wines.

HOW ARE BAROLO AND BARBARESCO DIFFERENT?

Despite being next-door neighbors, noticeable stylistic differences exist between Barolo and Barbaresco. Due to its lower elevation and closer proximity to the Tanaro River east of the town of Alba, Barbaresco's climate tends to be slightly warmer than Barolo's. Since grapes ripen a bit earlier there, yielding wines with relatively lighter tannins and a softer core of fruit, the conventional wisdom characterizes Barbaresco as fresher, more delicate, and easier to drink young. Barolo, by contrast, represents a more brooding, structured incarnation of nebbiolo, marked by an almost austere intensity in its youth. Hence, the perennial industry cliché that typecasts Barbaresco as the "feminine" counterpart to "masculine" Barolo.

In addition to being outdated and lame, these gender-based stereotypes are misleading. While typically not as muscular or tightly coiled as Barolo, Barbaresco is anything but dainty. We're still talking about nebbiolo here, folks; both wines will almost always benefit from some extra time in bottle before popping the cork.

THE WAKE OF THE "BAROLO WARS"

Not everyone will prove receptive to the idea of acquiring a cellar full of young Barolo or Barbaresco only to set it aside like some sort of drinkable 401(k) plan. For most of the twentieth century, however, it was taken for granted that if you wanted to enjoy your nebbiolo, you had no choice but to wait. That's not because consumers were more patient back in the predigital age (although they probably were). Rather, it's due to the nature of the wines themselves.

Until thirty or forty years ago, most Langhe producers still followed the same old-school production methods that their grandparents employed. Fermentations took place naturally and without temperature control—which is to say, slowly—in giant Slavonian oak casks, or *botti*, in the cold of northern Italian cellars. Thanks to these long maceration times, the wine would extract massive amounts of tannin from the grape skins, necessitating additional aging—again in large casks—which often imparted a touch of oxidation.

As a result, the prevalent style of Langhe nebbiolo was pale brick in color, high in acid, and severely tannic, requiring decades of ageing—think twenty years or more—before it could be enjoyed. If all went well, the greatest vintages would eventually evolve into mature wines of lean and subtle elegance, such as those that brought worldwide acclaim to icons such as Bartolo Mascarello, Giuseppe Rinaldi, and Giacomo Conterno. On the other hand, all didn't always go well; even after dozens of years in bottle, a great many wines never managed to relinquish their impenetrable armor of tannins.

Such was the state of affairs until the late 1980s, when a rebellious group of Langhe producers banded together to update this historical style of nebbiolo, convinced of its dwindling relevance to a global wine culture that increasingly demanded instant gratification. Much has been made of the so-called Barolo Wars that raged during that period, which pitted defenders of "traditional" winemaking against the young guard of "modernists" who introduced a new set of practices to tame the region's fierce tannins and generate softer, fruitier wines that could be consumed upon release.

By speeding up the winemaking process via temperature-controlled fermentations and high-tech gadgets, like rotary fermenters, modernist pioneers such as Angelo Gaja, Elio Altare, and Domenico Clerico dramatically shortened maceration times. Even more controversially, they ditched the rough-hewn quality of the old Slavonian oak *botti* in favor of flashy French *barriques*. The resulting crop of inkier, jammier, earlier-maturing wines shared little in common with the Barolo and Barbaresco of the past, but quickly racked up critical accolades, setting the stage for a region-wide schism that still reverberates today.

To the elder generation, all of this represented a form of heresy—an insult to tradition and a crass concession to commercial taste that threatened to transform the region's wines beyond recognition. The modernists, on the other hand, countered that they were simply raising quality standards and adjusting to a changing international market.

Such was the state of affairs in the region for the past several decades. But as Piedmont enters the next chapter of its development, the battle lines of the past have begun to blur. If we once automatically grouped the wines into opposite ideological camps, that old polarity no longer applies. As popular taste increasingly returns to an old-world sense of restraint, the modernists have dialed back the flashy new oak and extraction. At the same time, traditionalists have borrowed some of the technological advances that launched the region into the twenty-first century, replacing outdated equipment, improving hygiene in the cellar, and exerting greater control over the winemaking process.

In order to navigate through the region's wines, it's still important to understand the historical context for "modern" and "traditional" styles of nebbiolo. But consumers today should view those terms as the poles on either extreme of a highly nuanced continuum. No matter which side of the ideological fence you happen to be sitting on, one thing's for sure: Piedmont has only benefited from this struggle. Across the board, the wines have never been better, deftly synthesizing centuries of tradition with a restless spirit of modern innovation.

THE LAY OF THE LAND: GEOGRAPHICAL DISTINCTIONS IN NEBBIOLO

Now that the style wars of the 1980s and 1990s have started to subside, we're free to focus on the next chapter of the region's development: the further delineation of its terroirs and microclimates.

Far from monolithic in nature, Barolo and Barbaresco are each composed of several different villages, or communes (*comuni*): three in Barbaresco (Barbaresco, Neive, and Treiso) and eleven in Barolo, the most famous of which are La Morra, Serralunga d'Alba, Monforte d'Alba, Barolo, and Castiglione Falletto. Further complicating the situation, each of these communes boasts an array of single vineyards, or crus—the Cannubi vineyard in the namesake village of Barolo, for instance, or Brunate in La Morra, to name just two—that have earned reputations of their own.

Producers in the Langhe have always been familiar with the specific stylistic personalities of the area's various zones. Historically, however, winemakers would assemble their Barolo and Barbaresco wines from several sites and subregions, strategically blending them to achieve a specific result. It wasn't until the 1970s that producers began to create the village- and vineyard-designated bottlings that we now consider Piedmont's most important wines.

This being Italy, keeping track of the Langhe's chaotic mix of place-names is no easy task. But all things considered, Barbaresco's geography is relatively straightforward (*relative* being the operative word). The most powerful wines come from Neive, the warmest commune. The cooler vineyards of Treiso, on the other hand, impart more elegance and refinement. Finally, the commune of Barbaresco (yes, one of Barbaresco's subzones is called Barbaresco; this is admittedly confusing) combines the best of both. Fittingly, it's here that you'll find the greatest concentration of iconic crus, such as Asili, Rabajà, Pajè, Roncaglie, Rio Sordo, and Montestefano.

Most of these prized expressions fetch considerable sums. But the nine single-vineyard *riserva* bottlings produced by Produttori del Barbaresco, the region's celebrated cooperative, consistently rank among the greatest values to be found in the world of wine. Their basic flagship Barbaresco, sourced from an assortment of parcels, is also highly recommended as a textbook introduction to the category offered at prices that could only be considered a form of welfare for nebbiolo addicts.

For the sake of simplicity, Barolo can be divided into two main areas, corresponding to soil types formed during different geological eras. To the east, the Serralunga Valley covers the communes of Serralunga d'Alba, Monforte d'Alba, and Castiglione Falletto. Composed of a higher percentage of limestone, the area's Tortonian soils yield the most powerful and tannic expressions of Barolo, with the greatest capacity to age. By comparison, the Central Valley—located on the western side, encompassing the villages of Barolo and La Morra—is defined by fresher, more compact soils from the Helvetian epoch, which give a softer, velvety, more elegantly perfumed style of nebbiolo.

This familiar division offers a useful shorthand for contextualizing the region's terroir, but Barolo is ultimately a place of endless variables. Not only do the wines from each of the eleven communes differ from one another, but—just as in Burgundy—you could also easily fill up a life's worth of notebooks trying to document the subtle distinctions among crus.

While it's possible to detect La Morra's soft elegance in a bottle such as the Oddero estate's Brunate bottling, or the breadth and power of Serralunga d'Alba in a bottle such as Giacomo Conterno's legendary Cascina Francia (one of the region's benchmarks), the beauty of nebbiolo from this part of Italy is the way it resists ready-made formulas. There's always another layer to explore, another discovery to be made. It's this marvelous complexity—the ability to encompass endless shades of nuance and detail—that places Piedmont in the select company of just a few other regions on Earth.

Prices have steadily climbed over the years, but the simple truth of the matter is that wine rarely, if ever, gets better than Barolo and Barbaresco at their best. Yes, they're a splurge. But at a time when so many expensive trophy wines fall short of expectations, they're the rare sort of splurge that typically overdelivers.

THE OTHER PIEDMONT

By definition, the greatness of any wine culture is built upon a foundation of affordable yet delicious table wines. After all, if the local saying is true that Barolo is "the king of wines and the wine of kings," then there must be something left to drink for those of us without royal blood in our veins.

Fortunately, this less ambitious but no less important class of wine has been a foundation of daily life in Piedmont for generations. Here's where to look for these undersung values, which can usually be had for $30 or less.

LANGHE NEBBIOLO AND NEBBIOLO D'ALBA

Remember the name Langhe Nebbiolo and Nebbiolo d'Alba. The equivalent of the regional Bourgogne classification in Burgundy, this designation is reserved for any nebbiolo-based wine produced within the Langhe hills. However, many of the great estates of Barolo and Barbaresco (including Giacosa, Vajra, Vietti, Produtorri del Barbaresco, and Roagna) adopt it for their entry-level bottlings, making it one of the region's secret values. Usually sourced from younger vines or less heralded sites, they're akin to "baby" Barolo or Barbaresco, offering a glimpse of the glory at a fraction of the price (most fall in the $20 to $40 range).

BARBERA

Because nebbiolo gets all the attention, you'd reasonably assume that it is Piedmont's most widely planted variety. Far from it. That honor goes to the earlier-maturing barbera grape, which has traditionally played the role of quotidian thirst quencher. Far easier to grow than its finicky cousin, it thrives in cooler sites where nebbiolo would struggle to ripen. Full of herbal-tinged freshness and bright acidity, the grape has long been known for a juicy, slightly rustic style of red, perfect for washing down heaping bowls of *tajarin* pasta tossed with porcini mushrooms or sage brown butter. But a more recent push toward a premium, age-worthy expression—planted in prime vineyard land and matured in *barrique*—has broadened the stylistic playing field. The best examples of both styles come from the hillside vineyards surrounding the towns of Alba in the Langhe and Asti in the subregion of Monferrato: look for Barbera d'Alba or Barbera d'Asti on the label.

DOLCETTO

Meaning "little sweet one," due to its deliciousness straight off the vine, dolcetto has the distinction of being Piedmont's second-most important "minor" grape. Grown throughout the region, it's typically rendered in a softer, fruit-forward, drink-me-now style meant to be enjoyed while waiting around for your Barolo and Barbaresco. The plumpest and friendliest of the region's indigenous varieties, it thrives across Piedmont but represents the exclusive focus of the town of Dogliani, which is widely regarded as furnishing the finest dolcetto in the land. Here, as throughout the region, the grape yields brambly, purple-hued wines reminiscent of blackberries and violets, with a pleasant streak of licoricey bitterness and less stringent acidity than its more prestigious cousins.

FREISA AND GRIGNOLINO

Consider freisa and grignolino Piedmont's other "other reds." Once obscure local curiosities—the kinds of wines you'd never find outside the region itself—the freisa and grignolino grapes have started to gain traction among wine geeks, especially as lighter-bodied reds come into fashion. Of the two, the latter is by far the lightest and most idiosyncratic. Exceedingly pale (you could easily mistake it for a rosé) and yet often mouth-puckeringly tannic, with notes of spicy clove and cinnamon, grignolino isn't for everyone but can be just right after a quick dip in the ice bucket on a sweltering day. Freisa, on the other hand, is derived from a Latin word for "strawberry," which should give you some sense of its profile: floral, berryish, and aromatic.

Essential Producers: Bartolo Mascarello, Bruno Giacosa, Giacomo Conterno, Vietti, Roagna, Oddero, Barale Fratelli, G. B. Burlotto, Brovia, Cappelletti, Produttori del Barbaresco, G. D. Vajra, Crivelli, Castello di Verduno, Cantine Valpane, Renato Ratti, Giuseppe Mascarello, Elvio Cogno, Cavallotto, Francesco Rinaldi, De Forville

THE WINE LIST

◆ **Roagna Dolcetto d'Alba ($):** Luca Roagna's dolcetto reflects the same attention and care he directs toward his highly sought-after single-vineyard Barbarescos. With a sinewy streak of licorice and black currant, it's one of the region's finest examples—a testament to just how seriously Piedmont takes its supposedly unserious side.

◆ **Oddero Barbera d'Alba "Superiore" ($):** From a historic producer of Barolo, this is simply the archetypical barbera. The kind of earthy, racy, ruby-colored red that you can use to wash down pizza, it's still complex enough to keep things interesting.

◆ **De Forville Nebbiolo d'Alba "San Rocco" ($):** This modestly priced nebbiolo from Barbaresco's fifth-generation De Forville estate continues to be one of the region's best-kept secrets. Sourced from vines in the commune of San Rocco Seno d'Elvio, smack in the middle of Barolo and Barbaresco, it drinks a bit like a hybrid of the two—think roses, tar, sour cherry—minus the usual sticker shock.

◆ **Produttori del Barbaresco Barbaresco ($$$):** While the celebrated cooperative's lineup of single-vineyard crus might offer a more precise lens through which to pick apart the minutiae of Barbaresco's celebrated terroirs, there's something to be said for the way this blend of different sites speaks to the region as a whole. If you want to grasp the true meaning of Barbaresco, look no further.

◆ **G. D. Vajra Barolo "Albe" ($$):** For value, typicity of its terroir, and availability, it's hard to come up with a better introductory Barolo than Vajra's "Albe." Assembled from the vineyards of Coste di Vergne, Fossati, and La Volta, it offers a big-picture view of the region that sums up everything Barolo is supposed to be: firm tannins, dark cherries, and a licorice-tinted edge of bitterness.

ALTO PIEMONTE

The name Alto Piemonte (literally, "High Piedmont") serves as a useful catchall for the various nebbiolo-growing areas—most important, Gattinara, Ghemme, Lessona, and Boca—clustered in the mountainous provinces of Novara and Vercelli around one hundred miles north of the vineyards of the Langhe. It also includes the commune of Carema, located in metropolitan Turin, a bit closer to Valle d'Aosta.

The current vogue these wines enjoy, especially among the sommelier crowd, can be attributed to a kind of wine world version of gentrification. Increasingly priced out of Barolo and Barbaresco, nebbiolo lovers have been forced to explore the area's outer boroughs. That has meant trekking a bit higher up into the foothills of the Alps, where, it turns out, some pretty spectacular wines had been hiding.

Far more than "lite" versions of their southern neighbors, the wines of Alto Piedmonte offer a wholly unique perspective on the nebbiolo grape, which goes by the local name spanna. Leaner and more delicately perfumed (think strawberries, pine needles, and damp earth), spanna is commonly blended with small percentages of the local varieties croatina, uva rara, and vespolina.

As demand continues to grow, certain producers have become nearly as famous as any of their Langhe peers. Once a well-kept industry secret, the exquisite Carema-based wines of Luigi Ferrando, to cite just one example, have doubled in price over just a few short years. On the whole, though, Alto Piemonte remains a neglected bastion of distinctive, age-worthy nebbiolo at $40 or less. Look for bottles such as the nervy Ghemme from Antiche Vigneti di Cantalupo or any of the brilliant Gattinaras from Mario Petterino or Antonio Vallana, among many others.

Essential Producers: Antoniolo, Ferrando, Antiche Vigneti di Cantalupo, Petterino, Vallana, Monsecco

TUSCANY

······················

JUST THE HIGHLIGHTS

- ◆ **Tuscany is Italy's most emblematic wine region.** Historically, it is also the country's most commercially successful and widely exported region, having defined Italian wine for generations of American drinkers.

- ◆ **The heart and soul of Tuscany is the native sangiovese grape.** Italy's most widely planted variety, sangiovese provides the foundation for the region's leading wines, Chianti Classico and Brunello di Montalcino.

- ◆ **If Chianti is Tuscany's quintessential table wine, Brunello is its age-worthy heavy hitter.** But at their best, both highlight the sour-cherry brightness and earthiness of classic sangiovese that makes it one of the planet's greatest food wines.

- ◆ **Stylistically, Tuscany is a bit of a minefield.** After a period that favored a riper, oakier style of sangiovese—and, in Chianti's case, embraced international grapes, like cabernet and merlot—the region can be difficult to navigate, so sticking with the right producers is paramount.

We know it as Tuscany. To Italians, it's Toscana. But no matter the language, those three syllables conjure a platonic ideal of Italy that's perpetually awash in the same golden light the old masters so famously captured: the one to which we all dream of escaping when stuck in traffic or chained to our desks.

If Tuscany represents Italy at its most quintessentially Italian, the same is true of its wines. In addition to numbering among the country's most historic and prestigious, they positively radiate "Italianness." No other region more perfectly embodies what Italian wine is all about—not even Piedmont, Tuscany's great rival for national eminence.

Compared with Piedmont's cool-climate, northerly stoicism, Tuscany is the equivalent of a great big Italian hug, full of warmth, friendliness, and sunshine. This joyful quality has everything to do with sangiovese, the region's star grape. The most widely planted variety in Italy, it reaches its profoundest expression in the hillside vineyards surrounding the ancient cities of Florence and Siena. Enjoyed for centuries alongside the region's rich yet surprisingly simple country fare, sangiovese doesn't always command the same respect as nebbiolo, especially among snobby industry types, but in terms of sheer deliciousness and food friendliness, it has no equal.

Ruby red in the glass, the best examples play upon a vibrant tension between ripe sour cherries, licorice, and wet earth, often revealing a saliva-inducing edge of rusticity. Of course, there's plenty of richness and elegance as well. But whether it be a modest Chianti Classico or an aged Brunello—Tuscany's two most important reds—a good bottle of sangiovese should always remind you of the dirt from whence it came.

To find the grape in this optimal condition, however, isn't always easy. Why? Short answer, Tuscany is Italy's most successful and widely exported wine region. So it should shock no one that its modern history has been marked by the widest stylistic swings and concessions to market forces, resulting in a self-inflicted identity crisis from which it has only begun to emerge.

The contributing factors in that crisis—namely, the addition of nonnative grapes, like cabernet, merlot, and syrah; the use of new French *barriques*; and investment in a slew of high-tech cellar tools to push for a darker, more extracted cast of sangiovese—are hardly exclusive to Tuscany. But thanks to its long-established mercantile culture and concentration of wealthy families with no shortage of capital to burn, the region proved all too hospitable to such flash-in-the-pan trends. A case in point is the rise of the Super Tuscans, the blue-chip, Bordeaux-style blends that emerged in the 1980s and 1990s as totems of that era's globalized style.

This explains, in part, why Tuscany has lately lost a certain amount of cachet among fashion-conscious sommeliers and industry types. The constant hunt for the next big thing has largely steered them away from mainstream areas such as Tuscany in search of Italy's esoteric fringes.

Admittedly, words such as *fringe* and *obscure* aren't found in Tuscany's vocabulary. But the region offers something more important: timelessness. A foundational pillar of the Italian wine canon, the classic wines of Tuscany are simply required drinking for anyone hoping to understand what Italian wine means.

REINTRODUCING CHIANTI

Few Italian wines—or, for that matter, few wines period—loom larger in the American imagination than Chianti. Among the first to be exported to the United States, it has since been adopted as a universal symbol of Italian American culture, the perennial staple of pizza parlors and "red sauce" joints across the country.

Most regions could only dream of attaining a similar level of success. Mass popularity, however, doesn't exactly translate to cool or exciting. In fact, it often has the opposite effect, which might help to explain the paradoxical situation in which Chianti finds itself today.

It is Chianti's ironic fate to be both iconic and overlooked. Its ubiquity has, perversely, also been its downfall: the opposite of edgy, it has always just kind of *been there*, dismissed as a kitschy relic of red-checkered table-cloth days gone by. It doesn't help, moreover, that Americans generally encounter Chianti in its least persuasive forms, with wide inconsistencies in quality, price, and style. On the one hand, there's the glut of chemically farmed, mass-produced Chiantis stacked on supermarket shelves across the country; on the other, there's a rash of overly ambitious, lavishly oaked *riserva* and *gran selezione* versions, often blended with French grapes.

Frustratingly, both expressions run counter to what Chianti was always intended to be: Italy's archetypal table wine, beloved for its effortless compatibility with food. If any wine has championed these low-maintenance virtues across the generations, it's Chianti.

Fortunately, that platonic ideal of Chianti hasn't been forgotten. Of late, the area has experienced a return to form by emphasizing the attribute that elevated it to classic status in the first place: the juicy, bright typicity of Tuscan sangiovese stripped of the distracting varnish of French *barriques* and nonindigenous grapes.

The effects of this pendulum swing can be felt across the entire Chianti area, but ground zero for the current renaissance is the Chianti Classico subzone, the wine's historical center of production and home to many of its most traditional, quality-minded producers. It's here that you'll also uncover some of the best deals in Italian wine.

Today, old stalwarts such as Castell'in Villa, Fèlsina, and Fattoria di Rodáno—as well as relative newcomers, such as American winemaker Michael Schmelzer's Monte Bernardi and Silvio Messana's Montesecondo estates, both natural-wine-world darlings—are walking back the missteps of the past and realigning with a more traditional identity. In doing so, they're shedding light on the full spectrum of old-school sangiovese styles and proving why, even after all these years, Chianti still matters.

Essential Producers: Castell'in Villa, Fèlsina, Montevertine, Fattoria di Rodáno, Montesecondo, Monte Bernardi, Villa di Geggiano, Castagnoli, Podere Campriano, Montenidoli, Rocca di Montegrossi

BRUNELLO (AND ROSSO) DI MONTALCINO

If Chianti is the quintessential Italian table wine built for everyday drinkability, Brunello di Montalcino signals the fine-wine side of Tuscan sangiovese. Alongside Barolo and Barbaresco, it is widely regarded as Italy's major contribution to the pantheon of "big important" reds (clearly, there's something about the letter *B*).

With Brunello, the entire experience intensifies. The vineyards surrounding the village of Montalcino (which, in typical Tuscan fashion, comes complete with its own walled fortress and fourteenth-century cathedral) were originally planted with a different clone of sangiovese than Chianti's. This, plus the area's limestone-rich soils, results in a denser, fleshier take on the grape, with the tannic stuffing to mature for decades. Layered over the usual sangiovese fruit, acid, and floral aromas, it's customary to encounter flavors of a deeper pitch: aged balsamic, for instance, plus fig, leather, and tobacco leaf. When all of these components integrate into a seamless whole, there's no limit to how majestic the results can be.

But as you've probably guessed, they aren't always guaranteed. While regional regulations wisely prohibit the addition of international grapes, making Brunello the product of 100 percent Tuscan sangiovese, the region still fell prey to the same misguided ambitions that transformed Chianti's identity during the final decades of the twentieth century.

In fact, given Brunello's reputation as the supposedly "superior" expression of the grape, the luxury treatment went to even further extremes. Throughout the 1990s, a spate of hyper-exaggerated "modern" Brunello wines entered the market. The differences were obvious to anyone familiar with the graceful Brunellos of the past. Just imagine the lean, sinewy musculature of an Olympic wrestler versus the beefed-up WWE parody. This stylistic arms race culminated in the infamous Brunellogate scandal of 2008, when authorities investigated a handful of local producers for doctoring their wines with "performance enhancing" grapes, like cabernet and merlot—a serious no-no for a wine built on the premise of a single variety.

When it comes to Brunello's current range of styles, the good news is that many producers resisted the temptation to remake their wines in the previous era's self-indulgent image, or since returned to their senses. The greatest examples of Brunello—such as those from the legendary Biondi Santi estate, which many credit with creating the first Brunello wine back in the late nineteenth century—wield their power with a certain agility and restraint. The point isn't to clobber you over the head, but to achieve a dynamic energy between high-toned elegance and rich, savory depth that is the hallmark of authentic Brunello.

Several top producers can be found below. They range from arch traditionalists, like Sesti and Biondi Santi, to naturalists such as the biodynamically farmed Fonterenza estate. What all their efforts share is a transparent focus on sangiovese from the Montalcino hills with none of the modernist bells and whistles, typically aged in old Slavonian oak and sensitive to the subtleties of site and soil.

Given their distinguished pedigree, these top bottles deserve the steep sums they fetch (the cost of entry generally starts around $50 per bottle but climbs considerably higher). If your budget doesn't permit such splurges, don't worry. Most Brunello estates also produce a reasonably priced second wine in the form of Rosso di Montalcino, typically sourced from younger vines and aged for shorter periods prerelease. Often described as Brunello's "little sibling," the category offers the same earthy Montalcino terroir but in a lighter, earlier-drinking package.

Essential Producers: Sesti, Biondi Santi, Poggio di Soto, Campi di Fonterenza, Fattoria dei Barbi, San Polino, Stella di Compalto, Mocali, La Colombina, Poggio Nardone

THE WINE LIST

- Castell'in Villa Chianti Classico ($): A source of classic, age-worthy Chianti for decades, Castell'in Villa holds even their entry-level wines back before release to show their ability to age. Sourced from organic vineyards and aged for twenty-four months in Slavonian oak, this is intensely mineral, with a spine of red cherry fruit, smoked meat, and clove.

- Monte Bernardi Chianti Classico Retromarcia ($): Monte Bernardi's 100 percent sangiovese "Retromarcia" is, simply put, everything there is to love about Chianti delivered in an affordable package that feels as intense as it is lithe. There's no greater argument for the region's time-honored place on the table.

- Montesecondo Chianti Classico ($$): One of the poster children of natural wine in Tuscany, Silvio Messana's sangiovese-based wines, sourced from biodynamic vineyards, have become unlikely darlings of forward-thinking American sommeliers. Expect the usual red cherry fruit, wet earth, and a juicy acidity.

- Fonterenza Rosso di Montalcino ($$): Twin sisters Margherita and Francesca Padovani have repped Montalcino's cutting edge since 1997, when they founded their biodynamically farmed winery, dedicated to minimalist interpretations of the area's fabled soils. Aged in large Slavonian oak casks, their bright Rosso di Montalcino drinks like a manifesto for classic, untampered-with sangiovese.

- Castello di Argiano Sesti Brunello di Montalcino ($$$): While the celestial bodies that adorn his labels speak to winemaker Giuseppe Sesti's past as a scholar of astronomy, lately he's concerned with more terrestrial matters: his roughly thirty-two acres of vines in the southern slopes of Montalcino. One of Brunello's bright lights, his wines stand apart for their transparency and savory depth.

VENETO

· · · · · · · · · · · · · · · · ·

JUST THE HIGHLIGHTS

- Quantity, not quality, has defined the Veneto for much of the recent past. Responsible for pumping out more wine than anywhere else in the country, the region's bread and butter is bland supermarket pinot grigio, but that's hardly the full extent of its powers.

- The Veneto is where Prosecco is made. Yes, Prosecco is an actual place. For the best terroir-focused versions, look to the wine's original zones of production: the hilltop villages of Conegliano and Valdobbiadene.

- Paradoxically, the Veneto is also the source of one of Italy's biggest, most powerful reds. The blockbuster wines of Amarone della Valpolicella owe their massive concentration to the *appassimento* process, whereby the grapes are dried before fermentation to concentrate their sugars and boost alcohol content.

- The region's classic table wines, Soave and Valpolicella, have returned to form. No longer the cheap jokes they were in the 1970s, when ads for large brands such as Bolla ran on prime-time TV, these expressions offer some of the region's most intriguing everyday values.

The Italians produce more wine annually than any other country on the planet, including their great rival France. This distinction is largely owed to the Veneto, Italy's commercial powerhouse, which in 2018 accounted for nearly a quarter of the country's annual production.

That's an enormous quantity of wine. Quality, however, is another question. Sadly, on that front, the reality can't be denied: a dismally high percentage of the Veneto's output reflects the grand tradition of *vino italiano* about as faithfully as Chef Boyardee upholds the glories of the national cuisine.

If that analogy seems harsh, blame the oceans of brand-name pinot grigio that flow out of the Veneto each year, drowning the global wine market in a sea of sameness. Of course, there's a lot more to the Veneto than industrial pinot grigio, but the phenomenon illustrates one of the region's defining tensions. Big business has dominated the area since the 1960s, when massive conglomerates, like Bolla, Zonin, and Santa Margherita, first introduced American audiences to cheap commercialized versions of local wines such as Soave (the early forerunner of today's pinot grigio craze) and Valpolicella (the red version of the same).

As demand soared, so too did production. Unable to resist the lucrative combination of high yields and higher margins, winemakers in both areas quickly expanded beyond the classic hillside zones (where grapes had been carefully grown for ages) and into the surrounding flatlands. As business boomed, the fizzy wines of Prosecco followed suit (yes, *that* Prosecco; it's also part of the Veneto), the whole pinot grigio thing happened, and the rest is history.

Except the story doesn't end there. Since then, the Veneto has flashed glimmers of hope. That's true of Soave, where a handful of independent producers (for instance, Gini, Cantina Filippi, Prà, Azienda Masiero Masiero, and Angiolino Maule) have been rethinking their relationship to the land, making, under the Soave Classico designation, lively, complex whites that range from fresh and apple-y to rich, straw colored, and mineral.

Significant changes have also come to Valpolicella (a far more complex region than meets the eye) and Prosecco (it's not all just mindless bubbles) as well, guided by a desire to reclaim the identities of their original ancestral zones. As that evolution continues to unfold, quality remains somewhat dicey. The current challenge is figuring out how to find the growing number of bottles that prioritize place over product and speak to the historical importance of Veneto wine.

VALPOLICELLA

The Valpolicella region's popularity peaked during the 1970s and 1980s, when it couldn't crank out its cheap reds fast enough and commercials for the mass-market Bolla brand aired on network TV. Today, however, the region's most famous wine couldn't diverge any further from the cut-price image of decades past.

Monumentally rich, ripe, and powerful, Amarone della Valpolicella (often shortened to "Amarone") is to the Veneto what Brunello is to Tuscany and Barolo to Piedmont. In terms of greatness, it's also their equal—at least that's what the conventional wisdom has always maintained. Except now more than ever, wisdom can't keep up with the whiplash of changing public taste. So as the industry love affair with Barolo grows cozier by the day and Brunello revisits the elegance of old-school sangiovese, Amarone feels increasingly left out in the cold.

That has everything to do with the specific technique involved in its production. Unlike any number of big, mouth-coating reds, Amarone acquires its notorious heft thanks to a process called *appassimento*. The technique involves leaving the local corvina, rondinella, and molinara grapes to dry on large straw mats, concentrating their natural sugars to astronomical levels. Stop the fermentation early and you wind up with a world-class sweet wine. When left to ferment to near total dryness, the result is Amarone. Arguably the most decadent red in existence, it shares the ripeness and syrupy texture of many dessert wines while packing a mighty wallop of tannins, acids, and alcohol.

The effect is undeniably impressive. But at a time when nuance and site sensitivity have come to replace sheer power as the latest generational touchstones, Amarone's identity runs counter to the dominant less-is-more ethos. Dismissed as a wine of process over place, it tends to get pegged as a boomer-era relic: the sort of "steak house wine" (in the form of cult Napa cab or blue-chip Bordeaux) reserved for middle-aged suburban dads.

Regardless of preference or cachet, the style can be captivating, especially after some time in bottle, when only the faintest impression of sweetness remains and the wine's savory elements (leather, game, aged balsamic) step forward. If you ever have the opportunity to drink an older bottle made by one of the area's producers—such as Dal Forno or the late Giuseppe Quintarelli—consider yourself blessed.

The region as a whole is now putting a lighter foot forward. Producers are aiming for a fresher, more elegant style of Amarone, better attuned to modern taste, but basic everyday Valpolicella has seen a startling return to form. No longer the ersatz version of itself it became in the 1970s and 1980s, it has reemerged as the fresh, juicy table wine it was always meant to be. All sour cherry, bright acidity, and herbs, here is yet another food-friendly Italian red that does best with a slight chill. Look for the Valpolicella Classico label sourced from the hillside vineyards that comprise the area's historical home turf.

Essential Producers: Giuseppe Quintarelli, Dal Forno, Brigaldara, Le Ragose, Adalia, Corte Sant'Alda, Ca' del Monte, Massimago, Ilatium Morini

PROSECCO

The wedding reception and bridal shower, the gallery opening and complimentary "bottomless brunch" mimosa—these are the contexts in which most of our interactions with Prosecco take place. The quintessential inexpensive bubbly, the stuff has been flying off the shelves of late. In 2013, after several years of record-breaking sales, Prosecco surpassed Champagne as the bestselling sparkling wine in the world (by volume, if not by price) and hasn't looked back since.

But let's not begrudge Prosecco its success or, for that matter, its lack of fine wine ambition. No matter how incessantly it gets branded as an "alternative" to the Gallic original, the whole point of Prosecco is that it's categorically *not* Champagne. Rather than "chiseled" or "serious" or "austere," it's supposed to be a celebration of *la dolce vita*, the Italian art of everyday living: a sunset drink on the terrace of a Venetian café—or, somewhat less romantically, a cramped fire escape in Bushwick.

Stylistically, Prosecco's carefree appeal is directly related to the production methods that make it what it is. Unlike Champagne, which acquires its fizz through the so-called traditional method of re-fermentation in bottle, the vast majority of Prosecco is produced according to the Charmat method, whereby the secondary fermentation takes place in enormous pressurized tanks called autoclaves. In addition to preserving the delicate primary aromas of Prosecco's main grape, glera (think honeysuckle and peach versus Champagne's yeasty, brioche-like complexity), the Charmat treatment produces lighter, fruitier wines with softer bubbles meant to be popped open as soon as possible.

Prosecco's ubiquity as a product has all but blotted out its identity as a place. As sales continue to skyrocket, the area's future hinges on a crucial question: Will "Brand Prosecco" reign, or is there room for another way—one that, ideally, brings the land and its people back into the conversation?

If the answer to that question can be found anywhere, it's in the scenic tangle of vines that stretches between the hilltop villages of Conegliano and Valdobbiadene, Prosecco's original heart of production. Encompassing what's now known as the Prosecco Superiore zone, the area presents a welcome contrast to the gigantic corporate wineries that source their grapes by the truckload from the flat Treviso plains.

Sourced from the same steep, family-owned sites that the area's growers have tended for centuries, the top Superiore bottles that bear Conegliano and Valdobbiadene on the label taste like Prosecco was meant to taste: simple, perhaps, but in all the right ways, revealing crisp minerality, a soft froth of bubbles, and, in lieu of the usual synthetic fruit flavors, loads of ripe pear. While they're usually a bit more expensive than the garden-variety Prosecco—say, $15 to $20 per bottle versus $10 or $12—that's a small premium to pay for a wine that lets you know from the first sip that it came from an actual place.

Essential Producers: Adami, Bisol, Le Vigne di Alice, Ca' dei Zago, Bele Casel, Casa Coste Piane, Miotto, Costadilà, Col Vetoraz, Bisson, Sommariva, Masót, Sorelle Bronca, Nino Franco

THE WINE LIST

- **Prà Soave Classico "Otto" ($):** The Prà winery played an instrumental role in resuscitating Soave's image and demonstrating the underlying potential of the native garganega grape. The estate's introductory "Otto" is tank fermented and aged on the lees for four to five months, giving it a textural depth that so much of the conventional Soave lacks.

- **Casa Coste Piane Prosecco di Valdobbiadene "Sur Lie" ($):** One of the first examples of the unfiltered, bottle-fermented *col fondo* style to gain stateside attention, Casa Coste Piane's version remains a benchmark of the category. Hazy, frothy, and cider-like, with a slight whiff of funk, it's a liquid battle cry against industrial Prosecco.

- **Corte Sant'Alda Valpolicella "Ca' Fiui" ($):** Marinella Camerani makes the kind of crunchy, low-alcohol, ruby-hued Valpolicella that pays homage to the past. Her unusually elegant Amarone is worth a try as well.

PROSECCO COL FONDO

The backlash to boring, industrial Prosecco can be encapsulated in just two words: *col fondo*. Meaning "with its bottom," or "with sediment," the term refers to an unfiltered, ever-so-slightly effervescent, and notably cloudy style of Prosecco, fermented not in the massive stainless-steel tanks that dominate the region today but directly within the bottle, leaving the deposit of dead yeast cells intact. You'll also see it labeled as *sui lieviti*, meaning "on the lees."

This drier, yeastier version of the wine bears little resemblance to the conventional stuff we all know so well, but it has been produced for longer than anyone can remember in the areas surrounding Conegliano and Valdobbiadene.

Although many producers abandoned *col fondo* in the 1970s when the arrival of industrial-scale fermentation tanks transformed Prosecco into a million-dollar industry, lately the style has been bubbling up again, a specialty of the small family growers that have tended their vines over generations.

Today it's tempting to view the *col fondo* movement as the latest wave in a wider ripple of funky "ancestral method" sparkling wines (take France's *pétillant naturel* craze, for instance). For many *col fondistas*, however, the style's revival transcends mere fashion or farmhouse fetish. In its thirst-quenching simplicity and rough-edged rusticity, it offers a vehicle for telling the story of the land of their forebears and—crazy as it might sound—reclaiming Prosecco as a wine of place.

Essential Producers: Ca' dei Zago, Bele Casel, Casa Coste Piane, Miotto, Costadilà

FRIULI

· · · · · · · · · · · · · ·

JUST THE HIGHLIGHTS

- Friuli is one of the great white-wine-making regions of Italy. That's because it's the birthplace of Italy's modern white wine renassiance. In the 1970s, a new wave of winemakers invested in state-of-the-art technologies, making possible for the first time the kind of vibrant, steely whites we now take for granted.

- The region is home to a collection of native and international grapes that speak to its unique heritage. Here, local grapes, like ribolla gialla, friulano, malvasia, and verduzzo, plus others such as pinot grigo, sauvignon blanc, and even chardonnay, join forces to produce wines that are unmistakenly Friulian.

- Today, Friuli's most fashionable wines aren't white, or even red—they're orange. As the birthplace of Italy's orange wine revolution, Friuli's versions of the skin-contact category have become the stuff of natural wine legend; more than a passing trend, the early examples produced by such legends as Joško Gravner and Stanislao Radikon are now revered as classics of the style.

- Friuli's reds, though lesser known, are among northern Italy's most intriguing. The indigenous schioppettino and refosco grapes reflect the same combination of coastal freshness, earthiness, and high-altitude purity that makes Friulian whites so desirable.

French wine snobs sometimes take cheap shots at Italy, calling out its alleged lack of serious whites. Citing the usual roster of easy, breezy *vini bianchi* that we've come to associate with the country, they'll dare you to point out Italy's answer to white Burgundy or Alsatian riesling. Anyone willing to propogate such a muddled a notion, however, clearly hasn't had much experience with Friuli–Venezia Giulia (or just Friuli for short)—and for the record, that includes its excellent pinot grigios.

These days, most of us encounter this postage stamp of a region in the extreme northeast of Italy (any further east and you'd be in Slovenia) via the revival of its hyper-traditional skin-contact, or "macerated," whites popularly known as orange wines (see page 10). Ironically, the recent hype surrounding all things orange has all but obscured Friuli's original claim to fame as the birthplace of Italy's modern white wine renaissance.

Imagine, if you will, a time in Italian wine history when the bright, mineral whites we all take for granted had yet to come into existence. The dark ages in question weren't as far back as you might think; even as late as the 1950s and 1960s, most Italian winemakers still followed the same primitive playbook that had guided their ancestors for centuries. Highly alcoholic, murky, and prone to spoilage, the rustic examples of vintages past might have been fit for the local farmers, but that's where their relevance stopped.

It was in Friuli that everything changed. Buoyed by Italy's postwar economic miracle, a new generation of producers—guided by innovators such as Mario Schiopetto and Livio Felluga—sought to launch the region into the future. They replaced the dirty old barrels their grandparents had used and invested in cutting-edge cellar equipment, including the arrival of refrigerated stainless-steel fermentation tanks in the 1960s and 1970s. For the first time in the region's history, it was possible to prevent oxidation and preserve the underlying character of the grape. As if overnight, a new paradigm for Italian white wine was born—one of purity, transparency, and racy minerality ready for the worldwide market.

THE CLASSIC WINES OF COLLIO AND COLLI ORIENTALI

Today, it's widely acknowledged that Friuli's most complex whites hail from two adjacent subareas, Collio and Colli Orientali, which collectively form the region's main zone of production. It's here in the far east of Friuli, with Slovenia (often literally) in their backyards, that most of the area's benchmark producers call home.

Derived from the Italian word for "hills," the names Collio and Colli offer a topographical clue as to why this particular corner of Italy is such an ideal incubator for world-class whites. At the crossroads of the Adriatic Sea and the Julian Alps, the vineyards that unfurl along these scenic slopes are uniquely positioned to produce vibrant yet deeply structured whites that combine coastal salinity with bracing mountain freshness.

Equal parts "mountains" and "Mediterranean," the marvelous tension between these seemingly contradictory climes expresses itself across the area's multicultural array of grapes, which testify to Friuli's history as a spoil of war traded back and forth among empires—Venetian, French, Hapsburg, take your pick. Here, French and Teutonic grapes—including chardonnay, sauvignon blanc, and riesling—cohabitate with more generic northern Italian varieties, like pinot bianco and pinot grigio. It's the area's trove of native examples, however, that best translate Friuli's multifaceted identity.

If any of these deserves to call itself Friuli's signature variety, it would be friulano. While not technically indigenous (research has confirmed its French origin as a long-lost cousin of sauvignon blanc, but try telling that to the Friulians), the grape has thrived in its adopted homeland for centuries. Friuli's namesake white and preferred everyday drinking wine, friulano is what you're most likely to be served in the local *frasca*, or "wine tavern," with a plate of the area's famous *prosciutto di San Daniele*. Today, it encompasses a chameleon-like range of styles, from crisp and steely to full-bodied, with flavors of yellow apple, almond, and pear.

Less common but just as important are Friuli's other native delicacies, including the ever-popular ribolla gialla (another crisp, floral grape that combines delicate peach and citrus notes with a squeegee-like rinse of acidity), malvasia istriana (responsible for lush yet savory wines that virtually drip with fresh apricot and herbs), and the extremely rare verduzzo and picolit, which come in both dry and sweet versions.

Finally, though perpetually overlooked, Friuli's unique native red grapes, schioppettino and refosco, deserve a quick mention. Between the two, schioppettino, also known as ribolla nera, is slightly more interesting, yielding structured, high-acid wines that, in the right hands, call to mind the wild, floral, green peppercorn character of northern Rhône syrah. Although it contributes to plenty of innocuous table wines, the more serious side of refosco comes out in dense, dark-fruited reds with flavors of blackberry and plum.

After its first wave of commercially successful whites, Friuli has passed through several stages of development. During the 1980s and early 1990s, winemakers, like Silvio Jermann, Miani's Enzo Potoni, and Joško Gravner (more on him in a minute), pioneered a new breed of decadent, barrel-fermented whites modeled after Burgundy. Extensively aged in French *barriques*, these flashy Super Whites (white wine's answer to the Super Tuscan craze) added yet another style to the region's repertoire.

Whether bottled on their own or, as you'll sometimes find them, incorporated into blends, Friuli's panoply of grapes comes into sharpest relief through the "classic" tank-fermented style that paved the way for the subsequent flood of excellent white wines we can now enjoy from the Veneto and Alto Adige all the way down to the bottom of the Boot. While other styles tap into different aspects of the region, it was this ground breaking elegance and vibrancy that first put Friuli on the international map, proving once and for all that Italy deserved to stand alongside the great white-wine-making nations of the world.

JOŠKO GRAVNER AND THE
ORANGE WINE REVOLUTION

The funny thing is that the great benchmarks aren't the wines from Friuli that you're most likely to find on sommelier Instagram feeds or trend-setting wine lists. Given the cross section you're bound to encounter in your adventures through the twenty-first-century wine scene, you'd probably conclude that the region has only been known for one thing: its reactionary "orange wine" avant-garde.

The story of how that came to be—which has since passed into wine world legend—is in many ways that of a single visionary producer. Of course, the legend in question is Joško Gravner; yes, *that* Joško Gravner, who, earlier in his career, played such a pivotal role in Friuli's techno-logical transformation.

A perpetual iconoclast, Gravner sent shock waves throughout the Italian wine circuit in 2001 by rejecting everything he had learned about modern winemaking in favor of reviving the ancestral practices he first witnessed in the Republic of Georgia: namely, burying the wine underground in large clay vessels known as amphorae, where it's left to ferment—skins and all—for weeks and even months at a time, soaking up color and tannin.

His decision to apply this retro approach to his full range of whites in 2004 represented a watershed moment—not just for Friuli but also for Italy as a whole, signaling the deliberate sacrifice of technical perfec-tion in the service of a more authentic, rough-hewn order of beauty. Oxidative, amber hued, and powerfully raw, that first wave of macerated whites he ushered into existence—along with the benchmark examples created by his small band of followers, including Stanislao Radikon, Damijan Podversic, Paolo Vodopivec, and Slovenia's Aleš Kristančič—now invokes a religious reverence in the eyes of their legions of true believers.

The orange revolution has since spiraled into a viral sensation, spreading outward from Friuli to the rest of Italy. Far from fizzling out as the passing fad that skeptics first pegged it to be, the movement has only gained traction, adopted as an emblematic expression of the international natural wine scene.

Despite the category's global reach, the Friulian originals remain enduring touchstones of their genre. If examples of the style from other parts of the world sometimes feel kitschy, as if they exist only to capitalize on a trend, Friuli is where the movement first gained attention, and where its philosophy finds its most meaningful articulation, intimately tied to the history of the land itself.

Essential Producers: Venica & Venica, Joško Gravner, Stanislao Radikon, Edi Keber, Edi Kante, Ronchi di Cialla, Doro Princic, Petrussa, Ronco del Gnemiz, Villa Russiz, Borgo del Tiglio, i Clivi, Perusini, Vignai da Duline, Damijan Podversic, Paolo Vodopivec

THE WINE LIST

- ◆ i Clivi IGT Trevenezie Ribolla Gialla ($): Many of us now come to Friuli via the region's skin-contact orange expressions, which makes drinking clean, transparent wines such as i Clivi's an eye-opening experience. Clocking in at less than 12 percent alcohol, their hand-picked ribolla gialla exemplifies the grape's subtle, aromatic side, with notes of magnolia and a squeeze of lemon.

- ◆ Damijan Podversic Venezia Giulia Ribolla Gialla ($$): Although not as well known as some of the other saints of the orange wine hagiography, Podversic was one of Gravner's earliest disciples. Fermented on the skins for between sixty and ninety days using only natural yeasts, his ribolla demonstrates that macerated whites can still have a kind of aromatic delicacy and nuance, despite the obvious tannic grip.

- **Edi Kante Malvasia Carso ($$):** Located in the Carso distict in southeastern Friuli near the city of Trieste, Edi Kante makes one of the region's standout malvasias. Displaying the grape's intrinsic floral aromas with a saline coastal brightness and flavors of dried apricot, it's aged for a year in used barrels for added depth and complexity.

- **Ronco del Gnemiz Colli Orientali del Friuli Friulano "San Zuan" ($$):** Located in the heart of the Colli Orientali region on the hill of Rosazzo, Christian Patat and Serena Palazzolo of the organic Ronco del Gnemiz estate are producing some of the region's most distinctive and age-worthy wines, including this creamy yet laser-focused barrel-fermented friulano.

- **Ronchi di Cialla Colli Orientali Schioppettino ($$):** Schioppettino was effectively rescued from oblivion by the Ronchi di Cialla estate, so it's only fitting that they produce what is widely considered the benchmark example of the variety. If some versions render the grape in an easy-drinking style, Ronchi di Cialla's is built to last, exuding a raw, red-fruited energy that softens into a perfumed stoicism over time.

ALPINE ITALY

....

(VALLE D'AOSTA, LOMBARDY, AND TRENTINO–ALTO ADIGE)

JUST THE HIGHLIGHTS

◆ Alpine Italy isn't one region but several. At the crossroads of Italy, France, Switzerland, and Austria, the areas of the Valle d'Aosta, Lombardy, and Trentino–Alto Adige offer up a cross-cultural mix of native grapes and traditional wine styles that constitute a genre of their own.

◆ Each of these regions has its own unique identity. In Lombardy, for instance, the sparkling wines of Franciacorta coexist with Valtellina's high-elevation versions of nebbiolo, while Alto Adige shares a wine culture with neighboring Austria, highlighting lively white wines in a Teutonic mode. The tiny Valle d'Aosta, on the other hand, ekes out minuscule quantities of wine that reflect its distinctly Franco-Italian heritage.

◆ What unites all of Italy's alpine wines is a brilliant, nervy freshness. As drinkers increasingly favor purity and crystalline transparency, these "mountain wines" have gone from curious footnotes to contemporary classics, taking up space on wine lists all over the United States.

The enchantingly bucolic wine regions that spread out along Italy's northernmost borders are cultural melting pots where diverse languages, customs, and cuisines collide. Depending on where your bottle might call home, the label could just as easily be printed in French or German as Italian—proof that the cultural boundaries that make up the world of wine are far more fluid than the political lines drawn on the map.

Although they're all unique, laying claim to their own idiosyncratic mix of grapes, the regions of Valle d'Aosta, Lombardy, and Trentino–Alto Adige collectively form a pan-alpine alliance that has earned its place in the wider Italian repertoire. Despite their differences, they all share a specific high-altitude freshness that transmits their alpine origins with the clarity of a cowbell ringing through a field of wildflowers.

Until recently, wines from this part of the world were seldom encountered outside of their home turf. But as the Zeitgeist continues to celebrate the cool-climate virtues of all things lean and nervy, the distinctly alpine tension these bottles exhibit—a dazzling interplay among fruit, acid, and minerality—has put Italy's mountain wines on the industry radar. Few areas embody a sense of place with the same purity or precision, as if distilling the essence of the mountain air itself.

VALLE D'AOSTA

In the shadow of Mont Blanc, flush with France and Switzerland, the Valle d'Aosta (as Italians call it) just as often becomes the French Vallée d'Aoste. Home to some of Europe's highest-elevation vineyards, it's also Italy's smallest wine region, yielding minuscule quantities of white and red wine from its distinct combo of native and adopted Franco-Italian grapes.

Once considered as little more than pleasant après-ski quaffers, the brisk whites of Morgex et de la Salle, produced from the indigenous prié blanc variety, are now revealing their deeper potential as they gain a foothold on US wine lists.

Piercingly clear and pure, with a characteristic floral quality, the examples that have gained visibility stateside—such as those from the family-run Ermes Pavese estate—channel the chiseled delicacy of their extreme-altitude vineyards, which rise nearly four thousand feet above sea level. Equally idiosyncratic, the little-known petite arvine grape—native to Switzerland, just across the border—has found a second home in the Valle d'Aosta, giving fleshier wines with characteristics of grapefruit, pear, and bitter almond.

When it comes to the Valle d'Aosta, however, most drinkers fixate on its reds. These range from the humble petit rouge (historically considered a workhorse grape, it's most often made in a light, juicy style akin to Beaujolais) to fumin (a spicy, herbaceous, highly aromatic variety) to, the most structured of all, cornalin (distinguished by a smoky savoriness). Along with unique renditions of nebbiolo (known here as picotendro), gamay, and pinot noir, these can be bottled on their own as varietal wines or mixed into the region's traditional blends—all stamped with that signature alpine sheerness.

Essential Producers: Grosjean Frères, Ermes Pavese, Danilo Thomain, Ottin, Les Crêtes, Franco Noussan, La Kiuva, Cave Mont Blanc

LOMBARDY

To Italians, Lombardy—or Lombardia, as they refer to it—is synonymous with bubbles. The traditional method (or *metodo classico*) sparklers of Franciacortia, produced in Brescia Province near the resort-studded shores of Lake Iseo, represent Italian fizz at its most ambitious.

Developed during the 1960s and 1970s, the category sought to fill a gap in the Italian market for high-end bubbly by attempting to rival Champagne. That meant adopting the classic Champenois grapes of pinot noir and chardonnay (pinot blanc is also permitted) and, all too often, copying Champagne's luxury branding as well. At this stage, the category's identity is still in limbo. But a growing number of the area's producers (the Arcari e Danesi project is a clear standout) have come to view the Champagne comparison as more of a limitation than a leg up. Typically rounder, riper, and more fruit-forward than the Gallic original, the best Franciacorta wines make no attempt at mimicry but instead embrace their own unique "Franciacorta-ness," as it were.

Although Franciacortia is Lombardy's most famous wine region, its most distinctive is Valtellina, a tiny, under-the-radar area known for presenting nebbiolo in its lightest and most crystalline form. Centered in the town of Sondrio, directly across the border with Switzerland (to which it once belonged), Valtellina is the quintessential mountain wine, marking the northernmost frontier beyond which nebbiolo refuses to ripen.

Planted at heights of two thousand feet, the region's terraced vineyards appear to reject the laws of physics, jutting out from the rocky precipices as if they had been airlifted by helicopter and grafted onto the face of the granite cliffs themselves. You can taste that extreme verticality in the wines. Tart, high-toned, and crimson hued, the classic Valtellina style combines classic alpine transparency with nebbiolo's signature earthiness and tannic grip.

In fact, ripeness has historically been so elusive in these parts that it has long been local custom to make a deliberately richer style of Valtellina, known as *sforzato* or *sfursat*. Produced according to the same *appassimento* method that gives the wines of Amarone their high alcohol and over-the-top concentration (see How Wine Is Made, page 5), the category is more of a footnote today than an essential expression, but a weird and interesting one nevertheless.

Among locals, it's common knowledge that the most complex, age-worthy Valtellina wines come from five single-vineyard crus—Sassella, Grumello, Inferno, Maroggia, and Valgella—whose south-facing slopes allow the grapes to achieve peak ripeness. Production is extremely limited— remember, we're talking about only a handful of back-breakingly steep growing areas estate. But the producer to seek out is the venerable Ar.Pe.Pe., a sommelier favorite known for its awe-inspiring expressions of Sassella (prized for its richness and powerful structure) and Grumello (the finer, more mineral of the two), plus a teensy amount of brooding, muscular Inferno.

Essential Producers: Arcari e Danesi, Ar.Pe.Pe., Balgera, Aldo Rainoldi, Sandro Fay, Dirupi

TRENTINO–ALTO ADIGE

At the foot of the snow-capped peaks of the Dolomites, Italy and Austria meet. A magical landscape of mountain valleys and placid lakes (where you wouldn't feel at all self-conscious bursting into song Julie Andrews–style), Trentino–Alto Adige is the unique by-product of this cross-cultural fusion.

As you might guess from its hyphenated name, the region consists of two distinct areas that are, in fact, quite different from each other. To the south, in the lower half of the Adige Valley surrounding the village of Trento, Trentino Province is mainly Italian speaking, whereas the Teutonic-tongued residents of Alto Adige whose capital is Bolzano, still call the area Südtirol (South Tyrol), the Germanic name it bore before being annexed from Austria after World War I. What they have in common are wines of undeniable high-elevation energy made from any number of native grapes, plus others belonging equally to Austria and Germany.

In addition to a *metodo classico* bubbly tradition of its own under the Trentodoc designation, Trentino's main attraction is *vino rosso*. Of its indigenous varieties, the most compelling is undoubtedly the vibrant, dark-fruited teroldego, a specialty of the Campo Rotaliano in the northern plains of Trentino.

Historically produced in bulk according to a large cooperative model, it yielded thin wines of little interest outside the region. The grape's modern revival—and growing US acclaim—is a direct consequence of the work of one groundbreaking winemaker, Elisabetta Foradori. Her stunning teroldego wines—including several intensely mineral and savory single-vineyard versions—serve as standard bearers not just for Trentino but of all Italy.

If Trentino is still transitioning away from the legacy of its high-volume approach, the vertigo-inducing vineyards of Alto Adige make mechanical farming virtually impossible. Characterized by small family wineries operating on an artisanal scale, the wine culture here assumes a decidedly Germanic cast. That means crisp, acid-driven whites, including pinot blanc (bottled as either pinot bianco or Weissburgunder, depending on one's side of the linguistic divide) and surprisingly high-quality pinot grigio, as well as Austro-German grapes such as Müller-Thurgau, sylvaner, kerner, and gewürztraminer—the latter rendered in a much leaner frame than the signature versions from Alsace.

The area's most widely planted red, schiava, also known as Vernatsch, is experiencing a modest vogue; at its best, it delivers the kind of floral spice and berry-tinged brightness that will appeal to Beaujolais fans or recent converts to the fresh reds of the Jura. Also worth seeking out is its richer, meatier counterpart, lagrein, a native Alto Adige grape whose smokiness and intrinsic peppery, herbal streak shows its family resemblance to teroldego.

Essential Producers: Elisabetta Foradori, Muri-Gries, Weingut Köfererhof, Franz Gojer, Nusserhof, Alois Lageder, J. Hofstätter, Cantina Terlano, Erste+Neue, Markus Prackwieser Gump

THE WINE LIST

◆ **Arcari e Danesi Franciacorta "Dosaggio Zero" ($$):** This is the kind of grower of Franciacorta that shows the region at its most authentic. Committed to establishing Franciacorta's identity on its own terms, Giovanni Arcari and Nico Danesi bottle this without any *dosage* (added sugar), allowing its underlying richness and stone-fruit qualities to come forward.

◆ **Grosjean Frères Torrette Rouge Vallée d'Aoste ($):** The reference-point producer for the Valle d'Aosta, the Grosjean family's Tourrette is born of vineyards planted at heights of up to twenty-one hundred feet. A blend of 80 percent petit rouge with a smattering of assorted others (like fumin, doucet, and mayolet), it's as lithe and light-footed as red wine gets, with an earthy rusticity.

◆ **Elisabetta Foradori "Sgarzon" Teroldego Vigneti delle Dolomiti ($$):** A step up in complexity from her iconic entry-level terol-dego, Foradori's interpretation of the Sgarzon vineyard spends eight months fermenting in clay amphorae. It's typically the most delicate and finessed of her single-vineyard teroldego wines, a reflection of the site's cooler climate and sandy soils.

◆ **Ar.Pe.Pe. Rosso di Valtellina ($$):** Ar.Pe.Pe.'s acclaimed range of individual crus, such as Grumello or Sassella, represent the pinnacle of Valtellina's vertiginous style of chiavennasca (aka nebbiolo), but all of the estate's classic hallmarks are present in its crystalline entry-point *rosso*. A blend of different plots of younger vines, it's Italian red at its purest and most luminous.

◆ **Weingut Köfererhof Alto Adige Kerner ($):** The sort of steely, tank-fermented white that is Alto Adige's calling card, Köfererhof's incredibly fragrant Kerner—a cross between riesling and schiava—reflects owner Günther Kerschbaumer's commitment to making transparent wines of place that conjure the pristine beauty of the Dolomites through the prism of several Austro-Italian grapes.

EMILIA-ROMAGNA

JUST THE HIGHLIGHTS

◆ **Emilia-Romagna's best-known wine is Lambrusco, its signature sparkling red.** The category's reputation, however, has suffered thanks to the sweet, mass-market brands, like Riunite, that soared to popularity during the 1970s.

◆ **New to the market (but centuries old in spirit), the ancestral tradition of naturally sparkling farmhouse Lambrusco is coming back.** Rather than rely on the industrially scaled Charmat method, whereby the secondary fermentation takes place in giant steel tanks, today's "real" Lambrusco is fermented directly in bottle, yielding tart, dry wines of nuance and complexity.

◆ **Beyond the fizz, Emilia-Romagna has become Italy's "other" orange wine stronghold.** A mini naturalist revolution in the hills outside Bologna has ushered in a new wave of skin-contact whites, which have branched off into a weird little niche of their own.

Prosciutto from Parma. Balsamic vinegar of Modena. *Ragù bolognese.*
These are just a few of the delicacies that Emilia-Romagna, a storybook
stretch of vineyard land encircling the capital of Bologna, has bestowed
upon an eternally grateful public. Home to some of Italy's iconic
dishes, the area is a gastronomic wonderland, its creations as central
to the national identity as the operas of Verdi, Dante's epic jaunt through
the underworld, or any rippling physique carved by Michelangelo.

The local wines, on the other hand, haven't exactly shared the same
glory. Long aligned with a bulk production model, the region has struggled to cast off the lowbrow image it acquired in the 1970s, when a fizzy
red wave of supermarket Lambrusco—including, notoriously, the ubiquitous Riunite brand—colonized store shelves across the United States.

That cloyingly sweet, semi-sparkling invasion will long be remembered
as the shag carpeting of consumer wine trends, best relegated to history's trash heap. It would be a shame, however, to let its lingering bad
taste define perceptions of Emilia-Romagna's wines today, which have
made serious strides since their unfortunate disco-era heyday.

For one, as producers continue to explore traditional winemaking practices, Lambrusco is back and better than ever—or, at least, better than
it's been in recent memory, reimagined as the artisanal bottle-fermented
bubbly it was in days of yore. At the same time, a renewed interest in
the area's lesser-known indigenous grapes has given a growing network
of naturalists the materials to carve out an alternative ethos for the
region, centered on a mini-renaissance of savory skin-contact whites.

All of the above amounts to a welcome return to relevance for Emilia-
Romagna, offering drinkers hope that this essential swathe of Italy's
heartland will finally regain a meaningful wine culture to accompany
all the other bounty heaped on its table.

THE "REAL" LAMBRUSCO

The contrast between the artificial mass-produced Lambrusco that constituted America's initial introduction to Lambrusco and the authentic renditions you're likely to find in upscale stores and restaurants today couldn't be starker. It's like drinking your first glass of thirst-quenching, freshly squeezed lemonade after knowing nothing but the store-bought powder.

As always, the difference lies in the production details. On the one hand, there are the gigantic commercial cooperatives that bulk manufacture their product (because, let's face it, that's exactly what it is: a commodity) using the quick-and-easy Charmat method of secondary fermentation in enormous steel tanks. Then there's the real Lambrusco, handcrafted by the area's small growers according to the centuries-old *metodo ancestrale*, or "ancestral method," whereby the wine derives its fizz on a microscale through a naturally occurring refermentation in bottle.

If you've never experienced it, this new (to us, at least) breed of refreshingly tart, dry, bottle-fermented Lambrusco will come as a revelation, signaling a back-to-the-future throwback to what the wines resembled before big business took over. Occasionally giving off a pleasant whiff of farmhouse funk and a hint of sourness, it combines all of the cherry-meets-blackberry juiciness and bright acidity of the best everyday Italian reds with a soft froth of fizz that goes down with dangerous ease.

Consumed by the boatload in the cafés and taverns of Bologna, where the locals know a thing or two about a good meal, the wine is custom-built to cut through grease and fat. Just crack open a freshly chilled bottle alongside a hot, gooey pepperoni pizza and see for yourself.

Essential Producers: La Stoppa, Denavalo, Cà de Noci, Vigneto Saetti, Vittorio Graziano, Quarticello, Paltrinieri, Camillo Donati, Alberto Tedeschi

THE OTHER (ORANGE) EMILIA-ROMAGNA

Lambrusco has always been Emilia-Romagna's signature wine, and for good reason: it is not only delicious (provided you're drinking the old-growth ancestral method version) but also among the most versatile food wines imaginable. Some of the most compelling bottles from the region today represent the effort of a small but influential group of natural and lo-fi winemakers who interpret their terroirs through a completely different lens.

Notably, that translates to the rediscovery of Emilia-Romagna's grab bag of native whites, from the rich, aromatic malvasia (one of the area's most promising candidates) to such lesser-known obscurities as albana, pignoletto, spergola, and malbo gentile, previously reserved for rustic country wines that rarely left the region's home base. In the hands of such indie producers as La Stoppa, Denavalo, and Cà de Noci, however, these humble whites get the avant-garde treatment: farmed organically, fermented with native yeasts, and, increasingly, macerated on the skins, making the region Italy's second major breeding ground (after Friuli, of course) for orange wines.

THE WINE LIST

◆ **Camillo Donati IGT Emilia "Il Mio" ($):** A central figure in both the revival of authentic bottle-fermented Lambrusco and Italy's wider natural wine scene, Camillo Donati cultivates his vines using organic and biodynamic practices, ensuring that only the best raw materials make it into this tart, slurpable *frizzante* (that's Italian for "lightly fizzy"). Bottled unfiltered and closed with a crown cap, per local tradition, the wine often contains a haze of sediment—all part of the fun.

◆ **Vittorio Graziano Lambrusco "Fontana dei Boschi" ($):** Vittorio Graziano came to wine after initially working as an administrative accountant—a wise life choice if ever there was one. Today, he strenuously avoids the use of chemicals in his vineyard and raises all of his wines with the gentlest possible touch. His lightly sparkling red reveals the tannic grip and brambly, herbal complexity that gets entirely lost in the more conventional Charmat method versions of Lambrusco.

◆ **La Stoppa "Ageno" IGT Emilia Bianco ($$):** From one of Emilia's orange wine pioneers, La Stoppa's "Ageno" bottling spends three to six months macerating on the skins. This is always one of the most compelling macerated whites found outside of Friuli, combining tannic bitterness with a floral component (from the malvasia grape), fresh oregano, and burnt orange peel.

◆ **Alberto Tedeschi "Spungola Bellaria" IGT Emilia Pignoletto ($):** The little-known pignoletto grape is generally dismissed as forgettable, but in the hands of naturalist Alberto Tedeschi, who works exclusively with the variety, it's transformed into an unlikely masterpiece of the skin-contact style: slightly hazy, with flavors of baked apple, citrus, and walnut skins.

SICILY

············

JUST THE HIGHLIGHTS

- Sicily's wine industry has catapulted from a rustic source of bulk reds to the beating heart of Italy's new avant-garde. Now a staple of any self-respecting Italian wine list, it's regularly poured alongside classics such as Barolo and Brunello.

- The regions of Mount Etna and Vittoria are the driving forces behind Sicily's transformation. Each in its own way, these two areas helped to chart a completely new path for Sicilian wine, launching it into the modern era.

- Etna is one of Italy's most extreme terroirs. It is located thousands of feet up in the air on the slopes of Europe's tallest active volcano. All of the region's wines share the same smoky, ashen minerality.

- Known for reds of paradigm-changing freshness, Vittoria reveals the island's bright and chuggable side. That's most evident in its signature red, Cerasuolo di Vittoria, a juicy blend of the frappato and nero d'avola grapes.

- Sicilian whites are also having a moment. In particular, the western part of the island is emerging as a source of excellent whites from the catarratto and grillo grapes.

Just because wine has been made in Sicily since Roman times doesn't mean said wine was always good.

Historically famous as the home of Marsala, the fortified classic best known today for its namesake chicken dish, the region spent most of the twentieth century doing exactly what might be expected of a massive expanse of vines planted across the Mediterranean's largest island. In other words, Sicily served as Italy's bulk wine behemoth, reliably supplying millions of bottles of mass-market white and red, none of it particularly exciting. If any trace of this lowbrow image still remains, however, you'd never know it from the devotion Sicily inspires today.

At a time when the wine world proliferates with tales of regions rebounding from generations of high-volume mediocrity, the fact that Sicily salvaged its reputation isn't especially newsworthy. But beyond making amends for its wayward past and renewing its commitment to quality, the island has staged a comeback the likes of which no one could have predicted.

Within no more than a couple of decades, Sicily transformed itself from a rustic purveyor of industrial dreck into one of Italy's most innovative hotbeds of experimentation. Now a fixture of top wine lists across the United States, it stands alongside places such as Friuli and Alto Piemonte as emblems of the new Italian counterculture.

Sudden as it seemed at the time, the island's unlikely plunge into the avant-garde didn't come out of nowhere; it was driven by the discovery of two subregions, which are now synonymous with Sicily's revamped image. Each in its own way, the zones of Etna and Vittoria radically redefined expectations about Sicilian wine, bringing about the golden age the area is now enjoying.

ETNA

If there's truth to the cliché that all great wine tells a story, what more compelling tale could there be than making wine on the foothills of Mount Etna, Europe's tallest active volcano?

Located on the eastern side of the island, Etna surely ranks among the most extreme places on Earth to grow grapes. Every few years, the region's famous crater erupts, spewing up mounds of burning hot lava and lighting the night sky. Of course, this presents certain obstacles for the area's growers; all winemakers contend with climatic hazards of one kind or another, but the occasional drought or hailstorm is nothing compared to a river of molten rock flowing through your vineyard.

Based on weird factor alone, Etna couldn't have been better designed to appeal to a more curious generation of drinkers, for whom its idiosyncratic backstory presented an undeniable allure. When the region first started making headlines in the early aughts, Etna immediately went viral as the hottest thing in Italian wine.

It didn't hurt, of course, that Etna's volcanic origins make it one of the most singular terroirs on Earth. Climbing to heights of nearly four thousand feet above sea level, the region's otherworldly landscape of gnarled, ancient vines—many of which still survive on their own centuries-old rootstocks—yields wines of vibrancy and mineral intensity that couldn't come from anywhere else.

This fierce individuality runs through the entire spectrum of styles found on the volcano today, including sparkling, rosé, and some profoundly compelling whites. Etna's distinctive reds, however, produced from the obscure nerello mascalese and nerello cappuccio grapes, first launched the area to the height of fashion, offering the starkest contrast to the usual "big and clumsy" stereotypes about Sicilian wine.

Etna Rosso is a case study in all of the traits you wouldn't typically associate with sunbaked Sicily. The wines exude a palpable energy, offering bright flavors of sour cherry and blood orange, plus a signature smokiness and salty minerality that is the direct expression of its pumice-black soils. Stylistically, they most often draw comparisons to the cool-climate wines of Burgundy and Barbaresco (despite Sicily's proximity to Africa, Etna's high elevation preserves acidity and freshness) but with a wild volcanic streak that is uniquely Etna's.

Over the years, the area's fiery mystique has attracted several influential producers, including such important names as Belgian-born Frank Cornelissen, whose minimalist interpretations exemplify the area's alternative fringe, and Marc de Grazia of the Tenuta delle Terre Nere estate, whose wines strive for a more Burgundian model. Along with the classics from early pioneers, like Giuseppe Benanti and Salvo Foti, who first fomented the Etna revolution, the region now encompasses a wide range of styles and philosophies.

As Etna enters a more mature phase of development, the time has never been better to taste all the volcano has to offer. With its wild, almost feral intensity, Etna isn't the most obvious crowd-pleaser. But even if other Italian wines play more nicely with others, Etna's best achieve an inimitable complexity. What else would you expect from a fiery crater in the middle of the sea?

Essential Producers: Benanti, Salvo Foti (I Vigneri), Tenuta delle Terre Nere, Calabretta, Frank Cornelissen, Eduardo Torres Acosta, Biondi, Romeo del Castello, Graci

VITTORIA

For many early adapters to the world of natural wine, the first major sign that something exciting was happening in Vittoria—a comparatively flat, not especially acclaimed (at least not at the time) region in the boondocks of southeast Sicily—came in the form of a specific, highly symbolic bottle. From the moment it arrived on US shores back in 2006, the wine in question radically upended all of the conventional wisdom about Sicilian wine.

Made from an obscure local grape called frappato, it drank as if Sicily was imagined by the likes of Marcel Lapierre or Jean Foillard, the towering legends of Beaujolais: no hint of heaviness or overripe prunes, no high alcohol burn; just pure wild strawberry freshness and effortless drinkability. Adding to the hype, the winemaker responsible was none other than Arianna Occhipinti, an area native who, at the age of twenty-three, had already blazed her own path to natural wine superstardom.

With its obvious debt to that movement's aesthetics, Occhipinti's frappato struck just the right Zeitgeisty chord. Its runaway success not only propelled her to celebrity status but also brought renewed attention to her home of Vittoria, where, as it turned out, she wasn't the only one redefining the rules.

Over the years, rather than sticking to the beaten path of chunky, high-alcohol reds, a small but influential circle of producers—including, notably, the COS winery, cofounded in 1980 by Giusto Occhipinti, Arianna's uncle—have been steadily working to reshape perceptions of Sicilian wine. In addition to farming organically and implementing native yeast fermentations (often, as at COS, in alternative vessels, such as clay amphorae), they've also brought fresh attention to the area's main indigenous grapes: not just floral, light-bodied frappato but the richer, fleshier nero d'avola as well.

Although both varieties offer plenty to admire on their own, they're arguably at their best when combined in the area's classic blend, Cerasuolo di Vittoria. A variant on the Italian word for "cherry," the name of the style provides an accurate sense of what to expect while drinking it, embodying a perfect yin-yang between the red-berried snap of frappato and the brawnier structure of nero d'avola.

Essential Producers: COS, Arianna Occhipinti, Gulfi, Valle Dell'Acata, Portelli, Centonze

THE OTHER SICILY

It would be a shame to give the impression that Sicily's renaissance has extended only to its reds. Although they haven't yet received the same recognition, the island's whites are finally generating excitement among industry tastemakers. For one, Etna's whites, dedicated primarily on the savory carricante grape, reveal the same explosively mineral, volcanic components that have made its reds the object of such fawning industry adoration. But other parts of Sicily are also producing white wines from a range of native grapes—catarratto, grillo, and inzolia, among others—that can compete with Italy's finest.

Those three, in fact, comprise the traditional blending varieties used in Marsala, Sicily's historic fortified wine. It's here, on the westernmost edge of the island, that the late Marco de Bartoli, whose family estate is now run by his adult children, built a lasting name for himself based not only on his old-school renditions of Marsala but also on a lineup of dry whites that have become modern classics, including his fragrant, nervy "Grappoli del Grillo." Not too far away, near the city of Alcamo, natural winemaker Alessandro Viola also produces a standout dry white from grillo and catarratto, which has inspired a dedicated following.

THE WINE LIST

◆ **I Vigneri di Salvo Foti "Vinupetra" Etna Rosso ($$$):** Salvo Foti makes some of Etna's most riveting natural wines under his own I Vigneri label. The project's terroir-driven vision culminates in his flagship "Vinupetra," born of a single parcel of hundred-year-old vines planted twenty-three hundred feet above sea level on the northern side of Mount Etna.

- **Calabretta Nerello Mascalese "Vigne Vecchie" Sicilia IGT Valle dell'Acate ($$):** Massimiliano Calabretta only releases his wine after six to eight years of extensive aging. This unusual patience, plus the concentration he derives from his eighty-year-old nerello mascalese and cappuccio vines, imbues his flagship red with a visceral complexity that drinks the way nebbiolo might drink if planted in the volcanic ash of Mount Etna.

- **Agricola Arianna Occhipinti Il Frappato Sicilia IGT ($$):** One of the more ground-breaking reds of recent memory, Arianna Occhipinti's frappato put her corner of Sicily on the map. Several years later, it's still the defining reference point for the grape, displaying the same mix of rose-petal freshness and layers of pure berry fruit that made it an instant classic.

- **Azienda Agricola COS Cerasuolo di Vittoria Classico DOCG ($$):** Embodying the tension between nero d'avola's brambly concentration and frappato's strawberry-scented lift, COS's Cerasuolo di Vittoria is a textbook example of the style. Now a staple of natural wine lists across the country, it was one of the earliest examples to reach a wider audience.

- **Marco de Bartoli "Grappoli del Grillo" Sicilia IGT Terre Siciliane ($$):** Using a selection of the finest fruit of each harvest, Marco de Bartoli's generous yet vibrant grillo set the standard for dry renditions of that grape. Fermented with native yeasts and lees aged for an extra layer of depth, it's one of the island's most complex and sophisticated whites.

- **Alessandro Viola Catarratto "Il Mie Origini" ($$):** Viola first turned heads for his fleshy but laser-focused grillo wines, but this gently skin-fermented catarratto might just be his best wine yet. Rich almost to the point of creaminess, it backs up its full texture with the powerful salinity that is common to all Sicilian whites and a wash of mouthwatering acidity.

CAMPANIA AND BASILICATA

....

JUST THE HIGHLIGHTS

- The rugged regions of Campania and Basilicata are giving the iconic wines of northern Italy a run for their money. If it was once assumed that the bottom of the Boot had no answer to Barolo or Barbaresco, these southern Italian strongholds are quickly proving the conventional wisdom wrong.

- At the center of this transformation is a noble duo of native grapes. For reds, the thick-skinned aglianico has been dubbed the "nebbiolo of the south" for its intensity and ability to age. The textured, smoky fiano variety, native to Avellino, reveals a seriousness that's at odds with the usual stereotypes surrounding simple, easygoing Mediterreanean whites.

- The ascendance of Campania and Basilicata is one of Italian wine's great modern success stories. It's all part of the southern peninsula's wider rediscovery of its native grapes and growing regions.

Ever since Garibaldi united Italy in 1861, herding a chaotic mess of sovereign kingdoms and nation-states under one rule, a bitter rivalry has raged between the country's rich industrialized north and the stereotypically poor agricultural south. This central conflict extends to many aspects of Italian life, not least of all wine.

According to the accepted history, great wine comes from the north. While areas such as Piedmont and Friuli took full advantage of the country's postwar fiscal boom, investing in cutting-edge equipment and radically transforming quality, the bottom of the Boot missed out. Combating decades of economic hardship, its sparsely populated rural wine industries continued cranking out the same rustic country fare as before. Thus was born the age-old myth that there's no serious wine lurking below the Tuscan border.

Recently, however, a groundswell of artisanal winemaking has redefined the trajectory of Italy's entire southern peninsula. Of all the neglected, little-known areas to have clawed their way out of obscurity, none has shown as much promise or generated the same excitement as the wild, rugged regions of Campania, located on the volcanic slopes outside the capital of Naples, and Basilicata, another thrilling volcanic terroir in the foothills of Mount Vulture.

Fueling their success is the star power of a pair of native grapes, the potentials of which have only recently been realized. Every bit as impressive as their northern rivals, aglianico (responsible for rich, structured reds) and fiano (the next great southern white) have emerged as the crown jewels of the new Italian south.

THE REALMS OF AGLIANICO:
TAURASI, TABURNO, VULTURE

In an effort to express aglianico's nobility, critics have often described it as the "nebbiolo of the south." Of course, this comparison to the legendary grape of Barolo is flattering. But despite sharing some basic similarities (that is, fierce tannins, high acidity, and a serious capacity to age), it's the differences between the two varieties that highlight what aglianico ultimately brings to the table.

Big, bold, and built to last, everything about aglianico—from the volcanic soils in which it thrives to its full-bodied brawn and inky ripeness— speaks to its unambiguously southern identity. That shouldn't suggest, however, that aglianico wines are monolithic or lack transparency. At a time when we tend to equate balance with lightness and elegance, the powerful complexity of an age-worthy aglianico serves as an important reminder that finesse comes in many shapes and sizes.

To that end, aglianico expresses itself differently across each of its main growing areas. To many, it reaches its greatest heights (both literally and figuratively) in the mountainous vineyards of Taurasi, perched in Campania's Irpinia zone not far from Mount Vesuvius. Often painfully austere in their youth, the best Taurasi wines stand toe-to-toe with any top Barolo or Brunello in terms of longevity; over time, they soften into a savory, meaty elegance with the floral spice and smoky minerality that conjure the wine's genesis in the shadow of a volcano. For slightly softer, drink-me-now alternatives, the Taburno region in the province of Benevento showcases the grape's approachable side, full of brambly black-berry fruit without sacrificing any of that classic Campanian tar and ash.

Finally, the most lavish (but never to the point of jamminess, thanks to their high acidity) aglianico wines come from the region of Vulture, just across the border in Basilicata. Named after the extinct volcano that looms over the area's craggy landscape, Aglianico del Vulture combines the grape's heady fruit and licorice-inflected spice with the tannic struc-ture to improve for decades, all the while delivering that same blast of minerals it shares with its counterparts from Campania.

Essential Producers: Cantine Lonardo, De Conciliis, Cantine Guastaferro, Luigi Tecce, Salvatore Molettieri, Pietracupa, LeLùSi, Macarico, Musto Carmelitano

THE REALM OF FIANO: AVELLINO

If aglianico is the south's reigning red, then the ancient fiano variety is its essential white. And much like its deeply pigmented cousin, rich, luscious fiano makes no excuses for its full-bodied southern heritage.

Except that, from Italy's shin on downward, the dominant image for southern whites has long been that of the zippy coastal wine. To be sure, Campania has no shortage of examples to fit that description—notably, the falanghina grape, which enjoyed a modest vogue on Italian wine lists during the early aughts, as well as greco, a grape that grows up and down the country's southern coast. Fiano, however, has earned its world-class status by embodying a contrary idea of the south—one defined by a resinous density, texture, and savoriness.

Although it's grown across Campania (and other parts of the Italian south as well), the grape fares best not along the shoreline but up in the densely forested foothills of Avellino, where plantings survive at elevations of more than two thousand feet. These extreme heights not only retain freshness in the grapes but extend ripening times as well, resulting in a dynamic tension between chiseled acidity, briny salinity, and a nutty, almost honeyed weight on the tongue: think beeswax, wild herbs (especially basil), and a gunflint smokiness (are you beginning to see a pattern?) that tells you all you need to know about the area's ancient ashen soils.

Increasingly produced in a generous style (lees aged, fermented in concrete tank or old wood cask) designed to accentuate the grape's intrinsic richness rather than stifle it, fiano stands to benefit from the wider celebration of fleshy, textured whites that recently made sommelier darlings out of wines such as Loire chenin blanc (see page 84) and Greek assyrtiko (see page 268). At the very least, it has proved itself to be every bit as essential to the Italian repertoire as the classic whites of Alto Adige and Friuli, matching their northerly purity and precision with an extra helping of warm-blooded southern swagger.

Essential Producers: Ciro Picariello, De Conciliis, Pietracupa, Benito Ferrara, Clelia Romano, Cantina di Lisandro

THE WINE LIST

- **Pietracupa Fiano di Avellino ($$):** Ever since taking over his family vineyards three decades ago, Sabino Loffredo has built a reputation for ripe yet chiseled fiano (plus some greco and aglianico) from the mountainous terrain of Avellino. Aged for eight months in stainless-steel tanks, this has a briny, caper-like tang that melds into what might be called a honeyed richness if it weren't for the bright spike of acidity that seems to cleave the wine in two.

- **Ciro Picariello "Ciro 906" Fiano di Avellino ($$):** To understand how texture in white wine works, you need only experience Ciro Picariello's "Ciro 906." Its age-worthiest fiano, sourced from a single plot of old, high-elevation vines, the wine wears its golden apple fleshiness (the result of extended lees aging) over a backbone of smoky minerality, lemony acids, and a dense pine-sap quality that somehow makes it feel richer and more refreshing at the same time.

- **Cantine Lonardo Taurasi ($$):** In the heart of Taurasi, the family-run Cantine Lonardo has perfected a traditional style of aglianico that ignores the modern fashion for new oak and jammy fruit. Assembled from a selection of different parcels, the excellent standard-issue Taurasi (the estate also makes a handful of single-vineyard versions) is aged in a combination of stainless-steel tanks and large wooden casks.

- **Musto Carmelitano "Serra del Prete" Aglianico del Vulture ($$):** Basilicata's versions of aglianico can be even richer and inkier than their Campanian counterparts. Derived from fifty-year-old vines planted high up in the blackened soils of Mount Vulture, this example from the organic Musto Carmelitano estate doesn't lack in power or concentration, but it also has a savory earthiness and the smoky volcanic aspect that runs through all of the region's best wines.

SPAIN

Spanish wine has taken quite a long time to learn how to be traditional again. First, there was Franco. Under the general's rule, many of the country's family-owned vineyards fell into disrepair and the majority of Spanish wine was bulk manufactured by a handful of large cooperative wineries. The situation remained unchanged until the collapse of the fascist regime, when a fresh influx of capital from foreign investors attempted to catapult the nation's ailing wine industry into the modern era. This cry for modernization culminated in the 1980s and 1990s with the development of an unapologetically international style known as Alta Expresión.

Over recent decades, however, a new Spanish revolution has taken hold. Often taking its cues from France's natural wine movement—which embraces organic viticulture and a minimalist attitude in the cellar—a younger generation of winemakers has been busy resuscitating Spain's neglected local wine regions. This back-to-the-roots approach, which involves replanting local vineyards and rescuing indigenous grapes, aligns with the larger goal of reclaiming and articulating the diversity of the country's unsung terroirs.

RIOJA

· · · · · · · · · · · ·

JUST THE HIGHLIGHTS

- ◆ In the world of Spanish wine, it doesn't get any bigger or more important than Rioja. Ever since the nineteenth century, the region has almost single-handedly defined Spanish wine on the global front, thanks largely to the star power of tempranillo, its main indigenous grape.

- ◆ Rioja can be confusing. Between the so-called traditional style—mellow, savory, earthy, and full of sour cherries and leather—and the rise of a fruit-driven modern style in the 1980s and 1990s, it's often difficult to know what to expect when you open a bottle.

- ◆ Rioja is one of the greatest values in fine wine. Aged to perfection at the winery (often for several years), the celebrated *reserva* and *gran reserva* wines are released only when they're ready to drink—and at bargain prices compared to the top wines of France and Italy.

- ◆ Historically blended from grapes sourced from across the region, Rioja is evolving toward a greater understanding of terroir. The region recently approved several geographically specific designations, including a new wave of single-vineyard expressions.

What Bordeaux is to France and Tuscany is to Italy, Rioja is to Spain: the nation's leading and longest-established fine wine region. Ironically, it's often the classics, like Rioja, that prove hardest to pin down.

When you pull a bottle of Rioja off the shelf, it's not always obvious what you're about to get. Light, juicy reds meant for early consumption? Elegant, classically structured blends aged for years in old American oak? Sleek single-varietal wines of mouth-coating ripeness and velvety dark fruit? Rioja is all of these and more. While stylistic diversity is never a bad thing, this chameleon-like spectrum of possibilities makes Rioja's personality more than a little perplexing.

WHAT DOES CLASSIC RIOJA TASTE LIKE?

If Rioja represents an aesthetic minefield today, how it came to be that way is a familiar tale scripted by the usual factors: rapid commercial investment, the technological march of progress, and fluctuations in global taste. But what we generally consider to be Rioja's classical mode—the archetypal style upon which its reputation for greatness was initially built—emerged during the nineteenth century.

Devastated by the infamous phylloxera epidemic that would eventually decimate nearly all of Europe's vines, displaced winemakers from Bordeaux migrated south to Rioja, which had so far been spared. Catering to the sudden gap in the French market, they established a set of practices modeled after Bordeaux, including the careful blending of varieties—in this case, the region's star grape, tempranillo, alongside garnacha, mazuelo, and graciano—and extended aging in small barrels.

Thus was born the elegant, profoundly age-worthy expression of Rioja that we have come to define as traditional: earthy, perfumed, tempranillo-dominant blends with moderate alcohol levels and flavors of sour cherry and leather, all interwoven with a faint vanilla spice acquired over years of slow maturation in neutral American oak. Associated with iconic properties such as Bodegas Muga, La Rioja Alta,

CVNE, and the virtually frozen-in-time López de Heredia estate, this is the Rioja that canonically minded drinkers around the world celebrate as Spain's unrivaled benchmark.

In the CliffsNotes version of the region's history, this archetypal Rioja is upheld as a foil for the full-throttle cabernet-like versions—jammy, rich, and matured in new French *barriques*—that arose during Spain's version of the modern versus traditional style wars of the 1980s and 1990s. Custom-built for the export market, these wines often feature tempranillo as a single variety, smoothing out the grape's old-school rustic edges in favor of a commercial polish.

Regardless of personal preference, there's no reason a wine industry as large and robust as Rioja's shouldn't be able to incorporate different aesthetic camps. A few decades removed from the heart of that struggle, these two Riojas coexist, and, as in Barolo (see page 123), what once felt like a binary divide is giving way to a subtler stylistic spectrum. Today, however, a new form of identity politics is heating up in the region, fueling a different but arguably deeper debate that has the potential to reshape Rioja as we know it.

RETHINKING RIOJA'S TRADITIONAL STYLES

So central to Rioja's identity is the practice of barrel aging that it forms the basis of the region's traditional classification system. That system is not based on terroir distinctions as is Burgundy's, but on a hierarchy of aging requirements. Starting with the fresh unoaked *joven* wines at the bottom of the pyramid, it works its way up to the *crianza* and *reserva* levels, culminating in the rare *gran reserva* wines, released after no fewer than seven years of aging.

JOVEN

Without any aging requirements, joven wines are produced in a bright, fruity style designed for immediate consumption.

CRIANZA

Accessible and easy-drinking, crianzas offer a solid introduction to the region's cherry-and-spice charm. Assembled from a wide range of vineyards, they serve as Rioja's commercial backbone.

RESERVA

A step up in structure and seriousness, the *reserva* category is where Rioja properly becomes Rioja, revealing the secondary flavors and aromas (leather, tobacco, earth) that come with added age.

GRAN RESERVA

Only produced in exceptional vintages from the finest vineyards of a *bodega*, the large Rioja wineries, these are the crown jewels of Spanish wine. The best can continue to age for decades in bottle, offering wonderfully mellow, complex flavors that rival any of the great wines of the world.

These categories were originally conceived as indicators of quality; the implication being that the top grapes from the best sites would go into the most prestigious *reserva* and *gran reserva* designations. But the reality of the situation isn't so simple. When a low-end supermarket brand's $20 *gran reserva* shares shelf space with an iconic bottling from one of Rioja's leading estates, the standard of comparison risks losing all meaning.

A bigger question, however, is the system's relevance to consumers today. The traditional emphasis on time in barrel and bottle is increasingly at odds with a wine culture that places a premium on geographic specificity. The issue goes back to the region's long history of blending. As in brand-conscious Champagne, the *bodegas* would traditionally purchase grapes from across the region to be assembled into a consistent final product.

Unlike Champagne, however, which has directed more and more attention to the diversity of its terroirs, up until just a few years ago Rioja's labeling laws prohibited mentioning even the most basic geographical details. The extent of the terroir conversation rarely went beyond the usual rundown of the area's three main subregions, which contrasted the elegance of the cooler Rioja Alta and Rioja Alavesa zones with the warmer and somewhat less heralded Rioja Baja (recently renamed Rioja Oriental)—not that any of these designations were permitted to appear on the bottle.

But that's starting to change. Following a controversial campaign to petition the Rioja's regulatory body, in 2017 a new set of rules was approved to bring a fresh consciousness of terroir into the region, making possible not only village- and subregion-specific bottlings but also single-vineyard wines (or *vinedos singulares*). The passing of this legislation has empowered an exciting group of producers, including Olivier Rivière, Abel Mendoza, and Telmo Rodríguez, among many others, who are more interested in expressing the singularity of their soils than relying on the usual *crianza*, *reserva*, *gran reserva* model.

Emblematic of this shift, wines such as Rivière's "Losares" bottling—a field blend derived from a single vineyard of eighty-five-year-old vines in the village of Navaridas—are leaner, fresher, and brighter than either of Rioja's established styles (classic or modern), featuring noticeably less wood character. By breaking with tradition, they're inviting some far-reaching questions: Which is the truest expression of Rioja? A time-honored *gran reserva* sourced from a mosaic of terroirs and produced using the same techniques that have been handed down for generations? Or a wine that offers deeper insight into the nuances of a single site or subregion, introducing an entirely new place-based paradigm?

Lucky for us, there's no need to decide. The fact that we now have more than one lens through which to view the region only enriches our understanding of Rioja and expands the possibilities for what it's already in the midst of becoming.

Essential Producers: López de Heredia, Hermanos Peciña, CVNE, Olivier Rivière, Bodegas Muga, La Rioja Alta, Bodegas y Viñedos Artadi, Bodega Akutain, Bodegas Ostatu, Bodega Lanzaga

THE WINE LIST

◆ CVNE Monopole "Monopole Clásico" Rioja Blanco ($$): In sharp contrast to the winery's popular tank-fermented "Monopole" white, the recently released "Clásico" expression signals a remake of the wine as it existed more than forty years ago. Matured in wood and (believe it or not) topped up with manzanilla sherry purchased from the Hidalgo family of Sanlúcar de Barrameda, it's a history lesson in a glass.

◆ Hermanos Peciña Rioja Crianza ($): A baby by local standards, the Peciña estate was founded in 1992 but has quickly joined the ranks of Rioja's classically minded producers. Its affordable Crianza is everything the category should be: fresh and easy drinking but with a savory depth and just a hint of American oak.

◆ López de Heredia Rioja "Bosconia" Reserva ($$): All of the López de Heredia wines are beloved time capsules; but compared to the richer, dark-fruited "Tondonia" bottling, the classic "Bosconia" Reserva puts Rioja's leafy, sour cherry, high-toned aspect on full display. With five years of barrel age, it's as classic as Rioja gets.

◆ Olivier Rivière Rioja "Rayos Uva" ($$): Working with only bio-dynamically farmed vineyards, French-born Olivier Rivière is leading the charge of site-specific Rioja. His single-vineyard wines understandably command most of the attention, but for a completely different take on the region, this vibrant unoaked wine—sourced from younger vines in the Rioja Baja—is pure unadulterated fun.

WHAT TO MAKE OF RIBERA DEL DUERO?

Along with Priorat (see page 202) and Rioja, Ribera del Duero completes the holy trinity of heavy-hitting reds that rep Spain on the global stage. Located roughly two hours north of Madrid in the dry rocky hills of the autonomous community of Castile and León (Castilla y León), the region benefited from the same economic boom that transfigured so much of rural Spain during the 1980s and 1990s.

True to that era's "bigger is better" mentality, Ribera del Duero staked its reputation on the success of a blockbuster style of tempranillo—locally called *tinto fino*—engineered to upstage Rioja's classical expression. Inspired by the historic success of the area's renowned Vega Sicilia estate—which, to this day, produces Spain's most exorbitantly expensive wine, "Unico"—winemaker Alejandro Fernández of the celebrated Pesquera label was the first to adopt this powerhouse style. Once he started racking up scores, a rash of others soon followed, including the overnight sensation of Dutch-born Peter Sisseck's Dominio de Pingus, another highly coveted trophy.

Decades later, these top bottles share the same blue-chip status as any of France's or Italy's priciest collector's items. These days, a bottle of Pingus will easily set you back $1,000. But much has changed since Ribera del Duero's meteoric rise. In our brave new world of Spanish wine, comprising fresh discoveries such as Galician mencía and listán negro from the Canary Islands (see pages 188 and 206, respectively), one can't shake the sense that Ribera del Duero is lagging behind.

As it brushes up against the limitations of its original cult wine model, the lesson to be gleaned from Ribera del Duero is that even the most financially successful areas require fresh energy to adapt and evolve. So as Rioja embraces its traditional roots while rethinking its relationship to its soils, and Priorat works to redefine its notions of power and intensity, Ribera del Duero's future remains an open question.

Still, there's cause for hope. Although far from a cohesive movement, a small cohort of individual growers is actively challenging the status quo. Rather than push their wines in a predictable direction, winemakers such as Goyo García Viadero, Alfredo Maestro, and Dominio del Águila's Jorge Monzón are pursuing a less-is-more approach. By farming organically, harvesting earlier, fermenting with native yeasts, and avoiding the usual high jinks in the cellar, they're revealing what the region might be if stripped of its usual luxury trappings and reimagined as a wine of terroir.

For example, Goyo García Viadero's "Finca el Peruco" and Alfredo Maestro's stunning "La Asperilla" are both sourced from extremely old parcels planted to traditional blends of red and white grapes. Together, they conjure a previous chapter of the region's history, before its transformation into a commercial powerhouse. Pushing that retro spirit even further, Dominio del Águila's strawberry-colored "Clarete" was conceived as a modern homage to the light, almost rosé-like field blends the Ribero del Duero's farmers drank during harvest generations ago.

Wines such as these lay the foundations for a deeper connection to place and, in doing so, prove a salient point: to be truly modern requires a working knowledge of the past.

Essential Producers: Goyo García Viadero, Alfredo Maestro, Dominio del Águila

GALICIA

·················

JUST THE HIGHLIGHTS

- Cool, wet, and rainy, Galicia is known as "green Spain," and its wines directly reflect that suggestion of freshness. The maritime region, located in the northwest of the country, couldn't be more diametrically opposed to the popular image of Spanish wine, requiring an alternative vocabulary of brightness, purity, and minerality.

- If crisp, aromatic whites are your thing, they're Galicia's specialty. The region's star white, albariño from the Rías Baixas subregion, is the quintessential coastal wine, custom-built to pair with anything pulled from the sea.

- Galicia's native red, mencía, is responsible for some of Spain's freshest, high-acid reds. The grape's thrilling expressions from Ribeira Sacra have emerged as instant modern classics and drink a bit as if Beaujolais and northern Rhône syrah gave birth to a Spanish love child.

It's easy to think about Spanish wine in broad strokes. What comes to mind are big, robust reds from hot, dry places: Priorat, Rioja, Ribera del Duero. Then there's Galicia, the perennial exception.

Part of "green Spain," the cool, misty region unfurls along the country's eucalyptus-forested, sea-sprayed northwestern coast, where the influence of the chilly Atlantic is never far from mind. The local dialect is Gallego (closer to Portuguese), bagpipes erupt at a moment's notice (a legacy of Galicia's Celtic heritage), the diet is based heavily on the finned and crustaceous (the seafood is among the world's best), and wine is synonymous with vibrancy, high acid, and minerality.

In modern times, this outlier status has cemented Galicia's reputation as one of Spain's most promising destinations for wine. Attracted by the possibilities of its cooler microclimates and unique native varieties, an influx of winemaking talent has constellated there, generating the momentum and energy necessary to catch the eye of the industry in-crowd on this side of the Atlantic. To Galicia's ever-growing US fan base, whose taste aligns with the current vogue for brightness and transparency, the region represents the "other" Spain—the Spain for people who think they don't particularly care for Spanish wine.

RÍAS BAIXAS

If every aspiring region needs a star grape to hitch its fortunes to, for years it appeared that the answer to Galicia's prayers would be albariño. A specialty of the Rías Baixas subregion—named after the four finger-shaped estuaries that carve their way into the provinces of Pontevedra and Corunna—the lively, high-acid wine is traditionally imbibed young (and by the gallon) in the area's sleepy fishing villages.

Readers old enough to recall the Clinton impeachment trial might remember albariño's brief flirtation with fame. Back in the 1990s, after a decades-long effort to modernize and polish itself up for the international market, the variety rode a wave of hype billed as something like Spain's answer to Sancerre.

That initial surge of popularity, however, never quite achieved true staying power. Over time, albariño was relegated to the realm of perfectly reliable whites that wine writers typically prescribe as an antidote to the same old pinot grigio and sauvignon blanc. When it's overcropped and churned out in bulk, as is too often the case with albariño, that's basically all you can expect. But this simplistic image of Rías Baixas belies the saline pungency and herbal complexity that the variety is capable of attaining when held to more rigorous standards.

Above all, these are maritime wines; the seashore is part of their DNA. In drinking them, you want to taste those rocky miles of coastline, that tidal salinity and cool Atlantic breeze. So while certain producers have looked to French *barrique* and excessive *bâtonnage* as one way to deepen albariño's stylistic spectrum, their efforts miss the point of what Rías Baixas is geographically designed to be.

The examples revolutionizing the category today push the boundaries in a different way, magnifying the qualities that are unique to albariño from this foggy corner of Spain. This is accomplished not by fattening the wines up through tricks in the cellar, but by embracing a more conscientious approach to the vineyard. When low yields, sustainable farming, and small-scale production methods join forces, what comes into focus is one of the country's truest illustrations of place.

The classic example of Rías Baixas's deeper side is the celebrated Do Ferreiro estate's "Cepas Vellas" bottling. Sourced from a plot of two-hundred-year-old albariño vines in the Salnés Valley subzone, it offers a unique perspective on the region's terroir—all crushed rock, white flowers, lemon oil, and iodine sea air.

As the embodiment of a more expansive albariño paradigm, it's increasingly finding itself in good company. Through the work of influential importers such as José Pastor, who specializes in Spain's little-known independent grower-producers, a vibrant crop of artisanal albariños

GALICIA'S OTHER WHITE

While Rías Baixas albariño is Galicia's most famous white, lately a great deal of innovation is taking place outside of that region, focusing on an array of native whites. Chief among these are the areas of Valdeorras and Monterrei, where Galicia's second white grape, godello, takes center stage, alongside a supporting cast of grapes such as treixadura, albariño, and loureiro, which speak to the region's proximity to Vinho Verde just over the Portuguese border.

After a recent identity crisis, during which producers experimented with a glossy, Burgundian style of godello, the grape is now hitting its stride. When it manages to avoid flabbiness and excessive new oak, the results are captivating: a bit richer and more succulent than albariño, with a warm honeyed quality, floral aromatics, and Galicia's signature acidity.

Essential Producers: A. Coroa, Guímaro, Ronsel do Sil, Rafael Palacios, Viña Somoza has been washing up on US shores; by focusing on subtle nuances of site and microclimate, they offer a deeper look below the region's crisp and serviceable veneer.

Essential Producers: Do Ferreiro, Bodegas Albamar, Pedralonga, Nanclares y Prieto, Benito Santos

RIBEIRA SACRA

If albariño once promised to be Galicia's great white hope, the region's singular reds have since stolen the spotlight. At the center of this turnaround is the indigenous mencía grape. Once obscure, the variety now draws comparisons to some of the most beloved red wines in the world.

Imagine the juicy, lip-smacking transparency of gamay from Beaujolais combined with the brambly earthiness and peppery spice of northern Rhône syrah. Then imagine planting that grape in the steep terraced slopes of Ribeira Sacra, the variety's ancestral home in the forests of eastern Galicia, high above the winding Miño and Sil Rivers. Few red wines possess the depth, agility, and freshness that these ancient, rugged vines coax out of mencía, which has been cultivated in the area since the Roman era.

The fact that we've only recently discovered such exceptional wines shouldn't be surprising. As in most Spanish regions, the twentieth century didn't do the area any favors. First came civil war, then Franco's dictatorship and decades of economic depression. By the 1980s, most of Ribeira Sacra's vineyards had been long abandoned, the younger generation having fled to the cities, unwilling to perform the backbreaking labor of tending such precipitous plots.

The narrative of Ribeira Sacra's comeback, however, follows a slightly different arc than other parts of Spain. The usual story (at least the 1990s version of it) is characterized by foreign investment and the embrace of a more lucrative market-driven style (see Priorat, page 202). In Ribeira

Sacra, however, not only did the renaissance come from within—most of the region's stars, such as Pedro Rodríguez of the much-admired Guímaro winery, are native-born—but it largely avoided awkward concessions to international taste. So by the early aughts, when touchstones such as D. Ventura's single-vineyard "Viña Caneiro" bottling, for instance, or any of Guímaro's exhilarating expressions of old-vine mencía started to trickle into the market, the profile of Ribeira Sacra as we now know it was already fully manifest.

Although mencía thrives in other parts of Galicia (and in neighboring Bierzo as well), it's in Ribeira Sacra that the grape's reputation was first formed and where it continues to spark the most excitement. To discover it today is to catch one of the truly exceptional red wine regions in the process of coming into its own.

Essential Producers: Adega Algueira, Adegas Guímaro, D. Ventura, Castro Candaz, Ronsel do Sil, Dominio do Bibei, Luis A. Rodríguez Vázquez, Envínate

THE WINE LIST

- **Pedralonga Baixas Rías Albariño ($):** Pedralonga's "DoUmio" mencía has emerged as a sleeper sommelier hit, but the winery's specialty lies in incredibly saline, site-specific, native yeast–fermented albariños that burst with Atlantic freshness. A product of forty-year-old vines planted just ten miles from the ocean, this is the Galician coast in a glass.

- **Alberto Nanclares Albariño Rías Baixas ($$):** From several parcels of thirty- to sixty-year-old vines planted on decomposed clay and granite soils, this complex, structured organic albariño from Alberto Nanclares proves what that grape can do when given the chance to tell the whole story of Rías Baixas's maritime terroir.

- ◆ A. Coroa Valdeorras Godello ($): One of the most trusted godellos found on the market today, this organically farmed wine from hillside vineyards near the village of A Rúa is harvested by hand and fermented with natural yeasts. It exhibits some of the succulent roundness and tropical fruit associated with the grape, but its snappy acidity always saves the day.

- ◆ D. Ventura "Viña do Burato" Ribeira Sacra ($): Highlighting mencía's chuggable, easy-drinking side, the Viña do Burato is the value wine in D. Ventura's estimable lineup of site-specific Ribeira Sacra wines. Coming from a cooler, wetter site than the others, it's full of sea spray and tart cranberries.

- ◆ Guímaro Ribeira Sacra "Finca Meixeman" ($$): If you're going to try just one mencía, let it be Pedro Rodríguez's dazzling expression of the Meixeman vineyard's seventy-year-old vines. A more convincing case for Ribeira Sacra's greatness couldn't be made: like drinking a gamy, peppery old-school French syrah but with more verve and lift.

BASQUE COUNTRY

JUST THE HIGHLIGHTS

◆ Plenty of wines are more complex than txakoli, the most emblematic expression of Spain's Basque country, but few are more refreshing. As the thirst for all things clean and acid-driven reaches its peak, the shockingly crisp (almost to the point of astringency), ever-so-slightly effervescent Basque tavern wine has morphed into the latest summertime sensation.

◆ Txakoli comes in all colors. Most often you'll encounter the traditional lemony whites, but spritzy txakoli rosé is just as popular. There's even a small amount of red txakoli circulating through the market, notable for its low alcohol and herbaceous, berryish flavors.

◆ Drink txakoli as young as it comes. In their Basque homeland, these wines are consumed as early as possible, while they're at their prickly best.

Much easier to drink than to pronounce, txakoli is the official wine of the *pintxos* taverns of San Sebastián, the northerly Basque equivalent of the tapas bars that proliferate farther south in "sherry country" (aka Jerez; see page 209).

While the concept behind both traditions is essentially the same (eat, sip, swallow; repeat for as long as you can remain upright), txakoli couldn't be further removed from the fortified realm of sherry. Intensely lean, low ABV, and slightly frothy, it's not an aged wine to be sipped and savored but a young one to be gleefully chugged—ideally in traditional Basque fashion, after being poured from precariously high above one's head into the mouth of a tumbler several feet below.

This practice, known in Spanish as *escanciar*, is intended to emphasize the wine's natural effervescence. It would be hard, however, to repress txakoli's signature ability to refresh. Based on the searingly high-acid hondarrabi zuri and hondarrabi beltza grapes, the category arrived out of nowhere just a few years ago to secure its perennial place in the annual rotation of go-to summer pours. The wine has become so wildly popular that an annual txakoli fest is now held in its honor. So how did this unpronounceable beverage from a stretch of Spain better known as a tourist hot spot go on to become such a runaway hit here in the United States? That question can be answered in just three syllables: Ameztoi. One of the area's top producers, this modest family-run property almost single-handedly established txakoli's stateside reputation.

A viral sensation from the moment it hit the market, it was the now-legendary "Rubentis" rosé that first captured the trade's attention, riding into visibility on the larger "pink wave" that forced many adventurous somms to look beyond the familiar horizons of southern France to satisfy their rosé jones. Still the category's benchmark, all sea spray and raspberry Smarties, it now sells out almost instantly each year. Happily, other wines have followed in its wake, fashioned after the same addictively brisk, saliva-inducing mold.

Essential Producers: Ameztoi, Txomin Etxaniz, Bodegas Zudugarai, Rekalde

THE WINE LIST

◆ **Ameztoi Getariako Txakolina "Rubentis" Rosé ($):** Equal parts hondarrabi zuri and hondarrabi beltza, this is the breakout txakoli that started it all. The slight spritz of CO_2, the powdered rock minerality, the hint of grapefruit-skin bitterness—all of these aspects combine to form one of the most infectiously drinkable wines ever bottled under a screw cap.

◆ Txomin Etxaniz Getariako Txakolina ($): Every bit a classic in its own right, Txomin Etxaniz's white Txakolina is a textbook representation of the regional style. Made from vineyards located just a few hundred feet from the ocean, this is a "beach read" of a wine that drinks like bottled sea spray from the coast of San Sebastián.

CATALONIA

. . . .

JUST THE HIGHLIGHTS

♦ Catalonia is best known for Cava. The famous traditional method Spanish sparkler is produced mostly in the Catalonian region of Penedès, surrounding the region's capital of Barcelona.

♦ If you think of Cava as a cheap, mass-produced Champagne alternative, think again. The category is now being reinterpreted in light of an important question: What does it mean to make world-class Spanish bubbly with an identity of its own?

♦ Penedès is expanding beyond bubbly. Of late, the burgeoning natural wine scene has transformed the region into one of the most interesting and diverse in Spain, highlighting complex non-sparkling whites (plus a handful of fresh reds and rosés).

♦ Priorat is the most recent addition to Spain's roster of big, important reds. The region exploded out of obscurity in the 1980s and 1990s thanks to its massively extracted, boozy, in-your-face appeal. After making some of Spain's biggest and most expensive reds, it's now thinking seriously about terroir and putting a (relatively) lighter foot forward.

In the streets and bustling bars and cafés of Barcelona, Catalonia's capital, you hear the local Catalan dialect spoken more often than Spanish. As its recent bid for independence made clear, the region has always insisted on its own cultural and political autonomy from the rest of Spain. It's a bit of a paradox that no other region better encapsulates the story of modern Spanish wine.

The two major Catalan wine regions—Penedès, home to the multimillion-dollar sparkling wine industry of Cava, and Priorat, which arrived out of nowhere in the 1990s to storm Spain's pantheon of full-bodied reds—are both potent symbols of Spain's twentieth-century technological revolution. Today, confronted with the growing pains that come with different versions of rapid success, they're grappling with the same fundamental question: What comes next?

THE OTHER PENEDÈS

It was Cava, Spain's preeminent sparkling wine, that first put Penedès on the map. Or perhaps more accurately, Cava put *itself* on the map. Today, the bubbly represents one of Spain's most popular household names.

That recognition, however, has been slow to spread to the rest of the Penedès area. But lately, fueled in no small part by Barcelona's energetic natural wine scene, Penedès has emerged as a source for excellent still whites. As a result, Cava is now just one part of a far more diverse tale about the region's identity.

It's impossible to understand the story that is unfolding in the hills of Penedès without looking at the new (and, in most cases, natural) producers who are in the midst of writing it. Across the area, the up-and-coming generation has made it their mission to reject the dominant mode of industrial Cava and find out what else their soils can do. As in other parts of Spain, this ambition has taken the form of a renewed interest in indigenous grapes—namely, the main Cava varieties of macabeo, xarel·lo, and parellada, plus others such as garnacha blanca and the fresh red trepat—as well as a shift toward sustainable and low-impact practices.

At the center of this movement are rising stars such as Enric Soler, the former sommelier who is crafting some of the area's greatest whites from vines he inherited from his grandfather, Finca Parera's Rubén Parera, whose biodynamically farmed wines have become stateside sommelier darlings, and Toni Carbó of Celler La Salada, the talent behind a range of fresh, unsulfured single-vineyard expressions of xarel·lo.

Essential Producers: Enric Soler, Celler la Salada, Finca Parera, Celler de les Aus, Finca Sabaté i Coca, Celler Pardas

THE NEW CAVA

Even as Penedès continues to trespass beyond the familiar confines of Cava, the world-famous bubbly is wrestling with some existential questions of its own. Until the 1970s, when Champagne prohibited use of the term, sparkling wine from Spain was most often labeled as *champaña*. This brief lesson in nomenclature is relevant insofar as it speaks to Cava's origins as something of an off-brand knockoff—Champagne but with a Spanish "squiggle."

Fittingly, that's how Cava has been treated through most of its existence. Like Prosecco, its chief rival in the discount bubbly department, the category has been typecast into an extremely perfunctory role: to be there when you're in need of bubbles but aren't feeling terribly discriminating about it.

Unlike Prosecco, however, Cava is made according to the traditional (aka Champagne) method of secondary fermentation in bottle. If only for this reason, there have always been individual examples that entertained more serious ambitions—generally vintage-dated wines labeled as *reserva* or *gran reserva* and aged for months (or even years) on lees. But if the category is now poised to outgrow the mass-market image that first launched its career, it hasn't always been clear what premium

Cava should be. Is it just a higher-end version of Spanish Champagne? Or could Cava encompass something more—a sparkling wine idiom entirely its own?

This is the question that several of the area's more ambitious producers have been posing for over a decade now, culminating in the creation of the single-vineyard Cava de Paraje Calificado classification in 2017. Implementing stricter regulations to guide production, including limitations on yields and a minimum of thirty-six months aging in bottle, the new system aimed to uncover what Cava might offer not as a fizzy industrial fill-in but rather as a carefully made wine of terroir.

These site-specific examples have helped carve out the finer details of Cava's identity—a process that means highlighting it as a uniquely Iberian approach to sparkling wine rather than holding it up to the mirror of Champagne. This ambition definitely applies to wines such as biodynamic Recaredo estate's "Serral del Vell" bottling, which was among the first to receive the Cava de Paraje classification. Based on roughly equal parts macabeo and xarel•lo, it delivers a bright, foamy mouthful of sea spray and sun-drenched fruit, far removed in both style and spirit from the chilly cellars of northern France.

But there's always risk involved in chasing after a deliberately elevated style. To that end, Cava would do itself a favor by avoiding Champagne's time-honored affinity for luxury branding. When used as an excuse to charge more for an opulent "prestige" cuvée, premium designations such as Cava de Paraje can easily backfire. As interpreted by some of the region's larger commercial houses, the results occasionally veer in that direction, featuring over-the-top lees aging and excessive French oak. More often than not, this also means the inclusion of nonnative grapes (pinot noir and chardonnay) in addition to indigenous varieties, such as macabeo, xarel•lo, parellada, and trepat.

It's probably too early to speak of a full-fledged grower Cava movement, but the work being done on behalf of the region's independent producers could soon change that. At the very least, they're farm-ing their land with the goal of producing distinctly Spanish sparkling wines—fleshy, savory, herb tinged, and mineral—that couldn't be mis-taken as coming from anywhere else.

Essential Producers: German Gilabert, Fermí Bohigas, Castellroig, Cellers de Can Suriol, Raventós i Blanc, Recaredo, Clos Lentiscus

PRIORAT

The rugged, mountainous territory of Priorat, near the medieval city of Tarragona, was once the sort of frozen-in-time backwater found across much of the Spanish countryside.

Now one of Spain's most expensive and highly coveted trophy wines, Priorat (and its rags-to-riches backstory) speaks to the seismic changes that rocked the Spanish wine industry toward the end of the twenti-eth century. That history begins in the 1980s with a group of outside investors—chief among them René Barbier of the internationally renowned Clos Mogador estate and Álvaro Palacios, whose L'Ermita wines are now among the most sought after in Spain—who recog-nized hidden potential in the abandoned centuries-old garnacha and cariñena vines (in French, grenache and carignan) dotting the region's rocky precipices. Applying the latest winemaking techniques and new French *barriques* to the low yields eked out of the impoverished *llicorella* ("brown slate" in Catalan) soils, they pioneered a full-throttle, high-alcohol style—often incorporating new plantings of syrah and cabernet sauvignon—that would reinvent the region overnight.

In other words, balance wasn't exactly Priorat's strong suit. For this reason, ever since its heyday in the 1990s and early aughts, the region's cachet has waned among younger industry types, who tend to view Priorat as embodying all that's wrong with Spanish wine today. To those willing to experience its wines with an open mind, however, that cat-egorization isn't entirely fair. As Priorat embraces a fresher aesthetic, it faces the challenge of staying true to what it was always designed to be—the biggest and most impressive of Spain's big, impressive reds—while establishing a more enlightened definition of grandeur.

One of the most successful proponents of change, the Terroir al Limit project, founded in 2004 by German winemaker Dominik Huber, offers a glimpse of the new Priorat paradigm. Farming organically, employing whole cluster fermentation, and aging his wines in large oak *foudres*, Huber has helped to usher in a fresher, mineral-driven, yet still undeniably powerful style of Priorat that homes in on the subtler inflections of terroir.

Essential Producers: Terroir al Limit, Ferrer Bobet, Costers del Priorat, Fredi Torres, Familia Nin-Ortiz

MONTSANT

Priorat is a place defined by extremes: of altitude, terroir, stylistic intensity, and, unavoidably, cost. But it's possible to get a sense of the region's steep, high-elevation aesthetic without paying those equally steep prices. The wines of neighboring Montsant, which practically surrounds Priorat like a ring, capitalize equally on old garnacha and cariñena vines planted at just slightly lower elevations. You might not get the full effect of Priorat's fireworks, but these wines still pack plenty of sizzle.

Essential Producers: La Figuera, Joan D'Anguera, Orto Vins, Sindicat La Figuera

THE WINE LIST

◆ **Enric Soler "Nun Vinya dels Taus" Xarel•lo ($$):** A leader of Catalonia's contemporary avant-garde, Enric Soler proves the greatness of old-vine xarel•lo—nearly seventy years old to be precise—from the minuscule Nun vineyard, which he farms biodynamically as he does all of his parcels. Its lemony richness and mineral tension conjure great white Burgundy.

◆ **Recaredo "Terrers" Brut Nature Cava ($$):** All of the Recaredo estate's wines come highly recommended, but this, its flagship bottling, is the one that will make a believer out of any Cava skeptic. Aged five years on the lees yet without a trace of heaviness or pomp, it doesn't just transcend the category but points the way forward.

◆ **Raventós i Blanc "de Nit" Rosé Cava ($):** A Cava in all but name, Raventós no longer bottles its wines as such, opting instead for the newly created Conca del Riu Anoia designation. That said, its wines represent a pinnacle of the genre, as exemplified by its bone-dry, deeply savory rosé.

◆ **Terroir al Limit Priorat "Les Tosses" ($$):** Hand harvested from a steep ninety-year-old vineyard of pure cariñena, Dominik Huber's pure and vibrant "Les Tosses" bottling is a perfect example of Priorat's newfound ability to impress without the need to overwhelm.

SIERRA DE GREDOS

The hour-and-a-half drive due west from Madrid to the rugged Sierra de Gredos area feels like a form of time travel. What would constitute an average weekday commute in Boston or Los Angeles magically transports you to a remote wilderness of mountain villages that seem unchanged since the turn of the twentieth century. Climbing up the area's winding plots of gnarled centuries-old vines, planted at more than three thousand feet above sea level, you couldn't feel further removed from the Spanish capital—let alone the trendy wine bars of New York City and London, where tho Gredos has won an improbable cult following.

The ingredients involved in that success couldn't have been better designed to appeal to the alternative wine geek crowd: high-altitude terroir, extremely old plantings of indigenous grapes (garnacha and albillo real, the local white), and a tiny community of naturally minded producers who are taking over abandoned vineyards and reviving long-lost viticultural practices. That includes organic farming, ambient yeast fermentation, and the use of large oak barrels and hyper-traditional clay vessels known as *tinajas*.

Although this sort of rediscovery narrative is hardly unique to the Gredos, rarely are the results so complex or compelling as this wave of wines emerging from the hillside towns of El Tiemblo, El Barraco, and Cebreros. The reds, in particular, stand out for their unusual delicacy. Unlike the inky, high-octane garnachas from Priorat, for instance, the precipitous terroir of Gredos produces ruby-hued wines of a different order of intensity. Balancing supple mountain fruit and grippy tannins with pinot-like elegance, scrubby herbaceousness, and a core of granitic minerality, they represent a welcome addition to the expanding repertoire of overlooked but authentic regional wines of Spain.

Essential Producers: Daniel Landi, Bernabaleva, Rubén Díaz, RuBor Viticultores, Bodegas Comando G, Daniel Ramos (Zerberos Finca), 4 Monos Viticultores

CANARY ISLANDS

....

JUST THE HIGHLIGHTS

- Few of the wine world's recent revolutions rival the Canary Islands for sheer strangeness. But then again, that's what you would expect from a subtropical island chain marooned off the North African coast.

- "Off the beaten path" doesn't begin to describe the Canary Islands. Unknown to the modern world for decades, the first wave of Canary wines washed up on US shores in the early 2000s, perfectly timed to catch the interest of trendsetting somms.

- The Canary Islands are more than just a curiosity. You can taste the wildness of the area's landscape directly in its wines. Both its tangy, juicy reds and savory, aromatic whites burst with the smoky minerality that is the telltale sign of volcanic soils.

Do yourself a favor: perform a Google image search for the phrase "Canary Islands vineyard." In the few seconds it will take for the results to pop up on your screen, you'll grasp the otherworldly strangeness of *las Canarias*, as its Spanish colonizers called this remote subtropical archipelago that sits seventy miles off the Moroccan coast.

Yes, those are grapevines you see crawling out of the pits of black sand, known as *hoyos*, that stipple the ashen landscape like craters on the moon. Each surrounded by a small stone fence, they're traditionally dug to preserve moisture and protect the grapes from the harsh desert winds that blow in from Africa. Only adding to the surreal sense that pervades the region, during harvest it's not uncommon to spot the vineyard workers hauling grapes back to the winery with the help of camels, which were introduced to the Canaries in the fifteenth century.

Given the extreme measures required just to grow a few grapes, it's a miracle that wine of any level of quality could be eked out of this punishing terrain. But the seven main islands of the Canaries—Lanzarote, Tenerife, La Gomera, La Palma, Gran Canaria, El Hierro, and Fuerteventura—have been producing wine for centuries, historically in a semisweet fortified style that once enjoyed the same high regard as sherry or Madeira. This rich legacy, however, provides no clue to what the wines are like today, which number among Spain's most unflinchingly individualistic.

Because the phylloxera louse never infiltrated this island oasis, the Canaries are one of the few places on Earth where vines—many of which are more than a hundred years old—still grow on their original ungrafted rootstocks. Despite differences in elevation and microclimate, the signature trait that runs through all the wines is a smoky, ash-like minerality derived from the area's dark volcanic soils. While varieties such as malvasia, verdelho, albillo, and listán blanco (known as palomino fino in Jerez), among others, make up the region's complex, pungently saline whites, the major red of the Canaries, listán negro, has achieved modern success in a fresh style that drinks a bit like prehistoric Beaujolais.

Thanks to this unique backstory, and to the efforts of a handful of natural-leaning producers who serve as the region's benchmarks, the Canary Islands have quickly captured the imagination of cool-hunting somms across the country, joining fellow island wines from Sicily, Corsica, and Santorini as talismans of changing culture.

Essential Producers: Los Bermejos, Envínate, Viñátigo, Matias í Torres, Frontón de Oro, Ignios

THE WINE LIST

- **Los Bermejos Malvasia Seco ($):** Bermejos's malvasia—technically, malvasia volcánica, a local variant grown exclusively on the island of Lanzarote—represents an utterly unique take on the grape from one of the globe's distinctive terroirs, all sea spray, honkeysuckle, and smoke.

- **Frontón de Oro Tinto ($):** Vinified from estate-grown fruit on the island of Gran Canaria, this peppery, floral expression of listán negro buzzes with energy, combining an earthy astringency with flavors of blood orange, cranberry, and oolong tea.

- **Envínate "Benje" Tinto ($$):** Of all the Canary Islands wines to make a splash with the somm crowd, none has rippled to greater effect than those of the Envínate project, a collaboration among four friends focused on what they call "Atlantic wines" of freshness and transparency. The team's "Benje" Tinto is made from three old-vine parcels of high-elevation listán prieto vines, plus a touch of tintilla, and that verticality comes across in its high-toned, red-fruited purity and floral, pink peppercorn spice.

JEREZ

············

JUST THE HIGHLIGHTS

◆ **Misconceptions about sherry abound.** The biggest misunderstanding of all is that sherry is categorically cheap and sweet. But despite its fortified status, the vast majority is bone-dry and designed to accompany dinner.

◆ **Jerez has clawed its way back to relevance after decades of decline.** Now in the midst of a region-wide renaissance, the area's incredible array of wines is being discovered and celebrated anew.

◆ **Sherry overturns expectations about how wine should taste.** Unlike virtually all other wine styles, sherry's appeal has little to do with fruit; instead, the world of flavor that sherry inhabits revolves around the nutty, the savory, and the pungently umami.

◆ **En rama sherry has become Jerez's answer to natural wine.** This new crop of minimally filtered fino and manzanilla sherries, bottled *en rama*, or "raw," are some of the region's most vivid wines, speaking directly to the contemporary vogue for pure and unadulterated styles.

We all love a good comeback story, and in terms of dramatic plot twists and surprise endings, few rival the epic tale that is sherry. Produced for centuries in the Andalusian towns of Jerez de la Frontera, Sanlúcar de Barrameda, and El Puerto de Santa María—collectively known as *el marco de Jerez* (the sherry triangle)—the classic fortified wine has experienced both triumphant highs and soul-crushing lows the likes of which have left lesser regions in ruin.

Once the epicenter of the global wine trade, immortalized by none other than Shakespeare's Falstaff (who famously enumerated the virtues of "a good sherris sack"), sherry limped its way out of the twentieth century in a state of near total collapse. By the time the early 2000s rolled around, the region's prospects couldn't have seemed any bleaker.

Little did anyone expect that sherry was about to find an unlikely savior. Reclaimed as a star ingredient in the classic canon of pre-Prohibition cocktails, sherry came out of early retirement as an essential item in the mixologist's tool kit, quickly making the rounds of North America's top bar programs. Before long, interest spread to the right sommelier circles, the media took notice, and, all of a sudden, sherry was improbably, unironically hip.

If any wine deserves a wider audience, it's sherry. Once you're willing to embrace it on its own terms—which, on the most basic level, means simply treating it like any other wine—you immediately understand why it inspired such reverence in the first place. As a table wine, it's unmatched in its versatility with food, dazzling in its range of expressions, and (the one silver lining to its long history of neglect) ridiculously cheap for the quality it delivers.

Luckily, the market has never offered a wider assortment of authentic sherry to explore. Over the past ten years, we've witnessed an explosion of producers both classic and modern, large and small, who are not just reclaiming sherry's legitimacy as a wine but also renewing its long track record for greatness.

WHY HAS SHERRY BEEN SO MISUNDERSTOOD?

If sherry deserves the title of "world's most misunderstood wine," it's because, on virtually every level, it flies in the face of our commonly held beliefs about wine.

For one, sherry is fortified, meaning that a small amount of neutral grape spirit has been added to it to boost alcohol content. This fact is innocent enough in itself. In the court of public opinion, however, sherry's fortified status has sentenced it to life in the purgatory of "after dinner drinks" despite its traditional role on the table—or, as the case may be, the tapas bar. Remember, it was in the bustling restaurants and taverns of Jerez, Sanlúcar, and El Puerto that the tapas tradition was born, a practice that refers not to the size of the plate, as commonly assumed, but to a specific culture of eating and drinking. This symbiotic relationship between food and wine is a fact of life in sherry country.

Sherry's natural compatibility with food only puts into sharper relief the absurdity of another myth surrounding it: namely, that it's sweet. A legacy of the cheap blended sherries of the 1960s and 1970s, this mis-apprehension deserves to be cleared up once and for all. As any native Andalusian will tell you, the overwhelming majority of sherry consumed today is bone-dry—and unapologetically so.

No previous drinking experience fully prepares you for the alternate universe of flavor that sherry encompasses. Those reared on the notion that wine should express itself in predominantly fruity terms (that is, most Americans) quickly discover that sherry speaks a totally foreign dialect. Rejecting the standard white wine vocabulary, it converses with the brine of Spanish anchovy and olives, the intense savoriness of sliced *jamon*. To first-time drinkers, this sometimes makes sherry an acquired taste—a bit like drinking your first dirty martini after a lifetime of piña coladas.

Beyond these initial cultural and aesthetic barriers, however, there's a deeper explanation for sherry's aura of otherness, which is born out of the unique production methods involved in its creation.

THE SOLERA: PROCESS AS PLACE

Most wine exists as a composite snapshot of vineyard, vintage, and grape. Sherry, on the other hand, is predicated on a radically different psychology of place. Like Champagne, sherry is essentially a wine of process, requiring an enormous amount of skill and human intervention to become what it is. Historically, that's why terroir hasn't always meant the same thing in Jerez as in Burgundy, for example, where geographical specificity is the main modus operandi.

Not only is it unusual for the large sherry houses, or *bodegas*, to own their own land or farm their own grapes, but the very notions of site expression and varietal character require a shift in expectations as well. Palomino fino—the main indigenous variety of Jerez—is notoriously neutral, low acid, and bland. But it's this very lack of distinctiveness that makes it the ideal raw ingredient to be shaped by the *solera*, Jerez's elaborately intricate system of fractional blending and aging.

Through this carefully orchestrated process, which often takes place over several years, the wine is successively moved through a complex network of casks, or *criaderas,* each containing wine at a different stage of evolution. At every step, a small amount of younger wine is drawn from the first *criadera*, then blended into the next—and so on—so the wine bottled from the final *criadera* consists of a multivintage blend that bears the unique imprint of its journey from barrel to barrel.

This time-honored institution is what makes sherry *sherry*, a beverage that couldn't be more viscerally evocative of the culture and people of Jerez. It's an art form that the great sherry houses have perfected over generations, responsible for imparting the wine's seemingly infinite stylistic range—from the bracingly saline to the unctuously rich and nutty and, yes, on occasion, the dazzlingly sweet. For our purposes, however, it's the incredible dry styles that we'll be focusing on, as they have the most to offer modern drinkers.

FLOR POWER: THE STYLES OF SHERRY

In all its diversity, the full breadth of the sherry continuum can be accounted for by two fundamental approaches to this aging process. The differentiating factor is how much slow, controlled exposure to oxygen the wine receives during its long trip through the *solera*.

That's not simply a question of the amount of time the wine spends in barrel. Perhaps the most distinctive aspect of sherry production, which sets it apart from almost every wine in existence, is the practice of aging wine under a living veil of yeast, locally known as *flor*, the Spanish word for "flower." When allowed to bloom across the surface of the wine, this protective film prevents contact with oxygen, preserving transparency and freshness. For obvious reasons, this practice is referred to as "biological" aging. "Oxidative" aging, by contrast, refers to the time a wine spends developing in the *solera* without the influence of *flor*, during which it acquires a richer mahogany hue and nuttier, caramelized flavors.

Out of these two approaches to oxygen exposure—and often through a combination of both—the main categories of dry sherry are born. Together, they comprise a broad stylistic spectrum, ranging from the lightest purely biologically aged wines to the heaviest fully oxidative expressions that develop in the complete absence of *flor*.

FINO AND MANZANILLA

The product of complete biological aging, having spent their entire lives under a waxy veil of *flor*, fino and manzanilla sherries exit the cask bright and vibrant. Pungently yeasty and brisk, with a briny ocean-water tang, they're typically served chilled with the area's bounty of local seafood. A subspecies of the category, manzanilla is essentially a fino produced specifically in the ocean-side town of Sanlúcar de Barrameda, where the humid sea air encourages a thicker veil of yeast, yielding wines of enhanced elegance and delicacy.

AMONTILLADO

Every amontillado was once a young fino, shielded from oxygen under a layer of *flor*. But when that microbial barrier dies off—either naturally, after several years of age, or through additional fortification—the wine is transferred to a separate *solera* to continue developing oxidatively. In this way, amontillado embodies a thrilling hybrid of both poles of the sherry spectrum, revealing what author and *PUNCH* editor in chief Talia Baiocchi has described in her book *Sherry: A Modern Guide to the Wine World's Best-Kept Secret* as "an eternal sort of tension between the loud flavors of oxidation and the leanness and austerity that biological aging imparts."

PALO CORTADO

Ask five *bodega* owners to define palo cortado and you're likely to get five different answers. The most mysterious of all sherry styles—and therefore the object of intense cult appreciation—palo cortado was traditionally considered an accident of nature, occurring when a wine originally destined to become a fino would deviate from expectations, becoming more full-bodied and brawny over time. At this point, it would be refortified to eliminate its *flor*, then transferred to a separate *solera* and left to age oxidatively like an oloroso. According to the Consejo Regulador, the organization responsible for regulating sherry production, the category refers to "a wine of great complexity, which combines the delicate bouquet of an amontillado with the body and palate of an oloroso," but it's up to each individual bodega to arrive at its own definition of those criteria. For practical purposes, palo cortado can be understood as a midway point between amontillado and oloroso—fuller and more deeply pitched than the former but displaying a subtle refinement not always associated with the latter.

OLOROSO

If you could transform Barry White's resonant baritone into vinous form, you'd end up with something like oloroso, the richest and fullest wine on the sherry spectrum. Something similar to the reverse image of fino, it's initially fortified to levels exceeding 17 percent alcohol, beyond which *flor* can't survive. As such, oloroso is the product of pure oxidative aging, imparting a burnished amber color (think rye or bourbon) and intensely savory notes of roasted walnuts, orange peel, and dried fig. You can think of them as the red wines of the sherry triangle, where they're traditionally paired with braised meat and game. Pro tip: Because oloroso has already been vaccinated, in some sense, against oxidation, you can keep bottles of it open in the fridge for several months.

◆ ◆ ◆

To be clear, these expressions exist as subjective reference points within a vast continuum rather than precise classifications. It's impossible to pinpoint the exact moment a fino or manzanilla becomes an amontillado, or for that matter, what exactly qualifies as a palo cortado. Every bottling represents a winery's own interpretation of the intended style. Because of this—and the potentially infinite number of variations on the idea of "fino" or "oloroso"—sherry exists as an invitation to experiment and compare. The following suggested wines hardly begin to scratch the surface of what's possible in Jerez, but they do provide a basic introduction to the major styles to fuel further investigation.

Essential Producers: Equipos Navazos, Valdespino, Barbadillo, Hidalgo, César Florido Hidalgo, González-Byass, Lustau, Bodegas Tradición, Gutiérrez Colosía, Fernando de Castilla, El Maestro Sierra

THE WINE LIST

◆ **Valdespino Fino "Innocente" ($):** Based solely on the stats, it's a marvel that Valdespino's beloved "Innocente" doesn't cost three times the price. Fermented in wooden casks with natural yeasts (a rarity for the region) and sourced entirely from the acclaimed Macharnudo Alto vineyard, it's aged in *solera* for ten years. Pungent, briny, and incredibly complex, it is not only one of the iconic wines of Jerez but also one of the wine world's best values.

◆ **Barbadillo Solear Manzanilla En Rama ($$):** Barbadillo's beloved seasonally bottled *en rama* expressions of manzanilla are released four times annually (winter, spring, summer, and fall). Averaging eight years of age, they allow audiences to compare the fluctuating influence of the *flor* on the wine at different stages of the year. The project is yet another testament to sherry's extraordinary diversity and evidence of how the category has evolved.

◆ **Emilio Lustau Amontillado del Puerto "José Luis González Obregón" ($$):** The extremely limited wines in Lustau's Almacenista range are all purchased from small boutique sherry producers and bottled under the Lustau label. From a *solera* comprising just ten casks, this exceptional amontillado is bottled with an average age of twelve years. A textbook example of its kind, it expresses the salty pungency of its five years under *flor* and the nutty, toffee-like notes acquired through oxidative aging.

◆ **Fernando de Castilla Antique Palo Cortado ($$$):** The most elusive wine of the sherry continuum, certain palo cortados drink like fresher, tangier amontillados, whereas others skew more toward the richer, caramelized oloroso side of the spectrum. Fernando de Castilla's amber-hued interpretation combines the best of both worlds. Showing all the depth and complexity of its thirty years' average age, it exudes dried orange rind, Marcona almond, and salted caramel.

◆ **Gutiérrez Colosía Oloroso "Sangre y Trabajadero" ($):** For the money, there's no better go-to oloroso on the market. A perfect marriage of savory and sweet sensations—although technically completely dry—this full-bodied sherry spends an average of twelve years in *solera* and overflows with fig, walnut, and quince, all balanced by a salty tang.

THE EN RAMA REVOLUTION

One of the most compelling off-shoots of the recent sherry renaissance has been the emergence of a new—or at least new to the market—minimally filtered style known as *en rama*, which roughly translates to "on the branch" or "raw." Specifically pertaining to the biologically aged categories of fino and manzanilla, the *en rama* movement aligns with a wider embrace of unmediated and unadulterated styles.

Over the course of the twentieth century, as the wines of Jerez grew increasingly industrialized, it became common practice to heavily filter biologically aged sherries to remove the bits of *flor* and other sediments that develop during production. But this effort to ensure a more stable commodity often stripped the wines of their underlying flavors and aromas, frequently leaving a pale imitation in its place.

Up until just a decade ago, the only way to taste sherry in its natural state was to go to Jerez, visit the *bodegas*, and taste the wine poured directly from the cask. But thanks to a rash of *en rama* releases from several top producers—including, notably, the hugely influential Equpios Navazos project—that experience, or a close approximation of it, is now available to those of us not fortunate enough to make the annual pilgrimage to sherry country.

By scaling back filtration, the movement is rejecting the traditional view of sherry as a consistent product and proving that variation over standardization can—and should—be part of the sherry paradigm. Compared to their conventional counterparts, the *en rama* expressions of wines such as the González-Byass estate's popular "Tio Pepe" fino drink like HD versions of themselves. Or maybe it's more like listening to vinyl: you're treated to a deeper, more sonorous experience of the original track, keeping all its nuance and detail intact.

Essential Producers: Equipos Navazos, Lustau, Valdespino, Barbadillo, Hidalgo, Fernando de Castilla, González -Byass

PORTUGAL

Think of Portugal as the last frontier of the Old World. Finally coming out from under the shadows of France, Italy, and Spain, the Portuguese wine industry has transformed rapidly and dramatically over the past twenty years. For centuries, Portugal was synonymous with its most celebrated and historically significant product, fortified "port" wine. More recently, however, the image of Portuguese table wine has been cheap and value-driven, but many regions are now revealing greater ambitions, pushing the country out of the bargain bin and making Portuguese wine one of the most compelling categories to watch.

VINHO VERDE

JUST THE HIGHLIGHTS

◆ **Vinho Verde isn't a style but a place.** The wine you think you know—an inexpensive, lightly sparkling quaffer that goes down like adult 7Up—isn't all the northern Portuguese region has to offer.

◆ **For decades defined by a cheap high-volume model, Vinho Verde is now shifting gears.** A new wave of small artisanal producers is turning expectations upside down by showcasing the region's serious side.

◆ **Say good-bye to the fizz.** The new Vinho Verde is generally bottled without carbonation to better highlight the identities of the region's nine demarcated subregions and bring out the character of its many indigenous grapes.

◆ **It's still as refreshing as ever.** In assuming a more ambitious guise, this new crop of Vinho Verde doesn't sacrifice the qualities that always made it a hit: freshness, acidity, and incredible versatility with food.

Portugal's Vinho Verde region has forever been synonymous with zippy, lightly fizzy wines designed to be knocked back by the case at picnics, pools, and pretty much anywhere else day-drinking is encouraged. Imagine wine's answer to Key lime LaCroix and you'll have some sense of its goes-down-easy appeal.

Industrially scaled and globally exported, this popular commercial style first put Vinho Verde on the map and has defined perceptions of it ever since. A spritzy summertime staple? For sure. One of wine's most reliable ten-buck bargains? Absolutely. But a wine that rewards sustained contemplation? Not so much.

Long wed to this cheap high-volume model, Vinho Verde is the last place you would expect to be leading the charge of Portugal's twenty-first-century renaissance. But in stark contrast to the large corporate firms that still dominate production, a groundswell of independent producers is out to prove that the region is capable of so much more. Improbably, they're making the case for what still sounds like a contradiction in terms: the rebirth of Vinho Verde as a serious wine.

Say what you will about its cheap and cheerful mass-market image. From the standpoint of raw materials, Vinho Verde couldn't be better equipped to embody a new paradigm for Portuguese whites. Located in the lush green hills of the nation's rainy northwest (which give the wines their name), under the cooling influence of the Minho and Lima Rivers, the area seems climatically custom-built for high-acid wines.

Rather than reject these natural endowments, the area's rebranding efforts have wisely highlighted the qualities that made Vinho Verde so popular in the first place: in-your-face freshness and insane food friendliness. Combine that with a diverse arsenal of native grapes and several distinct subregions and microclimates to explore, and all the necessary ingredients for a modern revival are there.

IN SEARCH OF THE TRUE VINHO VERDE

Where the new Vinho Verde breaks with the artificially carbonated "classic" style, on the other hand, is that signature dose of fizz. A modern approximation of the region's original ancestral method traditions, dating back to when the wines were characterized by a natural prickle, the addition of CO_2 is conspicuously absent in the latest crop of vintage-dated, varietally specific expressions. This approach, the thinking goes, is better calibrated to transmit the unique details that make Vinho Verde what it is—or rather, what it is in the process of becoming.

It's also part of the wider effort to carve out the unique identities of Vinho Verde's nine demarcated subregions—Amarante, Ave, Baião, Basto, Cávado, Lima, Monção e Melgaço, Paiva, and Sousa—which decades of bulk production have all but obscured. The most prominent of these, Monção e Melgaço, just across the Minho River from Galicia, has long enjoyed a local reputation for its fleshy, mineral renditions of the alvarinho grape, better known as albariño over the Spanish border. It's here that pioneering producers such as Anselmo Mendes, along with the highly respected Quinta de Soalheiro, first established the variety's track record for crafting elegant and even age-worthy whites.

That vision informs the work currently under way in some of Vinho Verde's lesser-known subzones, whose potential is still being mined. If alvarinho from Monção e Melgaço has always been Vinho Verde's most prestigious expression, the little-known but highly aromatic loureiro grape, which thrives in the area of Lima, is quickly catching up, thanks to its riesling-like delicacy, salty tang, and signature scent of magnolias.

VINHO VERDE IS STILL A GREAT BARGAIN

What all of these next-gen Vinho Verdes share is mouthwatering acidity, low alcohol, and floral complexity. They pull off "serious" in the same way that certain Loire whites do (Sancerre, for one), delivering succulent fruit and mineral depth in a light and nimble frame. But even in this elevated form, they're still exceptional values. Top wines rarely exceed the $20 mark—a welcome reprieve from the price inflation that has engulfed so much of the "crisp white" competition from France, Italy, and Spain.

Essential Producers: Aphros, Anselmo Mendes, António Lopes, Quinta de Soalheiro

THE WINE LIST

- **Anselmo Mendes Vinho Verde Alvarinho "Contacto" ($):** No one has contributed more to Vinho Verde's revitalization than Anselmo Mendes, whose aptly named "Contacto" bottling reveals an extra layer of textural richness thanks to a brief period of maceration on the skins. Not at all overwhelming, it's just enough to magnify what alvarinho from Monção e Melgaço is all about: bright tropical fruit, a firm mineral bite, and acidity for days.

- **António Lopes Vinho Verde "Biotite" ($):** António Lopes always allows this loureiro-dominant, organically certified bottling to ferment spontaneously, stopping whenever nature dictates. As a result, sugar levels tend to vary from one vintage to the next— some years it finishes bone-dry, other years not so much—but the occasional touch of sweetness only highlights its riesling-like purity and lemon-lime lift.

- **Aphros Vinho Verde Loureiro ($):** In 2003, winemaker Vasco Croft set out to revive his family's abandoned estate and has since emerged as a darling of the natural wine scene on the basis of his biodynamically farmed interpretations of Lima's granitic terroir. Aged four months on the lees, this is quintessential loureiro, chock-full of white peach, honeysuckle, and lime, with the same core of salinity that runs through all his wines.

DOURO

·················

JUST THE HIGHLIGHTS

◆ **Historically famous for port, the Douro is increasingly focusing on dry table wines.** The earliest examples tended to be big, ripe, and oaky. But that's no longer the case. In recent years, the region is embracing a new aesthetic of freshness.

◆ **The Douro is now the epicenter of the Portuguese avant-garde.** It is experiencing a stylistic sea change as producers explore remote high-altitude parcels of extremely old vines that the big port shippers had previously neglected.

◆ **The fresh wave of Douro whites has exposed a whole new side of the region.** No longer reserved for the throwaway category of white port, the area's ancient vineyards are giving rise to a contemporary crop of mind-bending whites that are every bit as captivating as its reds.

The steep terraced vineyards that tower above the winding Douro River have long been famous for one thing and one thing only. Of course, we're talking about port, the historic fortified wine that has quenched the thirst of monarchs, graced the pages of Dickens and Trollope, and, in more recent times, struggled to shake off its Victorian stereotypes and find its place in a modern wine culture that prizes the savory, saline, and mineral.

The port industry will always be deeply entrenched in the Douro, encompassing hundreds of years of tradition. And who knows, maybe the category stands to benefit from the same reversal of fortunes that recently transformed sherry—a wine that had arguably fallen into even steeper decline—from dusty museum piece into a reclaimed industry darling.

Until that day comes, however, the Douro won't be satisfied to slouch off into stodgy irrelevance. Faced with declining sales and the growing indifference of younger consumers, the region has increasingly shifted focus to the production of dry table wines—a genre that's now in the midst of a fascinating evolution of its own.

When that first wave of Douro reds entered the market in the 1990s, critics hailed it as the next big thing in Portuguese wine. Unsurprisingly, the region's efforts capitalized on the same obvious qualities that made it famous for port: richness and high alcohol. For years, this big, boozy formula would remain the norm. And although there's no shortage of inky, oaky Douro reds in the market, the area is finally seeing signs of change.

Independent of the large port houses, a younger generation of winemakers is working to disrupt the dominant Douro narrative and chart a more nuanced way forward. Unlike their peers in other regions of Portugal, who struggled to improve quality after decades of industrial mediocrity, they face a fundamentally different challenge: how to create an alternative paradigm for a historically prestigious region that has always defined itself through ripeness and power.

THE ALTERNATIVE DOURO

It's rare, if not unprecedented, for a classic wine region (and few deserve that title more than the Douro, one of Europe's oldest demarcated wine-growing areas) to reinvent itself so radically. But the shift toward dry table wine has afforded the area an opportunity to examine itself anew—starting with the dirt.

From the moment you set foot in the sweeping vineyards of the Douro, it's obvious that the area is an extremely special place to make wine. With more than eighty indigenous varieties—most prominently, the meaty, violet-scented touriga nacional, tinta roriz (aka tempranillo), tinta barroca, and touriga franca—its singular high-elevation vineyards, and ancient wine culture, the Douro clearly has a meaningful story to tell. Ironically, it's largely thanks to the port industry that so much of the Douro's rich viticultural heritage remains intact. Port's commercially successful past inadvertently insulated the region from the pressures of globalization that forced many others to tear out old indigenous vineyards and convert them to international varieties such as cabernet and merlot. Today, these centuries-old parcels represent the Douro's most valuable cultural asset. Now it's simply a question of creating a new idiom through which to express what's been there all along.

RETHINKING THE VINEYARDS

This conversation about the Douro's evolving identity would never have taken place without winemaker Dirk Niepoort. Aside from running his family's generations-old port shipping business, he was among the first to champion a new Douro aesthetic centered around a set of guiding principles: picking earlier to retain acidity, dialing back the oak and extraction to allow terroir to shine through, and, critically, rethinking the region's old vineyard classification system, which, having been originally conceived in relation to port, favors warmer, low-elevation parcels that give maximum ripeness, color, and sugar levels. To Niepoort and those who have followed in his footsteps, the key to the region's future lies in seeking out the cooler, high-altitude plots whose potential for table wines—red and white alike—is only now being recognized.

Through a range of single-vineyard expressions such as his "Redoma Branco" (a high-altitude field blend that indisputably proved the region capable of crafting elegant, mineral-driven whites) and Burgundy-inspired "Charme" (sourced from extremely old vineyards in the Vale de Mendiz), Niepoort developed an approach that would inspire rising stars such as Tiago Sampaio of the Folias de Baco project, Luís Seabra, and Rita Ferreira Marques of the Conceito winery, among others.

Essential Producers: Folias de Baco, Dirk Niepoort, Quinta do Infantado, Luís Seabra, Conceito (Rita Ferreira Marques), Mateus Nicolau de Almeida

THE WINE LIST

+ **Luís Seabra "Xisto Ilimitado" Branco ($):** In 2012, Luís Seabra left his position as head enologist at Niepoort to launch his eponymous winery. This riveting entry-level effort—dense but bright and citrus kissed—offers an ideal point of entry to Douro whites.

+ **Conceito Bastardo ($$):** The poster child for the entire "Alt Douro" ethos, Rita Ferreira Marques's ethereally light, perfumed rendition of the necglected bastardo grape is sourced from a single block in the Douro Superior subregion.

+ **Folias de Baco "Uivo Renegado" ($):** A field blend of more than twenty-five traditional Douro varieties—approximately half white and half red—Tiago Sampaio's "Renegado" drinks like a tart, rainwater-fresh rosé and channels the schist and granite minerality of its high-altitude soils.

+ **Dirk Niepoort Redoma Tinto ($$):** This startlingly fresh blend of more than thirty-five grapes taken from a handful of old vineyards offers a glimpse of what makes Niepoort the main architect of the Alt-Douro movement.

BAIRRADA

Portugal is home to more than three hundred indigenous grapes, most of which you've probably never heard of before. Viosinho, anyone? Fernão pires? Rabigato? Thought so.

But that's to be expected. Beyond the tongue-twisting difficulty of pronouncing grapes such as the above, let alone committing them to memory, the greater obstacle is Portugal's traditional blending culture. Historically reliant on a safety-in-numbers approach to viticulture, the nation has long operated under the assumption that a miscellaneous mixture of local varieties will yield the best results.

Still, certain examples inevitably stand out from the crowd. Touriga nacional, for instance, has turned more than a few heads of late, and alvarinho (or what the Spaniards call albariño) represents a rare exception to the rule, boasting a long history as a single-varietal wine.

But if any up-and-coming grape warrants closer attention, it would have to be baga, a little-known but exceptionally promising red native to the region of Bairrada. It doesn't hurt, of course, that its name is simple enough to appear in a second-grade spelling bee.

Located at the north end of the country between the chilly Atlantic and the mountains of the Dão region, Bairrada owes what little fame it has historically enjoyed to the sparkling wine industry that developed there at the close of the nineteenth century. The region still churns out a fair share of reliable traditional method bubbly, plus a smattering of thought-provoking whites. But these days, red wine is the main attraction.

What sangiovese is to Tuscany and nebbiolo is to Piedmont, the thin-skinned, late-ripening baga has become to Bairrada. The comparison to those two noble examples isn't random. Once dismissed as lean and austere, the grape has out-grown its reputation for rusticity; today's high-end, quality-minded versions combine a surprising maritime freshness (that's the influence of the nearby Atlantic) with a core of earthy dark fruit, distinct minerality, and enough tannic muscle to mature for decades.

Over the past ten years, baga's siren song has lured such internationally acclaimed talents as Dirk Niepoort, who purchased the Quinta de Baixo estate in 2012. But long before anyone outside of the area had ever heard of Bairrada, the region's tireless champion was winemaker Luís Pato. Over his decades-long career he quietly crafted some of Portugal's most complex and long-lived wines; his legacy is that of the innovative traditionalist who single-handedly lifts an entire region out of obscurity.

Pato's daughter Filipa, however, is the one breathing fresh energy into Bairrada today and updating its identity for the twenty-first century. From her twelve hectares of biodynamically farmed vines, she produces pure, vibrant wines inspired by a low-intervention philosophy (*vinhos autênticos sem maquilagem*, or "authentic wines without makeup," as she calls them). Her flagship "Nossa Calcário" Tinto, sourced from a single vineyard in the southernmost reaches of Bairrada and fermented in old oak casks, is a marvel of textural delicacy and aromatic lift, epitomizing the best of Portugal's contemoprary golden age.

Essential Producers: Luís Pato, Filipa Pato, Vadio, Sidónio de Sousa, Caves São João, Lasa de Saima, Tigo Teles

MADEIRA

JUST THE HIGHLIGHTS

- **Madeira was America's first great wine crush.** Produced for hundreds of years on the island that bears its name, the fortified wine was the toast of colonial America, adored by the likes of Washington, Jefferson, and Franklin.

- **Madeira's days as a cheap cooking wine are over.** Dismissed for much of the twentieth century as a lowbrow pantry item, the category's comeback coincides with the growing fascination with overlooked antique styles.

- **Madeira is indestructible.** A central part of the production process involves deliberately heating the wine to mimic the nutty, roasted qualities it would acquire during the long sea voyages of olden days. This makes it impossible for Madeira to spoil, so you can keep a bottle on your countertop indefinitely.

At a time when we're obsessed with reclaiming historical styles, it's no wonder that Madeira—the fortified wine named after the subtropical island where it's made, some four hundred miles off the coast of Africa—is experiencing a comeback. No other wine is more intimately connected to its storied past, and it's hard to imagine a past more storied than Madeira's.

The most fashionable beverage of the early American colonies, Madeira once flowed freely into port cities across the Eastern Seaboard. From Boston and New York to Savannah and Charleston, Madeira parties were the rage of high society, and the wine's early groupies included none other than George Washington, Thomas Jefferson, and Ben Franklin. The founding fathers were so enamored of the drink, in fact, that the members of the Continental Congress used it to toast the signing of the Declaration of Independence.

It wasn't until Prohibition slammed the breaks on all the fun that the American love affair with Madeira came to an unfortunate end. By the time repeal rolled around, the public had already moved on to that other great national pastime, the cocktail. Over the coming decades, Madeira's reputation would dwindle to that of a cheap cooking wine, buried in the back of the pantry except when called for to deglaze a pan in a Julia Child recipe.

If Madeira now finds itself on the rise, the uptick is partially due to the way the American palate has come to embrace more grown-up flavors. Although pigeonholed as a dessert wine, Madeira's sweetness is just one aspect of its profile. It's equally about pungent umami, burnt-sugar bitterness, and the savory depth of intentional oxidation.

Although not as widespread as sherry's twenty-first-century renaissance, the Madeira revival has followed a similar path to popular acceptance. First introduced through the strainer of a cocktail shaker, it's increasingly being embraced for what it is: one of the world's most idiosyncratic wines.

FEELING THE HEAT: THE PRODUCTION OF MADEIRA

Producers on the craggy, lushly forested island of Madeira have been shipping off its namesake wine to all corners of the globe ever since the fifteenth century. In those days, long before refrigerated shipping containers, the commercial viability of Madeira (just like that of port and sherry) depended on its ability to withstand months in the dank bowels of a ship, exposed to sweltering heat and lashed by wind and wave. Fortifying the wine with neutral grape spirit or brandy was necessary to stabilize it for its long ocean voyage.

In the case of Madeira, however, the wine did more than just survive the journey. It actually improved. Colonial audiences quickly developed a taste for the mellow, nutty character the wine developed during its tropical cruise. Before long, merchants began deliberately sending barrels of Madeira across the farthest reaches of the spice route, often to India and back, to maximize this specific set of flavors.

To replicate the effects of a swashbuckling adventure on the high seas, a crucial step in Madeira production involves deliberately heating the wine. But rather than resulting in flabby, cooked flavors that bear the foul effects of heat damage, in Madeira's case, the "maderization" process, as it's called, yields wonderfully complex multidimensional wines reminiscent of candied dates and figs, plus hints of salted caramel, sea spray, roasted walnuts, ginger, and baking spice. Critically, the wine is kept fresh with freakishly high acidity, allowing you to drink far more of it in a single sitting than might be advised.

This brings us to the coolest thing about Madeira. Because it has already, in effect, been inoculated against oxidation and temperature variation, the stuff is practically invincible. Even the longest-lived French and Italian reds will start to fade after a half century or so. Madeira, on the other hand, offers the rare opportunity to drink bottles with more than a hundred years of age. For this reason, exceptionally old Madeira has become something of a fetish for collectors of a certain antiquarian persuasion; it's a surreal and humbling experience to drink a wine that has outlived every last person alive at the time it was bottled.

Fortunately, there's plenty of delicious Madeira to be had that doesn't predate the Civil War. Even the most basic bottles will last on your kitchen counter indefinitely, although you'll probably find it vanishes far more quickly than you thought.

THE STYLES OF MADEIRA

Madeira's usefulness extends well beyond the postprandial purposes it usually serves. Classified by grape variety from lightest and driest and richest and sweetest, the category encompasses an entire continuum of styles. Although other expressions exist—the ambrosial terrantez grape, for example, is highly prized among connoisseurs, having once come close to extinction—they're best viewed as collector's items, rarely spotted in the wild. Most of the wines you're likely to encounter, leaving aside cheap bottlings simply labeled "Madeira," will be classified according to the following grape varieties.

SERCIAL

Sourced from the island's highest-elevation vineyards, sercial is the leanest, palest, and driest style of Madeira, exhibiting a bracing yin-yang tension between tangy salinity and delicate sweetness. Traditionally served slightly chilled as an aperitif, it can segue brilliantly into a soup or even a salad course, giving the impression of dryness thanks to its bracing spine of acidity.

VERDEHLO

A step up in richness and concentration, verdehlo is considered semidry, meaning that it definitely has a sugary side but won't clobber you over the head with it, finishing crisp and clean despite its added viscosity and weight. Also best when served chilled, it's one of the world's great cheese wines, but if you really want to play up its historical dinner-party associations, try it with savory dishes, like roast game birds or chestnut soup.

BUAL

Here's where Madeira enters proper dessert-wine territory. The bual grape produces sumptuous, mahogany-colored wines that balance their notable sweetness with secondary and tertiary flavors of wood smoke, toasted almond, clove, and bitter orange—always with that signature jolt of acidity.

MALMSEY

The most unctuous, lushest expression of the Madeira spectrum, malmsey—known as malvasia in most other places where the grape is grown—is the wine equivalent of reading a heavy leather-bound book by the fireplace. Easily a dessert unto itself, it's what you want to be drinking with chocolate.

Essential Producers: Henriques & Henriques, Rare Wine Co. Historic Series, Broadbent, D'Oliveiras, Blandy's, Barbeito

THE WINE LIST

◆ **Henriques & Henriques 10 Years Old Sercial Madeira ($$):** In the Madeira business since 1925, Henriques & Henriques lacks the name recognition of some of the island's bigger brands but enjoys a special appreciation among Madeira connoisseurs. Although lightly sweet (the burnt-sugar crust of crème brûlée comes to mind), their ten-year-old sercial's screeching acidity and saltiness keep everything in check.

◆ **Rare Wine Co. New York Malmsey Special Reserve Madeira ($$$):** The Rare Wine Co. Historic Series attempts to re-create the diverse styles of Madeira that were so popular in American cities during the eighteenth and nineteenth centuries. All of their releases deserve attention, but their rich, raisiny malmsey—the sweetest of the series—showcases Madeira's greatness as a full-on dessert wine, emulating the decadent style prized by colonial-era New Yorkers.

GERMANY AND AUSTRIA

Together, Germany and Austria form the wine world's grand Teutonic tradition—a legacy that, though it differs in both style and substance from the rest of Western Europe, once competed with the classic whites of France for global pre-eminence. In addition to a typically Germanic commitment to quality and precision, as well as a common cast of grapes, what defines both countries is a struggle to overcome the stigmas of the late twentieth century, a time when consumers typecast any wine with a German or Austrian label as cheap and sweet. Today, each in its own way, Germany and Austria have emerged as global innovators, reclaiming the historic grandeur and diversity of their centuries-old wine cultures while welcoming a new era of experimentation.

GERMANY

························

JUST THE HIGHLIGHTS

◆ No wine-producing nation strikes fear in the hearts of American drinkers quite like Germany. Infinitely complex and confusing, German riesling is also infinitely rewarding. To be intimidated by German wine is to miss out on what many believe to be the most nuanced white wine in existence.

◆ As a conduit for terroir, German riesling has no peer. The meticulous level of detail and transparency the grape achieves in Germany's historic vineyards has made it an object of endless study and debate. What's more, Germany's producers typically turn out several different wines from a single site, allowing drinkers to compare multiple overlapping interpretations of the same terroir.

◆ The conversation about German wine style is more complex than "dry versus sweet." For as long as anyone can remember, wine nerds have been arguing over which style represents Germany's "true" or "classic" expression: dry or sweet? Today, many of the country's most compelling rieslings split the difference, reflecting what has come to be known as the *feinherb* style: not fully dry, they possess an almost imperceptible level of sweetness.

◆ Incomprehensible though they may seem, German wine labels actually tell you a lot. If you want to drink dry, look for *trocken* on the label. Wines labeled with a Prädikat level (the traditional German ripeness scale), such as Kabinett, Spätlese, and Auslese, will typically possess some residual sugar.

Before we try to unpack the layers of misinformation and confusion that have accumulated over the years, a disclaimer is in order: For our purposes, "German wine" is understood to mean German riesling, the country's most celebrated and important variety.

This riesling-centric focus might invite controversy. German wine-makers are quick to point out that their talents extend beyond just one variety—and they're not wrong. Especially over the past few years, the country has had success with a whole host of other grapes, red and white alike, including a recent hot streak with pinot noir, or spätbur-gunder as they call it. Even so, there's no denying that Germany's claim to fame, both past and present, has always rested on the incomparable greatness of its riesling. The apotheosis of cool-climate transparency, purity, and site specificity, it's Germany's ultimate achievement.

Unfortunately, there's no easy guide to the category. You could spend the better part of your life trying to master the ins and outs of German riesling and still feel as if you've barely scratched the surface. On the upside, the challenges only amplify the potential rewards. If you're will-ing to wade into the depths and tolerate a bit of initial uncertainty, you'll be treated to some of the most transcendent wines in existence. For many, it marks the beginning of a lifelong obsession.

TYPICITY AND DIVERSITY IN GERMAN RIESLING

"Some German words are so long that they have a perspective," Mark Twain once quipped. The same is true of German wine labels. Pity the poor consumer who, having innocently wandered into the German wine section, now finds herself staring down a wall of names such as "Weiser-Künstler Trabener Gaispfad Riesling Kabinett Feinherb" and "Franz Künstler Hochheimer Hölle Riesling Grosses Gewächs."

All those intimidating umlauts would make anyone want to curl up and hide under the nearest bottle of chardonnay. But the intricate Teutonic terminology plastered across the typical German label is actually a testa-ment to the category's nuance and diversity.

Among its legions of die-hard fans, there's no doubting that Germany is the greatest white-wine-producing nation on Earth. From a historical perspective, this view is nothing new; during its nineteenth-century golden age, German hock regularly graced the tables of royalty, fetching higher prices than Champagne or Bordeaux.

Today, the country's wine culture remains among the world's most storied and significant, encompassing a seemingly infinite range of styles. Ever since Prussian officials began ranking the top vineyards of the country's two most prominent riesling regions—the Mosel and the Rheingau— wine lovers have worshipped sites such as Wehlener Sonnenuhr and Rüdesheimer Berg Schlossberg with the same cultish devotion as any of Burgundy's grand crus.

Unlike their Burgundian counterparts, however, world-renowned German vineyards such as these would traditionally produce not just one exemplary wine but several, ranging from light and dry to unctuously sweet. At once Germany's greatest asset and its biggest lability, this mind-boggling complexity is what makes its wine so utterly unique and so exasperatingly difficult to wrap one's mind around.

THE STIGMA OF "SWEETNESS"

It's no secret that many Americans still operate under the assumption that German wine is sweet. A legacy of the cloying, mass-market brands of the 1970s—the infamous Blue Nun is the most flagrant offender— this misapprehension is only compounded by our deep-seated national prejudice against residual sugar in wine.

Having been indoctrinated by decades of Cold Duck and white zinfandel, we still haven't shed the misconception that sweetness is somehow lowbrow. To combat this widespread suspicion, wine professionals across the United States have spent at least the last decade insisting that #notallriesling is sweet. As evidence, they've pointed to the incredible wave of bone-dry—or *trocken*—expressions that Germans have been drinking for decades, but which only began washing up on US shores since the latter part of the last decade.

Lately, it has become a favorite pastime among German wine geeks to debate which of these styles—the dry or the sweet—represents the "true" or "classic" version. But sidestepping that philosophical can of worms, here's a more relevant question: What do we want German wine to be today?

The correct answer is "all of the above." The entire appeal of German wine—its definitive personality trait—is its chameleon-like ability to occupy a dizzying spectrum of styles. In a way, it's the Prince of the wine world (as in "the artist formerly known as," not William or Harry), capable of seamlessly modulating from falsetto to baritone, hitting every register in between. To acquire a broader perspective, then, requires looking beyond the usual dry versus sweet binary and embracing the totality of German riesling in all of its many guises.

THE STYLISTIC CAMPS OF GERMAN RIESLING

When we talk about a sweet style of German wine, the terminology is inherently misleading. That's because sweetness has always been a relative proposition in Germany.

On one extreme, the country has a rich legacy of powerfully sticky, concentrated dessert wines; picked as late as possible and often shriveled by botrytis, the grapes finish fermentation with massive amounts of sugar remaining.

For the last sixty years or so, however, Germany has built its reputation around its traditional off-dry table wines. To avoid confusion, the word Germans now use for this style—not necessarily sweet but still possessing plenty of residual sugar—is *fruchtig*, or fruity. Classified according to the famous Prädikat scale of ripeness levels at harvest (that is, Kabinett, Spätlese, Auslese, and so on), which ascend in order of intensity from lightest to richest (and usually, but not always, sweetest), it's what many German wine drinkers consider to be the grape's classic expression.

Unless you specifically see the word *trocken* on the label, indicating a strictly dry wine, it's a safe bet that any bottle bearing one of these Prädikat classifications will drink with a touch (or more) of sweetness. Don't let that prevent you from giving it a chance. The finest examples of this fruity style rank among the most exquisite and long-lived wines ever captured in bottle.

Possessing a riveting tension—the perpetual push-pull between sweetness and spine-tingling acidity, ripeness, and chiseled-from-the-earth minerality—a vibrant yet featherweight Kabinett or Spätlese embodies a conception of balance that is, without exaggeration, unique among the wines of the world. Rarely surpassing alcohol levels of 10 or 11 percent, they're also incredibly versatile with food—especially as a foil for spice. After a decade or two in bottle, their noticeable sweetness dries out into a sort of honeyed richness, often acquiring a telltale whiff of gasoline aromas (no, really: it's a good thing) that make collectors swoon.

Until just a couple of decades ago, this fruity incarnation epitomized German wine for American audiences. Since the 1990s, however, the country's wines have grown more *trocken* by the day. Partially boosted by global warming—it's no longer such a struggle to achieve the necessary ripeness levels for quality dry whites—this push toward drier wines, known as the *Trockenwelle*, or "dry wave," has become synonymous with a specific category: *Grosses Gewächs*, or "GG" for short. Translating to "great growth"—the German equivalent of Burgundy's grand crus—the designation was created in 2002 to present the country's best individual vineyards in a new and savory light.

Despite some initial growing pains (namely, an early predisposition toward overripeness and high alcohol), these deluxe ambassadors of dryness have emerged as a new benchmark for seriousness in German wine. With time and experience, producers have homed in on a more elegant strain of GG, which telegraphs its respective terroirs with the same laser-like precision as any top white Burgundy.

With GG's ascendancy, Germany's dry versus sweet debate has only deepened. At the same time, however, some of the most compelling bottles to emerge from our Teutonic friends of late have refused to take sides, opting to explore the ambiguous territory in between. Once called *halbtrocken*, or "half dry," the going name for this new crop of not-quite-dry riesling is *feinherb*—a label with no exact definition or legal requirements, but which critic David Schildknecht has described in terms of "hidden sweetness." Neither obviously sweet nor fully dry, they share the best of both templates, using sugar not as a sweetener but as a seasoning to accentuate flavor and soften a wine's sharp edges.

For a country stereotypically defined by technical precision, the pursuit of this middle path represents a surprising embrace of intuition and chance. By allowing sweetness to be determined by vintage and vineyard, rather than a predetermined stylistic formula, these wines arguably come closer to what German wine must have resembled centuries ago, before techniques such as temperature control and sterile filtration enabled winemakers to carefully regulate fermentations.

Fittingly, then, the *feinherb* trend has emerged as a specialty of traditionally minded and naturally inclined producers, like Florian Lauer, Günther Steinmetz, and Clemens Busch, who are willing to sacrifice a bit of control to make wines more or less as their grandparents did. Priced for everyday enjoyment (examples rarely surpass $25) and refreshingly unpretentious, they exemplify all that's joyfully drinkable about German wine today.

THE MAJOR RIESLING REGIONS

Hypersensitive to subtleties of soil and climate, riesling acts like a tuning fork for terroir. While you might not always be able to pick out the differences between a Mosel example and another from the Rheingau, an important criterion to keep in mind is ripeness. When making wine this far north, even the smallest shifts in latitude, elevation, and exposure profoundly impact the end results.

MOSEL, SAAR, AND RUWER

When members of the trade rhapsodize over German riesling, they're often referring to the legendary wines grown on the steep, terraced slopes of the Mosel and its two tributaries, the Saar and Ruwer. Germany's most famous growing area, it exists at the extreme northern limits of European viticulture.

Although climate change has called into question the cool-climate identity of other areas, in the Mosel, the struggle for ripeness is real. While its fully *trocken* wines have, at times, been accused of austerity, that's increasingly no longer the case. Still, it's here that the traditional off-dry or fruity style reaches a spiritual apotheosis. Benefiting from that extra dose of residual sugar to tame their powerful acidity, the area's classic Kabinett, Spätlese, and Auslese wines typify the weightless intensity and mouthful-of-rock minerality that inspires such rabid devotion among riesling's true believers.

Essential Producers: Joh. Jos. Prüm, Weiser-Künstler, Hofgut, Falksenstein, Willi Schaefer, Clemens Busch, Peter Lauer, Immich-Batterieberg, Karthäuserhof, Günther Steinmetz, A. J. Adam, Zilliken, Julian Haart, Selbach-Oster

RHEINGAU

If the Mosel is Germany's most famous region today, throughout most of its history that honor belonged to the Rheingau. A commercial center of the global wine trade since at least the twelfth century, the area's celebrity reached its peak during the nineteenth century, when iconic estates such as Schloss Johannisberg and Kloster Eberbach were the toast of Europe. Now, after a decades-long slump of large-scale winemaking, the Rheingau is quickly regaining its former glory, thanks to its significant role in Germany's modern push toward dryness.

Because of the Rheingau's location a bit farther south, ripeness here comes as more of a given than in the Mosel. As a result, the area's riesling assumes a noticeably rounder and more voluptuous cast. Compared to the Mosel's lemon-lime and green apple flavors, expect juicy peach and apricot; in place of gossamer-like delicacy, Rheingau riesling is more about amplitude and breadth. Balancing their signature power with hair-raising acidity, the region's top single-vineyard GGs represent tours de force of mineral tension and depth.

Essential Producers: Johannes Leitz, Eva Fricke, J. B. Becker, Franz Künstler, Peter Jakob Kühn, Georg Breuer

THE OTHER RIESLING HOT SPOTS: THE NAHE, PFALZ, AND RHEINHESSEN

The Mosel and the Rheingau might be Germany's two biggest heavy hitters, but they hold no monopoly over world-class riesling.

Less well known than either, the Nahe region is often described as a delectable mash-up of classic Mosel vibrancy with the Rheingau's extra oomph (for a textbook example, keep an eye out for Weingut Dönhoff, one of Germany's finest estates).

The country's warmest region, bordering France's Vosges Mountains, the Pfalz reveals the grape's exotic side; its best wines, whether sweet or dry, practically drip with ripe, sunny fruit.

Last, there's Germany's next big up-and-comer, the Rheinhessen. Once a lake of cheap, industrially made bulk wine, the area is now churning out incredibly chiseled, fully *trocken* rieslings that deserve to be placed among the country's best.

Essential Producers: Donhöff, Von Winning, Von Buhl, Müller-Catoir, Ökonomierat Rebholz, Koehler-Ruprecht, Schlossgut Diel

THE WINE LIST

◆ **Peter Lauer "Barrel X" Mosel Riesling ($):** The master of German riesling's middle style of almost imperceptible sweetness, Florian Lauer's value-minded "Barrel X" is a blend of fruit from three different Saar villages. Full of lime zest, a kiss of sugar, and an almost aggressive minerality, it's emblematic of Germany's new wave.

◆ **A. J. Adam Dhron Hofberg Riesling Kabinett ($):** Rising star Andreas Adam has brought renewed attention to the Dhron, a neglected yet historically significant slice of the Mosel. This Kabinett from the Hofberg vineyard shows his dexterity with Germany's classic residually sweet incarnations.

◆ **Clemens Busch vom Roten Schiefer Mosel Riesling ($$):** Titans of Germany's natural wine scene, Clemens and Rita Busch bottle an assortment of biodynamically farmed wines from the Marienburg vineyard in the village of Pünderich. This example, from red slate soils (or *roten schiefer*), typically turns out dry, but exactly how dry depends on the vintage.

◆ **Ökonomierat Rebholz Riesling "Estate" Dry ($):** Hansjörg Rebholz's dense, savory rieslings from the Pfalz region—especially his celebrated GGs—show the impressive breadth and mineral intensity that the grape is capable of expressing in its top dry forms. Unusually, the grapes for his humble "Estate" riesling are sourced from his top holdings, making it more than just a basic introduction.

◆ **Eva Fricke Kiedrich Riesling Trocken ($$):** Eva Fricke has made it her life's mission to lovingly restore a handful of exceptional single-vineyard parcels in her subregion of Lorch. Considered one of her "grand crus," her Krone bottling, from vines partially planted in 1955, is a bracingly pure homage to the site's slate and quartzite soils.

AUSTRIA

. . . .

JUST THE HIGHLIGHTS

◆ **Austria doesn't make bad wine.** Mass production was never part of the country's grand plan. As a result, the average level of quality is remarkably high, with a focus on small-scale family estates.

◆ **Austria is riesling's second homeland.** Almost always fermented to complete dryness, Austrian riesling occupies a middle ground between Germany's ethereal transparency and the over-the-top opulence of Alsace.

◆ **Grüner veltliner, Austria's national grape, is capable of greatness.** Although you might recognize it from the popular liter-size bottles that line the $15-and-less shelf of your local shop, the grape covers a wide spectrum of styles, and is responsible for many of the country's age-worthiest wines.

◆ **Austrian reds are the next big thing.** Known almost exclusively for its white wines, Austria's indigenous red grapes, like blaufränkisch and zweigelt, are quickly gaining traction on US wine lists, riding the wave of interest in fresher, elegant styles.

Austrian wine's popular image, to the extent that it has one at all, is of the liter-size, screw-capped bottles of grüner veltliner that, without fail, materialize on store shelves each summer.

This phenomenon has been observed since the late 1990s, when grüner veltliner—or, as industry pros of a certain generation still call it, "groo-vee"—skyrocketed to celebrity, hyped as the Gen X alternative to the same old boring chardonnay or savignon blanc.

By the mid-aughts that momentum began to fizzle, but the grape's legacy lives on in the enduring popularity of this light, zippy expression. To this day, it accounts for most drinkers' first encounters with Austria.

The country's more serious side, on the other hand, has remained something of an industry secret. Slowly but surely, however, a new generation is discovering what Austria has been all along: one of Europe's oldest and richest wine cultures. From the Romans to the Hapsburgs, the country has slaked the thirst of countless generations of drinkers. It doesn't hurt that its wines have never been better.

Paradoxically, we have the Austrian wine scandal of 1985 to thank for that. In the summer of that year, the nation's wine industry shuddered to a halt when it was discovered that a handful of crooked merchants illegally added diethyleine glycol, a common ingredient in antifreeze, to sweeten a bunch of wines headed for the German market. The public backlash was swift and fierce, sending the nation's entire wine industry into a decades-long tailspin.

Today, you'd be hard-pressed to come across a legitimately bad bottle of Austrian wine. Hellbent upon repairing the damage to its reputation, Austria rebounded with some of Europe's strictest production standards and an unwavering focus on quality. This is evident across all price points—after all, that's the reason why those oversize liters of grüner continue to fly off store shelves.

Perhaps it's because Austria has consistently churned out some of the highest-quality, low-budget wines in the market that most of us never get around to discovering its full potential. But it's in the fine wine arena that the country truly comes into its own. Not that it's necessary to have the purse of a Hapsburg prince to get a sense of what Austrian wine is all about. The point is this: As you move beyond the entry-level segment of the market, the return on your investment exponentially grows. Once you hit the $25 to $50 range—generally, that's the sweet spot beyond which you start to enter world-class territory—you're getting not only great value but also some of Europe's most uniquely expressive wines.

WHAT IS AUSTRIA KNOWN FOR?

For most of its history, Austria's international reputation has long rested on its capacity for producing intricate, powerfully complex white wines based off its two headlining varieties.

Riesling, of course, is that perennial sommelier darling. After the whiplash of Germany's head-spinning renditions of the grape, here's some good news: except when explicitly used for dessert wines, riesling from Austria is, by definition, bone-dry. Not to be outclassed by its famous neighbor, Austrian riesling stands toe-to-toe with Germany's finest, while offering a completely different perspective on the grape: fleshy, taut, and muscular but without sacrificing the variety's signature raciness.

Then there's grüner veltliner. Reanointed as a national classic, the grape is once again returning to fashion—this time taken seriously as a dense, mineral-driven transmitter of terroir with the ability to age for decades. Savory and structured with a characteristic streak of grass and white pepper, it is extremely versatile with food.

As for what the future holds for Austrian wine, the next chapter of the country's evolution is still being written. From its emergent natural wine scene to the revival of its traditional indigenous field blends, there's plenty to get excited about. That's especially true of the next generation of Austrian reds. After years of middling obscurity, varieties such as the earthy, succulent blaufränkisch are now gaining a foothold on forward-thinking wine lists across the United States.

This flowering of innovation is present throughout Austria. As it continues to unfold, the country is shaking off its formerly staid and conservative image and embracing a new spirit of experimentation. Here are the major regions that are defining it today.

LOWER AUSTRIA

Lower Austria—or Neiderösterrich in the original German—is located not at the bottom of the country, as its name would suggest, but all the way up in the northeast, bordering Slovakia and the Czech Republic. Geographically, this makes little sense until you realize that the name refers to the lower part of the Danube, which flows right through the middle of it.

As you follow the river from west to east, through an enchanted landscape of rolling meadows and storybook castles, among the first vineyards you encounter are those of the Lower Austrian subregions of Wachau, Kamptal, and Kremstal. Holy ground for Austrian wine lovers, here riesling and grüner veltliner reach their national apogee.

Encompassing a who's who of Austrian wine royalty, these three neighboring areas boast an enviable number of the country's most celebrated estates. Most famous of all, however, is the Wachau. Long viewed as Austria's preeminent wine region, the Wachau produces not only the country's most prestigious wines but also its most flamboyant.

During the 1980s, the Wachau's producers introduced an internal classification system organized around a three-tiered hierarchy of ripeness. It's helpful to think of them in terms of weight class. Starting with the crisp, lightweight Steinfeder designation (capped at 11.5 percent alcohol for easy drinking), then ascending to the more structured, midweight Federspiel (possessing a maximum of 12.5 percent alcohol but still lithe and sinewy), the system culminates in the heavywieght Smaragd category (at a minimum 12.5 percent alcohol), produced from the ripest grapes with the highest concentration of sugars.

Because these showstopping Smaragd bottles tended to fetch the highest scores (and price tags), the market has recently rewarded producers for chasing the flashiest, most hyperbolic style possible.

Fortunately, this era of oversaturation appears to be on the wane. Facing a critical backlash, producers in the Wachau have started to recalibrate their ambitions, wielding the region's ingrained capacity for power with ever-increasing restraint. In the process, the virtues of precision and transparency are coming back into focus.

Finally, it's worth mentioning that the Kamptal and Kremstal regions were spared much of the stylistic excesses that infiltrated the Wachau. As a result, their slightly lesser-known rieslings and grüners tend to skew a bit leaner and brighter, at relatively gentler prices.

Essential Producers: Alzinger, Knoll, Hirtzberger, Rudi Pichler, Prager, Nigl, Bründlmayer, Hirsch, Schloss Gobelsburg, Nikolaihof

BURGENLAND

Bordering Hungary, just south of idyllic Lake Neusiedl (a popular tourist attraction), Burgenland has long been a source of nobly sweet wines made from botrytized grapes (see "Botrytis," page 14) in the same manner as Hungarian Tokaji. While it still excels in this capacity (if you want proof, just try any of the legendary Alois Kracher estate's sticky-sweet masterpieces), in modern times, Burgenland has emerged as ground zero for what once seemed like a contradiction in terms: Austrian reds.

The driving force behind this transformation can be summed up in just one word: blaufränkisch. Austria's second-most widely planted red grape after the juicy zweigelt (also worth checking out), blaufränkisch was once relegated to the wine world's fringes, dismissed as a curiosity at best. But it is now making inroads as Austria's standout red.

Structured, meaty, and dark fruited but delivering a one-two punch of minerals and herbs, the variety can be rendered in many forms, whether as a snappy, goes-down-easy *vin de soif*, perfect with a slight chill, or a cellar-worthy fine wine, combining the acidity of Burgundian pinot noir (or perhaps more accurately, Loire cabernet franc) with a rugged, central European wild streak.

For most blaufränkisch fans, their first great epiphany about the variety came via winemaker Roland Velich's Moric estate. Founded in 2001, the winery has already achieved classic status; its range of organically farmed, spontaneously fermented expressions of the grape—including a handful of exquisite single-vineyard bottlings—are regarded as regional touchstones. Others quickly entered the spotlight, most notably a strong naturalist contingent that has attracted the attention of several boutique importers specializing in lo-fi and minimal-intervention wines.

Essential Producers: Moric, Claus Preisinger, Gutt Oggau, Wachter-Weisler, Christian Tschida, Meinklang, Rosi Schuster, Jagini, Alexander Koppitsch

VIENNA

Once upon a time, the outskirts of many European capitals were fringed with vines. What remains of them today, however, is generally a few ceremonial plantings reserved for tourism's sake rather than any legitimate commercial purpose. But the vineyards surrounding the city of Vienna are no gimmick. These historic hillsides have been a central feature of the city's life for centuries.

Nowhere is the city's vibrant wine culture more evident than at the *Heuriger*, or traditional wine tavern, which has allowed generations of growers to sell their wine directly to the public—a perfect exchange of homespun supply and demand. At a time when we romanticize the idea of local wine, it's increasingly difficult to find the genuine article. In Vienna, however, the custom of the *Heuriger* provides the rare example of local wine in the literal sense—grown, produced, and consumed within a single capital.

Although Vienna offers a range of single-varietal wines—from grüner veltliner and riesling to pinot blanc, chardonnay, and pinot gris—its most authentically local expression is the indigenous Viennese field blend known as Gemischter Satz, or "mixed set," which predates the rise of Austria's mono-varietal wine culture by hundreds of years. The style was originally born of necessity; before the arrival of modern viticultural advances, the practice of co-planting several different grapes (with their varied acidity and ripeness levels) in the same vineyard afforded growers a built-in insurance policy against poor vintages.

Of late, the category is being reinterpreted by an ambitious band of growers who are eager to share a more serious version of it with the world. These range from fresh, classically styled versions fermented in stainless steel to preserve the wine's brisk acidity and bright orchard fruit to powerfully complex and age-worthy single-vineyard bottles such as Fritz Wieninger's "Rosengartl," a blend of five different varieties planted in a single south-facing parcel within the larger cru of Nussberg.

It's a paradox that Gemischter Satz, the archetypal local wine, is now developing a following in international cities, like New York, Sydney, and Tokyo. But in another way, it makes perfect sense. In our increasingly globalized, homogenized world, we look to traditional expressions such as Gemischter Satz to satisfy a deeper kind of thirst.

Essential Producers: Weingut Wieninger, Weingut Christ, Weingut Zahel, Jutta Ambrositsch, Mayer am Pfarrplatz

THE WINE LIST

◆ **Alzinger "Dürnstein" Federspiel Wachau Riesling ($$):** The riper Smaragd expressions of the Wachau tend to rack up the critical accolades, but when it comes to sheer drinkability (and value for the money), it's the sleek, racy Federspiel category that always outperforms expectations. The storied Alzinger estate's riesling "Dürnsteiner" displays an intriguing tension between crunchy stone fruits, a tarragon herbaceousness, and an electric jolt of acidity.

◆ **Nikolaihof Grüner Veltliner "Hefeabzug" ($$):** This grüner veltliner has become one of the organic Nikolaihof estate's main calling cards. Aged on the lees and displaying plenty of oyster-shell minerality, it's often compared to top Muscadet, but also displays the white-pepper spice and herbal character that could only come from Austria's national grape.

◆ **Jutta Ambrositsch Wien Stammersdorfer Gemischter Satz Satellit ($$):** Former graphic designer Jutta Ambrositsch puts a cotemporary naturalist spin on the traditional Viennese field blend via her captivating range of Gemischter Satz wines. From the Bisamberg vineyard in Vienna's twenty-first district, this consists of riesling, chardonnay, grüner veltliner, and sauvignon blanc, co-planted and co-fermented into the kind of fresh, goes-down-easy white that the city's residents have been enjoying for generations.

◆ **Moric Burgenland Blaufränkisch ($$):** When it comes to Austrian reds, it doesn't get more essential than Roland Velich's Moric estate. Still Burgenland's leading producer and a touchstone for the region, Moric's profoundly expressive renditions of blaufränkisch firmly established that grape's reputation as a worthy addition to the new pantheon of great reds. Even his basic blaüfrankisch is a dazzling meld of blackberry, violets, and a meaty, soil-driven complexity.

CENTRAL AND EASTERN EUROPE

For most of the twentieth century, to speak of the great wines of Europe implicitly meant Western Europe. But during the three decades that have passed since the collapse of the Soviet Union, the winemaking nations of Central and Eastern Europe have rebounded dramatically, increasingly driven by a younger generation of minimalist producers who are eager to reclaim their relationship to their land. At a time when it feels as though we've overturned every last stone in our perpetual pursuit of the new, the ability to tap into such uncharted territory as plavac mali, native to Croatia's Dalmatian coast, or juhfark, from Hungary's Somló region, among many others, proves to even the most jaded among us that there's always another horizon to explore.

HUNGARY, CROATIA, CZECH REPUBLIC, REPUBLIC OF GEORGIA, AND SLOVENIA

....

JUST THE HIGHLIGHTS

- **We think of the countries of Central and Eastern Europe as wine wastelands, where vodka and beer rule.** Historically speaking, however, this part of the world once boasted a winemaking tradition as rich as any other.

- **Communism changed everything.** Under Soviet control, wine production fell to large nationalized cooperatives tasked with manufacturing as much wine as possible for the Russian market. In the process, generations of tradition were nearly erased.

- **After the fall of the Berlin Wall, progress came quickly.** Today, the revived wine industries of Hungary, Croatia, the Czech Republic, the Republic of Georgia, and Slovenia have emerged as an unexpected epicenter of quality (and increasingly natural) winemaking.

- **There's a whole new Old World to discover.** Thanks to a handful of intrepid US importers, we're able to taste things such as Georgian rkatsiteli and Croatian plavac mali for the first time.

Throughout the eighteenth and nineteenth centuries (essentially, until the Hapsburg monarchy crumbled post-World War I), many of the world's most coveted wines originated not just in France and Germany but also in the vast vineyard areas of the Austro-Hungarian Empire. In fact, the imperial capital of Vienna merely represented the starting point of a wine culture that extended into modern-day Slovenia, Croatia, the Czech Republic, Hungary, and beyond. So what happened?

In a word, communism. Under Soviet rule, these local wine industries fell under state control. The mandate to deliver wine to the masses required a massive scale of production, hence the proliferation of gigantic nationalized cooperatives that all but obliterated generations of local tradition.

In the three decades that have passed since the fall of the Iron Curtain, progress has come quickly. After a period of rapid investment and modernization, the current generation of ex–Eastern Bloc winemakers is determined to reverse this epidemic of cultural amnesia and reconnect with the land of their ancestors. They're driving this renaissance, moreover, through a revived focus on native grapes (so brace yourself for oddities such as hárslevelu, rkatsiteli, and malvazija istarska) and, increasingly, by following the same natural playbook that has injected fresh life into so many forgotten corners of the continent.

Fueled by newfound interest from US importers and American audiences' unquenchable thirst for the fringe and obscure, these eastern offerings are quickly wrestling their way onto trendy wine lists and wine shop shelves. You'll want to start with the following areas, which have generated the greatest share of stateside attention.

HUNGARY

In 1730, more than a century before the famous 1855 classification of Bordeaux, Hungary's Tokaj-Hegyalja area became the world's first wine region to establish its own vineyard classification system, which should tell you all you need to know about the sophistication of its wine culture.

Back in the Hapsburg era, the area's signature wine—the decadently sweet, amber-hued Tokaji Aszú (or Tokaji for short)—was the toast of royal courts throughout Europe. Given this impressive history, it's only natural that Hungary figured among the first ex-Soviet nations to act as a magnet for private investors, who set their sites on the storied region of Tokaj: for instance, Anthony Hwang of the celebrated Királyudvar estate (his family also owns Vouvray's iconic Domaine Huet) and wine writer Hugh Johnson, cofounder of the Royal Tokaji company.

The area's specialty remains its traditional dessert wines, produced using shriveled-up late-harvest grapes infected with the fungus botrytis (see page 14). But ever since the 1990s, the region of Tokaji has shifted its focus to dry styles that showcase the incredible versatility of furmint, its main indigenous variety, which is often featured alongside the lesser-known hárslevelű. Displaying the same synthesis of waxy richness, razor-sharp acidity, and smoky minerality that brings to mind Loire chenin blanc, furmint, like chenin, is capable of assuming every conceivable stylistic parameter—from sweet, of course, to sparkling, semidry, and bone-dry.

While Tokaji understandably dominates the conversation about Hungarian wine, other parts of the country have recently stepped into the spotlight. Notable among these are the pungently dry whites of the Somló region, home to the densely textured juhfark variety (a personal favorite of Emperor Joseph II), as well as Sopron, where the kékfrankos grape (known as blaufränkisch in neighboring Burgenland, just across the border in Austria) is being channeled into vibrant, elegant reds.

Essential Producers: Fekete, Samuel Tinon, Royal Tokaji, Királyudvar, István Szepsy, Péter Wetzer, Árvay, Gábor Kardos, Bodrog Borműhely

CROATIA

After surviving the horrors of the Serbo-Croatian war of the 1990s, Croatia quickly rebuilt itself, for better or for worse, into one of Europe's fastest-growing tourist destinations, and the remarkable revival of its wine industry continues to play a significant role in that recovery. Just as the country's rugged beaches have lured travelers as an off-the-beaten-path alternative to the Italian side of the Adriatic, Croatian wine continues to benefit from the current vogue for coastal whites and reds that has long been Italy's specialty.

So while there's no shortage of quality wine being made in Croatia's inland area of Slavonia (not to be confused with Slovenia, which we'll address shortly), it's the seaside regions of the Istrian Peninsula and the Dalmatian coast that have won the country most of its recent admirers.

Istria's main attraction is the aromatic malvazija istarska. A unique local strain of malvasia, it comes in a range of styles, from crisp, floral tank-fermented versions to honeyed, deeply textured skin-contact expressions, often aged in clay amphorae; running through all of these permutations, however, is the area's signature salinity, a reminder that the sea is never far from view of the vineyards. That same briny quality manifests in the burly, earthy reds produced from the plavac mali grape, a relative of zinfandel that thrives high above the Adriatic on the craggy cliffside slopes of Dalmatia.

Essential Producers: Androvic, Vinarija Dingač, Giorgio Clai, Bura, Bibich, Frano Miloš, Matošević, Josipa Marinov, Bura Mrgudić, Vinarija Križ, Piquentum

CZECH REPUBLIC

Beer, not wine, is the beverage that immediately springs to mind in connection with the Czech Republic, the birthplace of the original Pilsner (made by the Urquell Brewery in 1842). But the country's vineyards have been cultivated for wine production since the Roman era and once enjoyed widespread renown.

Today, after decades of state ownership, those vineyards are thriving once again, even if US audiences have only recently started to take notice. Compared to the earlier hype surrounding places such as Slovenia, Croatia, or the Republic of Georgia, Czech wine took a bit longer to gather stateside momentum. In a short span of time, however, it has left an indelible mark.

That's due almost entirely to a small group of winemakers based in Moravia, the country's main growing region, who have gathered under the banner of the Autentisté (or "Authenticists") movement, a native offshoot of the global natural wine scene. Issued by cofounders Bogdan Trojak, Richard Stávek, and Ota Ševčík, the Autentisté manifesto effectively parallels the wider natural wine philosophy of organic farming and minimal intervention, emphasizing the return to terroir.

In their case, that means focusing on local varieties that bear the country's rich Central European heritage of its shared lineage with Austria. Take, for instance, Richard Stávek's "Veselý Oranžové," an electrifying skin-fermented field blend of riesling italico, grüner veltliner, traminer, and malvasia (plus a handful of others), or any of rising star Milan Nestarec's irreverently titled bottlings, including his chuggable "TRBLMKR" neuburger (a grape also found in Austria), or his liter-size "Nach" red, a Beaujolais-like blend of pinot noir and zweigelt.

Essential Producers: Milan Nestarec, Bogdan Trojak, Richard Stávek, Ota Ševčík, Dobrá Vinice, Jaroslav Osička, Porta Bohemica

REPUBLIC OF GEORGIA

Just a few years ago, asking for Georgian wine would have elicited a blank stare (or perhaps a polite inquiry as to whether you were visiting from Atlanta or Savannah). Today, however, the country's profoundly rustic whites and reds have emerged as popular emblems of wine's retro avant-garde.

The irony about referring to Georgian wine as hip or cutting edge is that the country lays claim to what is widely considered the world's oldest wine culture; archaeological evidence of viticulture in this part of the Caucasus dates back to around 6000 BCE.

For more than eight thousand vintages, wine has played an almost sacramental role in the area, deeply woven into the fabric of daily life. Exceptionally, that stayed true even during the Soviet era. While the area's industrial-scale collectivized cooperatives provided a steady stream of cheap, sweet wine for the Russian market, Georgia largely maintained its uninterrupted tradition of home winemaking, which has proceeded in the same preindustrial manner for centuries.

Much has since been made of Georgia's ancient winemaking practices, whereby grapes are left to ferment on their skins while buried underground in giant clay amphorae, known locally as *qvevri*. Although the country's reds—made primarily from the savory, highly tannic saperavi grape—have attracted attention, it's Georgia's oxidative, skin-fermented whites—derived from indigenous grapes such as rkatsiteli, chinuri, mtsvane, kisi, and tsolikouri—that have emerged as the country's signature expression. In fact, their discovery by Friulian winemaking legend Joško Gravner during his travels through the region in the 1990s launched the modern orange wine revolution, bringing Georgia international attention as the style's ancestral point of origin.

It's not difficult, then, to connect the dots between the public's newfound infatuation with the natural and orange categories and Georgian wine's growing US visibility. Lending credence to the notion that converts to a religion always become its most zealous practitioners, the individual who bears most of the responsibility for introducing Georgian wine to stateside audiences is American-born Jonathan Wurdeman, who moved to Georgia in 1996. His Pheasant's Tears winery, located in the Kakheti region near the medieval town of Sighnaghi, specializes exclusively in *qvevri*-influenced expressions of the country's native grapes. They still number among the most widely available examples found in the market today.

Essential Producers: Pheasant's Tears, Gia Togonidze, Tedo Gzirishvili, Gotsa, Makaridze, Niklas Marani, Zurab Topuridze, Okro's Wines, Archil Guniava

SLOVENIA

Among the first former Soviet countries to rebuild its wine industry, Slovenia owes much of its present-day fame to its proximity to Friuli, the source of many of northern Italy's most exciting and innovative wines. The westernmost Slovenian region of Primorski, for example, shares both a contiguous vineyard area and a common wine culture with Friuli.

Although Friulian producers such as Joško Gravner and Stanislao Radikon receive most of the credit for kickstarting the area's orange wine renaissance, a handful of winemakers across the Slovenian border, such as Aleš Kristančič (of Movia winery fame), Dario Prinčič, Branko & Vasja Čotar, and Aleks Klinec, played an equally instrumental role. Legends in their own right, their pungent, amber-hued whites—made from the usual Friulian mix of grapes such as ribolla gialla (here called rebula), tocai friulano, and pinot grigio—command as dedicated a cult following as any from the great Friulian masters.

Essential Producers: Čotar, Movia, Dario Prinčič, Aleks Klinec, Štoka

THE WINE LIST

◆ **Királyudvar Tokaji Furmint Sec ($):** Given furmint's similarities with chenin blanc, it's not hard to understand what inspired Domaine Huet's Anthony Hwang to acquire one of the most historic properties in Tokaji. Under his helm, Királyudvar has positioned itself at the center of the region's dry wine renaissance, and this golden, enveloping, high-acid white reveals why.

- **Milan Nestarec "Forks and Knives" White Moravia ($):** Milan Nestarec has emerged as the enfant terrible of Central Europe's naturalist fringe. Despite their playful names (such as "WTF" and "GinTonic"), these are some of the Czech Republic's most serious wines. His cidery, skin-fermented "Forks and Knives," made from organically farmed Müller-Thurgau, is as joyously drinkable as any natty *vin de soif* from the Loire.

- **Pheasant's Tears Rkatsiteli Amber Wine ($):** American-born Jonathan Wurdeman founded Pheasant's Tears in 2007 with the mission of paying homage to Georgia's ancient art of *qvevri* winemaking. Fermented on the skins like all of his whites, this golden-hued rkatsiteli comes across remarkably fresh, leading with bright pear fruit, honeycomb, and roasted walnut.

- **Frano Miloš Plavac Mali ($):** *Friškina* is a local word to describe the scent of the sea that defines coastal Croatian wines, and it's exactly what you'll encounter in Frano Miloš's rugged interpretations of plavac mali. Naturally fermented and aged in traditional Slavonian oak casks, this is one full of brambly black fruit, green olive, and scrubby herbs.

- **Movia Rebula Primorska ($$):** One of Slovenia's pioneers of biodynamic agriculture and a major player in the Brda region's orange wine scene, Movia's Aleš Kristančič is regularly mentioned in the same breath as Friulian legends Joško Gravner and Stanislao Radikon. This skin-fermented rebula speaks to the regions' shared cultural ties, revealing the lively, nutty complexity of the best Italian versions.

GREECE

Grapes have been grown, harvested, and fermented into wine in Greece since the age of Homer, so one can't help but appreciate the irony of describing Greek wine as an up and coming discovery. But after decades of mediocrity, that's precisely what the category represents today. From the country's northern border down to its sun-drenched islands, the latest generation of Greek winemakers has refocused its attention on the country's unique roll call of native grapes and growing areas. Together, they've kicked off a quality revival not unlike the one currently under way in Portugal, which also swept through Spain and southern Italy only a couple of decades earlier.

SANTORINI AND MACEDONIA

·····························

JUST THE HIGHLIGHTS

- Greece's wine culture is paradoxically ancient and brand-new. On one level, wine has been a fact of life on the Greek peninsula since the dawn of civilization. But in many ways, the country only recently entered the modern era.

- Greece is rewriting its identity. From its northern border down to its scenic islands, the country's winemakers are rediscovering their terroirs through the unique prism of native grapes.

- Two star expressions have emerged as the heroes of modern Greek wine. Assyrtiko, the white grape central to the sunny island of Santorini, and xinomavro, the full-bodied red that thrives in the remote mountains of Macedonia, show the greatest potential for mainstream success.

Despite having existed for millennia, Greek wine is still struggling to define its identity in relation to its mythic past.

If that past is prologue to the present, you could say that the country's wine industry has been acting out its own modern version of the great Homeric epic. Like the wandering hero Odysseus, for much of the previous century, Greece had lost its way. Beset by large-scale cooperative winemaking and the proliferation of international grapes, like cabernet and syrah, it only recently embarked on its journey home.

By all accounts, that perilous voyage is now coming full circle. No longer relegated to house wine status at kitschy gyro restaurants and Greek diners, the country's offerings are quickly capturing the attention of big-name importers and carving out a place on top US wine lists. As a result, many stateside drinkers are discovering Greece's ancient wine regions for the very first time.

Of these, highlights include the rugged, mountainous region of Nemea, tucked in the northeastern corner of the Peloponnese, where the agiorgitiko grape is channeled into rich, plummy reds that drink a bit like merlot's swarthy Mediterranean cousin. There's also Mantineia, known for crisp, aromatic whites made from the pink-skinned moschofilero, plus a handful of fascinating examples from Crete and Cephalonia, among others.

While all of these wines deserve attention, the country has invested its greatest hopes in two uncontested standouts—the red xinomavro, hailing from the hills of Macedonia, and the white assyrtiko, from the tourist mecca of Santorini—that have already been pegged as Greece's modern crown jewels.

SANTORINI

To many of us, the island of Santorini conjures luxury villas, private yachts, and white-domed villages perched above the radiant Aegean Sea. But after just a short drive from the airport, you begin to see signs of the other Santorini: the scattered patches of ancient, bush-trained vines growing out of the sand right along the side of the road.

No one who has ever set foot in the island's vineyards could deny that Santorini possesses all the raw materials to achieve the kind of greatness we associate with just a handful of places. Unlike almost everywhere else in Europe, Santorini's sandy, volcanic soils miraculously resisted the nineteenth-century phylloxera epidemic that wiped out most of the continent's vines. As a result, the island survives (along with the Canary Islands) as one of the few European growing regions still using its original, ungrafted rootstock. Adding to this sense of geographical uniqueness, the island's growers adopt a unique training system called *kouloura*, whereby vines are woven into nest-like baskets close to the ground to retain moisture and shelter the grapes from wind.

All of this, combined with the star assyrtiko grape's powerful mineral bite, has earned Santorini its reputation as one of the Mediterranean's most mind-bendingly unique wines: an electric yet deeply textured white with the potential to age like great Chablis or German riesling, but full of a brooding, volcanic intensity (you can literally taste the smoky, ashen minerality of its soils).

Because of its small size (it's possible to traverse the island by car in less than an hour), Santorini is home to no more than fifteen producers, so global demand increasingly outstrips supply. While Santorini is no longer as wildly undervalued as it once was, its top wines still overdeliver.

Essential Producers: Sigalas, Hatzidakis, Argyros, Koutsoyannopoulos, Gaia, Santo Wines

MACEDONIA

The red equivalent to Santorini's star assyrtiko grape, the aromatic, late-ripening xinomavro variety is increasingly hyped as Greece's answer to nebbiolo.

The grape's name roughly translates to "acid black," which should give you some sense of its appeal to fans of the great wines of Piedmont. Native to the semi-mountainous foothills of Macedonia in the zones of Naoussa, Amyndeon, and Goumenissa, it exhibits a similar balance between piercing acidity, astringent tannins, and the classic rose-petal and tar aromatics that make Barolo drinkers drool.

While this comparison has helped bring attention to xinomavro's complexity and extreme capacity to age, it has been cultivated in northern Greece for more than fifteen hundred years—long before anyone had ever heard of its more famous neighbors across the Adriatic. So, no matter how much traction it gained as a value-driven Barolo alternative (and to be fair, even the most acclaimed bottlings sell for a fraction of the price), it ultimately deserves to be taken on its own terms. Fortunately, you don't have to be able to pronounce it in order to drink it.

Essential Producers: Kir-Yianni, Domaine Nerantzi, Domaine Tatsis, Elinos, Dalamára

THE WINE LIST

◆ **Hatzidakis Assyrtiko Santorini ($):** When Haridimos Hatzidakis tragically passed away in 2017, the future of his beloved organically farmed estate seemed uncertain. Fortunately, the bottles coming out of the winery today remain true to his original uncompromising vision. Slightly richer and more rustic than some of the island's other expressions, this entry-level assyrtiko is a perfect tribute to the classic Hatzidakis style—all smoke, salinity, and ripe yellow fruit.

◆ **Domaine Sigalas Assyrtiko Santorini ($$):** Cleaner and more polished than the Hatzidakis version, the Sigalas' take on assyrtiko is every bit as essential and age-worthy, showcasing the estate's brighter, more reductive (that is, nonoxidative) approach in the cellar. Often compared to Chablis for its briny depth and lemony richness, it's ultimately pure Santorini: an indispensable benchmark of the new white wine canon.

◆ **Kir-Yianni Estate "Ramnista" Naoussa ($):** The expression of 100 percent xinomavro from the slopes of Naoussa's Mount Vermion, Kir-Yianni's "Ramnista" has emerged as the gold standard for that grape's regional profile. It's easy to understand the frequent comparisons to nebbiolo—it has a similar high-acid bite and leathery, floral intensity—but there's also a tomato-leaf herbal quality and southerly rusticity that places it firmly in the Mediterranean.

- **Domaine Tatsis Goumenissa ($$):** A big, burly beast of a red, this hyper-traditional biodynamically farmed blend of xinomavro and negoska from Macedonia's Goumenissa region is released only after several years of bottle aging—all the better to tame its fierce tannins. This allows mature aromas and flavors to emerge (think decayed leaves, balsamic, moist earth) alongside its rich core of black currant and leather: truly one of the most compelling and authentic expressions of its northern Greek terroir.

PART TWO

THE NEW WORLD

Encompassing North and South America, Australia, New Zealand, and South Africa, the "New World" refers to pretty much everywhere wine is grown outside of Europe. With few, if any, traditions of their own to guide them, New World winemakers took the only logical approach: copying the classics of the great European canon.

At the time that most of these areas began (literally) putting down roots and courting the global market, France represented the apex of wine world greatness. It's no wonder, then, that French grapes largely provided the inspiration for their early ambitions.

Just think about it. California embraced cabernet sauvignon, modeling itself to Bordeaux. Oregon chose pinot noir, in imitation of Burgundy. For Australia, it was syrah (or shiraz, as locals call it) that first earned the country fame, whereas New Zealand appropriated sauvignon blanc; and South Africa, chenin blanc. These days, Argentina is synonymous with malbec—a grape that originated in the Cahors region of southwestern France. And Chile . . . well, Chile has tried its hand at any number of Gallic varieties, from sauvignon blanc to cabernet to pinot noir and even the little-known carménère.

But over time, and through plenty of trial and error, even the most fledgling wine regions evolve. As they move toward greater self-awareness, they outgrow the need to rely upon external comparisons—what does sunny California have in common with rainy, maritime Bordeaux, anyway?—and begin to cultivate an identity of their own.

That's the condition in which we find so many New World regions today: on the cusp of becoming fuller, more mature versions of themselves. This evolution assumes any number of forms, depending upon the place, but it's evident across all of the regions that follow. To that end, these final chapters should be taken as preliminary snapshots of a wider process that's still coming into view.

THE UNITED STATES OF AMERICA

For a country whose wine culture can be measured in mere centuries (as opposed to Europe's millennia), the United States has come remarkably far in a shockingly short period of time. Even as late as the 1950s and 1960s, the question of whether it was possible to achieve greatness had yet to be tested. Then, circa the mid-1970s, an aspirational band of California vintners put the state on the viticultural map, setting into motion an evolution that has led to the astonishing diversity of today's domestic wine scene.

The Golden State still reigns as our most essential wine region. Thanks to the current generation's constant quest for reinvention, this is unlikely to change anytime soon. But if the story of American wine once started and ended in California, that's no longer the case. Originally conceived as a haven for top-notch (that is, Burgundy-inspired) pinot noir, Oregon is now turning out some of the country's most thought-provoking wines from a range of grapes. And unlikely as it might seem, a similar spirit of experimentation has come to New York's Finger Lakes and Long Island regions as they embrace a decidedly northeastern paradigm—one that, follows a completely different logic than sun-kissed California's.

CALIFORNIA

....

JUST THE HIGHLIGHTS

◆ **California is by far North America's major wine region.** The state accounts for 90 percent of US production and it's where we created our first great benchmarks: the classic Napa wines of the 1960s and 1970s.

◆ **Napa cabernet is (still) the quintessential American wine.** After a wave of ripe, oaky examples that turned off many classically minded drinkers, the area has seen a "return to form," focusing upon the Old World–inspired balance and restraint of Napa's pioneering midcentury wines.

◆ **The old California map is being rewritten.** The New California movement, as it is popularly called, isn't only predicated upon a shift toward fresher, lighter wines. It's also about exploring the state's lesser-known grapes and growing regions.

◆ **In California, producer matters most.** Given their current mandate to uncover a more diverse idea of California, many of today's top winemakers source grapes from all over the state. As such, the best way to explore what California has to offer is to stick to the winemakers who are actively shaping that conversation.

Once upon a time, not so long ago, throwing shade at California wine constituted a rite of passage in snobby (read: Eurocentric) New York wine circles. To order the proverbial "big Napa cab" or buttery chardonnay symbolized supporting the slick mainstream over all things soulful, artisanal, and authentic.

Fortunately, attitudes have since evolved. For one, the landscape of California wine has matured exponentially. And in the process, we've learned to appreciate North America's largest and most important wine region in a much more nuanced way, no longer conflating it with its most exaggerated stereotypes.

Thanks are due to a younger generation of winemakers, along with a handful of early pioneers, who have pushed the conversation forward by radically rethinking the possibilities of what California wine can be. These days, as it navigates away from the bombastic, high-octane style that defined it during the 1990s, California is the source of many of the country's most thought-provoking wines. But to envision the future of this New California—the umbrella term coined by author Jon Bonné to describe the reactionary changes sweeping through the Golden State—we need to revisit California's origin story.

That tale, as it turns out, overlaps with the birth of The Unites States' own emerging wine culture, holding up a mirror to our national taste and our shifting sensibilities about wine. After all, it was in the sunny, promised land of California that the dream of American wine first became a reality. By proving to the world that we could compete with the grand European classics, we ended up inventing a classic of our own.

THE RISE AND FALL OF "CLASSIC" CALIFORNIA CABERNET

It may be hard today to appreciate just how audacious that early dream was. But back in the state's formative years, when legendary players such as Mondavi, Heitz, and Ridge were just ramshackle upstarts, greatness was still assumed to be the exclusive province of France. It wasn't until the landmark 1976 Judgment of Paris tasting, when a lineup of California cabernets and chardonnays outscored an elite roster of red Bordeaux and white Burgundies, that California gained widespread legitimacy.

Thus was born what we now call the golden age of California wine. Modeled after benchmark Bordeaux, the lean, grippy cabernets that reigned during the 1970s and 1980s rarely topped 13 percent alcohol. Prizing elegance and vibrancy over blunt power, they didn't shy away from the grape's inherent herbal streak, which provided a savory counterpoint to the state's natural proclivity for ripe, sunny fruit. All of this gave the wines of this classic period an incredible capacity to age: even four decades on, the best examples remain remarkably light on their feet and full of dark brambly fruit, high acidity, and earthy complexity, hence the renewed interest in early California cab among serious collectors and sommeliers today.

As history teaches, however, every golden age is followed by one of decadence and excess. With the rising influence of critics such as Robert Parker, whose famous one-hundred-point scale fueled a push toward increasingly oaky, opulent wines, California's ambitions quickly shifted. No longer desiring merely to imitate Bordeaux, it soon tried to out-muscle and overpower it.

This is when California wine jumped off the deep end, so to speak, turning its greatest assets (warmth, sunshine, a seemingly endless penchant for ripeness) into an overblown parody of itself. Although these effects were felt across California's growing regions, no other part of the state embraced the bigger-is-better mantra more brazenly than Napa.

By the 1990s, the transformation from "classic" to "cult" Napa cabernet was complete. As if overnight, a fresh crop of stylish, high-scoring, and exorbitantly priced Napa wines arrived on the scene, funded by wealthy investors. These trophy bottles bore little resemblance to the classic cabernets of decades gone by. Totems of the period's myopic style, they existed not so much to be drunk as to be conspicuously consumed.

THE CLASSIC HOLDOUTS

This commodified image of Napa has defined perceptions of California for a whole generation of drinkers. But in the revisionist history of California wine that is being written today, the heroes have turned out to be a small but influential band of original visionaries—both in Napa and in other parts of the state—who refused to stray from the righteous path of the classic style.

Over the years, producers such as Corison Winery, Edmunds St. John, Smith-Madrone, Dunn Vineyards, and Ridge Vineyards, among several others, never swerved from their original vision of crafting precise wines of place—often in the face of an indifferent public. The ongoing reappraisal of their legacies points to an alternative paradigm for California wine, which the new class of Golden State winemakers has eagerly seized upon.

THE NEW CALIFORNIA (AND BEYOND)

California's return to balance is a major talking point these days. Often pegged as a kind of back-to-the-future reclamation of the restrained aesthetic of the 1960s and 1970s, the movement toward brighter, more elegant wines is a defining feature of the state's new wave. But to view the changes that have transformed California over the past decade in purely stylistic terms is to miss the bigger picture.

Sure, the backlash against what Jon Bonné has called California's era of "big flavor" has inspired winemakers across the state to harvest earlier (for sharper acidity and lower alcohol) and tone down the heavy-handed oak and extraction. But beyond simply making brighter, fresher wines, today's top producers are asking big existential questions about where California is headed.

If California's founding mothers and fathers sought to emulate Bordeaux—their generation's esteemed benchmark—the most meaningful wines coming out of the Golden State today reflect our own era's postmodern kaleidoscope of influences. Early New California reference points—the tangy Jura-inspired trousseau from the Arnot-Roberts projects, for example, or Steve Matthiasson's skin-fermented homage to Friulian ribolla gialla—conjure a far more expansive idea of California, measured against a new template of global influences.

What unites California's current avant-garde is the conviction that there's more to the state's identity than has previously been expressed, and that the next phase of its evolution will depend on a willingness to explore its fringes: the obscure and typically unsung grapes and growing regions that are revising expectations about what California means.

REWRITING THE OLD CALIFORNIA MAP

Maybe *willingness* isn't the most accurate word. Fact is, most newcomers had no choice but to venture into California's margins and peripheries. No amount of bright-eyed enthusiasm can change the fact that land in California is outrageously expensive. Unless you're a tech or hedge-fund billionaire with unlimited capital to burn, you're probably not going to be consolidating thirty acres in prime Napa Valley anytime soon.

This brings us to the biggest challenge facing California's younger generation: the struggle to find an economically sustainable formula for making wine on a smaller scale. In fact, many have abandoned the prospect of land ownership altogether, opting to follow what we might call the Steve Edmunds model. Ever since founding his seminal Edmunds St. John winery in 1985, Edmunds has purchased fruit from a handful of sites in the craggy ranges of the Sierra Foothills. These raw materials form the basis for his acclaimed range of Rhône-inspired wines, which he crafts in a warehouse in an industrial section of Berkeley.

In the same spirit, faced with the lack of affordable land, many of California's most promising winemakers now double as vineyard scouts, scavenging the state in search of uniquely compelling sites—a patch of high-elevation aglianico here, some old-vine carignan there—that somehow slipped off the radar. As if that weren't enough, they're acting as vineyard managers as well: in order to obtain the highest-quality fruit, they typically work directly with the growers to oversee all aspects of the farming. As a result, it's not at all uncommon for a single winemaker to produce separate bottlings from an assortment of vineyards scattered across the state, often separated from one another by hundreds of miles.

Take, for example, the acclaimed Sandlands project from Tegan and Olivia Passalacqua. In the words of the Sandlands mission statement, the winery focuses on "the forgotten classic California varieties" sourced from little-known areas that have "remained the outliers of California viticulture."

On paper, the Passalacquas' range of single-vineyard expressions reads like a CliffsNotes guide to the New California. In addition to a juicy Sonoma Coast trousseau, they make a pair of textured chenin blancs from Amador County and Lodi, respectively, along with two different takes on old-vine mourvèdre (here known as mataro) from San Benito and Contra Costa Counties. Other highlights include a rendition of the neglected mission grape from California's oldest productive vineyard, planted in 1854 in the Shenandoah Valley of the Sierra Foothills, and a refosco—Friuli's signature red grape—from Napa, of all places.

Sandlands is just one example of many. All over California, like-minded peers are bringing visibility to corners of the state that never registered on the mainstream radar. At the same time, they're presenting established areas in a radical new light. Napa ribolla gialla is now becoming a thing; even more conventional grapes such as chardonnay are getting a makeover. Consider the version that the Berkeley-based Donkey & Goat project makes from Napa's Linda Vista Vineyard: bearing the signature of winemaker Jared Brandt's "hands-off" sensibility (that is, naturally fermented, unfiltered, and slightly hazy), it couldn't break more radically from the Napa status quo.

By the numbers, teensy-production wines such as these represent a drop in the proverbial bucket of California's total output, but their influence can't be overestimated. As dispatches from a deeper and far more diverse vision of California, they reveal the ways that the Old California map is being rewritten right before our eyes.

A ROUGH GUIDE TO THE REGIONS

As this statewide excavation of California's identity continues to unfold, one thing is clear: at this stage, a region-by-region breakdown isn't the most useful way to delineate what's relevant in California wine today. Unlike France or Italy, where regional wine styles developed out of centuries of trial and error, California (like the rest of the United States) is still a work in progress. And like any adolescent, it's going through its awkward phase, trying to figure out which grapes should be planted where and which specific sites hold the potential for greatness.

So rather than cover the geography on a micro level, dissecting the minute distinctions between every subregion of Santa Barbara County, we'll take a big-picture view of the state, highlighting the major pockets of excitement where producers are pushing the conversation forward. To that end, since many of California's most influential winemakers are sourcing fruit from all over the state, instead of including the essential producers for each individual region, they've been grouped together into a single statewide list (separated into two categories, the Classics and the New Wave) at the end of this chapter (see pages 296–297).

We can begin by dividing the state into three extremely broad zones: the North Coast, the Central Coast, and the inland areas of Lodi—the most prominent AVA (American viticultural area) in the vast tract of vineyard land known as the Central Valley—and the Sierra Foothills. Each of these enormous zones, of course, boasts a multitude of smaller AVAs, making it almost impossible to generalize about wine styles.

That said, we can establish some preliminary guidelines. On the most basic level, a natural division exists between the cooler coastal parts of the state, which tend to favor lighter-bodied grapes (like pinot noir) and yield brighter, fresher wines, and the warmer inland areas, where the dominant style becomes richer and the varietal mix shifts toward cabernet sauvignon and zinfandel and, depending on the area, native Rhône and other Mediterranean grapes, whether Italian, Iberian, or French.

THE NORTH COAST SUBREGIONS

The North Coast (meaning north of San Francisco) is the seat of California's winemaking aristocracy, culminating in the crown jewels of Napa and Sonoma. A veritable who's who of winemaking legends, this is the California most of us think of when the subject turns to California wine. Accordingly, we'll limit our discussion to those two titans, but it's worth mentioning that Mendocino County—best known as America's cannabis capital—is quickly emerging as a hot spot for compelling pinot noir and chardonnay.

NAPA VALLEY

It's easy to make Napa a scapegoat for California's slip to the dark side. But no matter how frequently it gets called out for its luxury trappings, there's a much wider stylistic spectrum on display in Napa than haters give it credit for.

In fact, there has always been another side of Napa. By definition, where there's a valley, there must be peaks. In Napa's case, there are five: Howell Mountain, Spring Mountain, Diamond Mountain, Mount Veeder, and Atlas Peak. With higher elevation and thinner, rockier soils comes a leaner, more muscular style of cabernet than the plush examples grown in the fertile benchland (valley floor) vineyards of areas such as Rutherford and Oakville.

The change in altitude signals one in attitude as well. Historically, the hills have exuded a different culture of winemaking, more attuned to nuances of soil and place. It's no coincidence that many of the iconic individualists who delight old-school California fans are tucked away in the winding country roads of Napa's mountain districts.

On Spring Mountain, for example, the family-operated Smith-Madrone estate has been producing taut, linear cabernets for decades; their steely riesling and complex chardonnay also offer excellent values within a classic Napa vein. Similarly, nearby Stony Hill has long been worshipped as the source of some of California's great classically structured whites.

Other members of this same club include Diamond Mountain's Diamond Creek Vineyards and Mount Veeder's legendary Mayacamas estate. And at Spring Mountain's Cain Vineyard & Winery, winemaker Chris Howell—one of Napa's great overlooked originals—continually pushes the boundaries of what Napa wine can be: see, for example, his profoundly earthy and savory Cain Five, a blend of traditional Bordeaux grapes from the steep, organically farmed slopes of Cain's namesake vineyard.

SONOMA

Just across the Mayacamas mountain range to the west of Napa, Sonoma is also home to some first-class cabernet and a historic home for zinfandel. (To that end, don't miss Morgan Twain-Peterson's riffs on several ancient zinfandel field blends under the Bedrock label, as well as Ridge Vineyards' classic "Lytton Springs" and "Geyserville" bottlings). But ever since the 1970s, when several producers went hunting for a perfect place to plant pinot noir, the noble grape of Burgundy has been the region's calling card.

Closer to the coast than Napa, the thinking went, Sonoma's main growing regions—notably the Russian River Valley—offered a cooler climate that would be just right for that notoriously fickle grape. Of course, *cooler* is always a relative term in California. Packed with black fruit and cola-like sweetness, the lavish style of Russian River pinot popularized during the 1990s took full advantage of the area's abundant sunshine. While that era's lush, higher-alcohol pinots will always have fans, if you ask pinot purists, they'll tell you that what tends to get lost under all that exaggerated fruit is the grape's heightened sensitivity to the intricacies of terroir.

Over time, the quest for elegance in California pinot has taken the shape of a migration west, pushing vinters to explore the farthest reaches of the chilly, fog-haunted Pacific Coast. Here, on the remote ridges of the West Sonoma Coast (or what insiders call the "true" or "far" Sonoma Coast, to differentiate it from the glut of bottles masquerading under the ubiquitous "Sonoma Coast" designation), a handful of fanatics and true believers are testing the very limits of the grape's ability to grow.

If Burgundy's genius with pinot is predicated upon an epic struggle for ripeness, then the same kind of climatic adversity has brought attention to outposts such as Fort Ross–Seaview, Annapolis, and Occidental, long considered too marginal for red wine production. Led by the pioneering David Hirsch of Hirsch Vineyards, who first arrived in 1978, producers such as Peay, Littorai, and Failla have honed a shimmering expression of pinot noir—red fruited, tart, and hauntingly mineral—that feels born of the salty ocean breeze.

THE CENTRAL COAST SUBREGIONS

Heading south, the Central Coast unfurls for nearly three hundred miles from the San Francisco Bay way down to the Santa Ynez Valley, a tiny area in the southernmost tip of Santa Barbara County. Although its many growing areas lack the name recognition of Napa or Sonoma, it nevertheless claims some of California's most historically prized sites and estates. Due to its vast size, it's impossible to cover in its entirety, but following are some of the highlights worth seeking out.

SANTA CRUZ MOUNTAINS

It's odd that the Santa Cruz Mountains area, nestled just south of San Francisco between the Pacific Ocean and Silicon Valley, isn't better known. If nothing else, the reputation of Ridge Vineyards' iconic "Monte Bello" cabernet—the closest thing to an American answer to "first growth" Bordeaux (see page 52)—should be enough to ensure lasting fame. Due to its diverse mosaic of soil types and microclimates, it's also one of California's most versatile regions, equally adept with pinot noir and chardonnay (typically grown nearer to the coast) as it is with its savory, angular renditions of cabernet sauvignon. And yet the area remains something of an inside secret, flying under the radar of the general public.

Those privy to that secret, however, can attest to Santa Cruz's status as California's great overlooked classic—a haven for traditionally minded drinkers who have found themselves alienated by some of California's more hyperbolic tendencies. Although it might lack the experimentalism that has launched other parts of the state into the spotlight, it consistently delivers on the initial promise that first lured such early legends as Martin Ray to its foothills back in the 1940s.

As a destination for world-class cab, the Santa Cruz Mountains boast a lineage as hallowed as Napa's. Beyond Ridge's flagship "Monte Bello," the longtime standard bearer, the winery's more basic "Estate" bottling represents one of the best values in California wine, offering a taste of the same famous dirt in a far more affordable package. These iconic examples aside, Santa Cruz continues to demonstrate its greatness in the form of wines such as the Arnot-Roberts "Fellom Ranch," produced since 2007 from a vineyard just above Monte Bello in the town of Cupertino, or the Ghostwriter project's minimalist interpretation of the "Bates Ranch" vineyard.

Despite the region's illustrious history with cabernet, the grape that generates the most hype for the Santa Cruz Mountains today is (you guessed it) pinot noir. To California purists, the defining Santa Cruz style—bright, focused, and floral—has always been synonymous with the historic Mount Eden Vineyards. Under the tenure of winemaker Jeffrey Patterson, the property never wavered from its fundamental commitment to soil over style, even at the height of pinot's flashy high-alcohol phase. The same vision informs Patterson's approach to what is indisputably one of California's iconic chardonnays, a case study in balancing California's innate richness with a spine of nervy acidity.

No conversation about pinot's role in the Santa Cruz foothills would be complete, however, without paying respect to Kevin Harvey, the ex–Silicon Valley entrepreneur who left the corporate world behind after planting some pinot noir in his own backyard to stunning results. Encouraged by this early experiment, he founded Rhys Vineyards in 2004. Ever since, he has pursued the singular mission of ferreting out the region's greatest sites for pure, mineral-driven pinot noir, plus some equally fantastic chardonnay and syrah.

Paragons of nuance and site sensitivity, the range of wines that Harvey produces from his six Santa Cruz Mountains vineyards (and another in Anderson Valley) embody a transparency of place rarely seen outside of Europe. There could be no better rebuke to the skeptical Burgundy drinkers in your midst who claim California pinot lacks terroir.

SANTA RITA HILLS

California's ever-expanding exploration of its coastal extremes brings us, finally, to the Santa Rita Hills AVA, a tiny bastion of cool-climate winemaking at the westernmost tip of Santa Barbara County's Santa Ynez Valley.

To be clear, Santa Rita is just one of several parts of Santa Barbara where winemakers have been chasing greatness. To the north, the Santa Maria Valley first cemented its reputation for stellar pinot and chardonnay back in the 1980s, largely thanks to Au Bon Climat winemaker Jim Clendenen. At the eastern portion of the Santa Ynez Valley, the warmer (read: farther from the ocean) AVAs of Happy Canyon and Ballard Canyon fare well with cabernet (not just sauvignon but also franc). For two of the best, look for Broc Cellars' elegantly floral take on the grape and Mike Roth's crunchy, carbonically macerated version from the Coquelicot vineyard, bottled under his Lo-Fi label. (Seek out Rhône varieties as well; top examples include Two Shepherds and A Tribute to Grace.)

For much of recent history, the Santa Rita Hills were lumped in with the rest of the Santa Ynez Valley. But over the past couple of decades, the area has made a convincing argument for its geographical distinctiveness from the neighboring AVAs to the east. Ask any winemaker in the area and you'll be guaranteed to hear how the foggy Pacific breezes that funnel through the area's transverse (east-to-west-running) valleys make it a perfect incubator for world-class pinot noir and chardonnay.

In fact, for a while, some might have called it too perfect. If that maritime influence cools the area, allowing for a slow, steady growing season, the flip side is that grapes can ripen almost indefinitely, leading to a rash of bombastic, high-alcohol wines that lapped up accolades during the early 2000s. That's what makes the stylistic shift that is redefining the area today so surprising. Not only are winemakers picking their grapes weeks earlier than before, but, as in the far Sonoma Coast, where the westward push has brought to light a whole new set of terroirs, they're also working toward a more nuanced delineation of Santa Rita's soils—specifically, the far western fringes of the AVA, where climatic conditions become all the more extreme.

No one has fought harder to advance this dirt-centric aesthetic than winemakers Sashi Moorman and Rajat Parr. Ever since 2007, the year they founded Sandhi Wines—a *négociant* project that sources grapes from a handful of singular sites, including the historic Sanford & Benedict Vineyard—the pair has set out to make a case for the Santa Rita Hills as one of the world's premier sources of Burgundy varieties. Further evidence came in 2013, with Domaine de la Côte, their collection of six estate pinot noir vineyards planted within seven miles of the Pacific Ocean.

Fresh and structured without trying to repress California's signature ripeness, Sandhi's wines exist as prototypes of the direction in which California appears to be heading—or, perhaps more accurately, of the ways that classic grapes, like pinot noir and chardonnay, are becoming truly Californian. As tempting as it may be to call Sandhi's site-specific approach "Burgundian," they're ultimately striving for a different goal. The endgame isn't to imitate or even surpass Burgundy but to apply the

A BRIEF WORD ON PASO ROBLES

For the warmer inland area of Paso Robles, always something of a Central Coast outlier, the South of France has historically provided the prism through which to understand its potential—at least insofar as "historically" applies to the late 1980s, when Tablas Creek, one of California's earliest specialists in Rhône-styled blends, established roots in the area.

That legacy continues in the form of oddities such as Broc Cellars' take on picpoul blanc, a tangy lesser-known white native to France's southern Languedoc region, to cite just one example.

More recently, however, Paso Robles is also making a name for itself with Italian grapes: Stephanie and Brian Terrizzi's exclusively Italo-focused Giornata project comes to mind (particularly their work with nebbiolo, not the most obvious fit for the area's sunbaked soils), as does Ryme Cellars' savory aglianico from the Luna Matta Vineyard.

same meticulous philosophy of place to their own little corner of the globe and figure out what it has to say.

INLAND CALIFORNIA: LODI AND THE SIERRA FOOTHILLS

If places such as the Santa Cruz Mountains and far western Sonoma draw inspiration from Bordeaux's Left Bank (the original coastal cabernet) and the thrilling marginality of Burgundy, then the rugged, inland areas of Lodi and the Sierra Foothills conjure a completely different set of reference points. The polar opposite of Napa's romanticized dream of California wine country, the areas have mostly toiled in obscurity while their fancier coastal counterparts dominated the headlines. But the promise of centenarian vineyards and the freedom that comes with less-expensive land have combined to transform Lodi and the Sierra Foothills into unexpected hotbeds of experimentation.

LODI

The enormous grape-growing area of Lodi, sandwiched between the cities of Sacramento and Stockton, is the last place anyone expected to emerge as one of New California's major capitals. Long known for supplying low-cost fruit to giant brands such as Sutter Home and Mondavi's Woodbridge label, the region served for decades as California's bulk wine epicenter. When it finally started to aspire beyond the usual table wine stereotypes, circa the 1990s, Lodi was pegged as a place for burl and brawn rather than finesse, known for oaky, high-alcohol zinfandel.

But through it all, Lodi remained in possession of one of California's great historical assets, even if it lacked the means to realize its potential: a scattered treasure trove of gnarled, heirloom vines planted by Italian and Portuguese immigrants during the nineteenth and early twentieth centuries. Consisting primarily of zinfandel (with its usual entourage of backup grapes such as petite syrah, carignan, mourvèdre, and alicante bouschet), most of these early field blends were torn out during the transition to high-volume production. Yet somehow, despite all odds, a handful of these relics managed to survive, their precious grapes typically destined for cheap white zinfandel blends and other ignoble purposes.

Just as in Europe, where a younger wave of winemakers has been seeking out abandoned plots of extremely old vines and restoring their potential, the movement to recognize California's irreplaceable heritage vineyards has reshaped Lodi's trajectory. Within the span of just a decade or so, a flood of top talent has arrived on the scene, eager to express sites such as Bechthold Vineyard, a plot of knobby, tangled cinsault vines planted in 1886 by German emigrant Joseph Spenker in the region's Mokelumne River area. Sourced by such fashionable names as Birichino, Turley, and Abe Schoener's Scholium Project, the vineyard—and the pale, highly perfumed wines they draw forth from it—has become an unlikely emblem of Lodi's reversal of fortunes.

If what attracts winemakers to places such as Bechthold is a glimpse into Lodi's past, others have taken a more experimental route. For example, Markus Bokisch of Bokisch Vineyards has built a name for himself by interpreting Lodi through the lens of Spain via plantings of Iberian varieties, like tempranillo, garnacha, and albariño. Similarly, the boundary-pushing expressions that Markus Wine Co.'s Markus Niggli channels from Lodi's Mokelumne Glen Vineyards, planted exclusively to Germanic grapes such as kerner, grüner veltliner, and blaufränkisch, presents the region through an unexpected paradigm of vibrant acid-driven whites and juicy, fragrant reds.

SIERRA FOOTHILLS

The discovery of gold in the hills of California's Sierra Nevada mountain range in 1849 ushered in a steady stream of grizzled prospectors seeking to strike it rich. Most of them, as we know, found only hardship, sorrow, and broken dreams. At the very least, however, your standard down-and-out gold hunter could find solace in what would quickly become the area's other booming industry: wine.

First planted under vine by the European emigrant miners who arrived in the area and realized its potential for growing grapes, today the Sierra Foothills has attracted a new cohort of fortune hunters in search of a very different form of currency: a slice of some of California's most distinctive terroirs.

In fact, the list of winemakers who have flocked to the area's Amador and El Dorado Counties reads like a roll call of California wine's current in-crowd. Sommelier favorites such as La Clarine Farm's Hank Beckmeyer and Matthew Rorick of the Forlorn Hope label both established wineries in the foothills, where they developed their own less-is-more spin on the area via offbeat grapes, like albariño, barbera, mondeuse, trousseau, vermentino, and more. The foothills are also the source of experimental bottles such as Donkey & Goat's "Stone Crusher" (a skin-fermented, minimally sulfured take on the Rhône's roussanne variety) and Jolie-Laide's juicy, carbonically macerated "Barsotti Vineyard" gamay noir (inspired as much by Steve Edmunds's classic expression of the grape, "Bone-Jolly," as the wines of Beaujolais).

◆ ◆ ◆

Any attempt to reduce California wine to a user-friendly list of producers (or for that matter, an inventory of wines) is bound to backfire; no matter how thoughtfully assembled, it will never be complete. Although cursory at best, the selections that follow represent a good-faith effort to carve out a representative cross section of the people, places, and bottles that are essential to California today.

Essential Producers: The Classics— Corison Winery, Edmunds St. John, Tablas Creek, Heitz Cellar, Ridge Vineyards, Mount Eden Vineyards, Hirsch Vineyards, Cain Vineyard & Winery, Diamond Creek, Smith-Madrone, Larkmead, Mayacamas, Au Bon Climat, Calera, Turley Wine Cellars, Stony Hill, Porter Creek

The New Wave— Forlorn Hope, Broc Cellars, Dirty & Rowdy, Birichino, Lo-Fi Wines, Cruse Wine Co., Ryme Cellars, Scholium Project, La Clarine Farm, Markus Wine Co., Bokisch Vineyards, Giornata, Ceritas, Sandhi, Domaine de la Côte, A Tribute to Grace, Rhys Vineyards, Arnot-Roberts, Failla, Peay Vineyards, Littorai, Sandlands, Matthiasson

THE WINE LIST

- ◆ **Matthiasson Napa Valley White Wine ($$):** Why shouldn't Friuli offer a model for what Napa whites can be? Matthiasson's groundbreaking blend of sauvignon blanc, ribolla gialla, sémillon, and tocai friulano offers proof that even California's most mainstream region is capable of reinvention.

- ◆ **Ridge Vineyards Estate Cabernet Sauvignon ($$):** As an argument for cabernet's life beyond Napa, it doesn't get more convincing than Ridge's basic "Estate" bottling. High-toned and tangy, with firm tannins and a core of dark berries and herbs, it's the classic expression of the Santa Cruz style (priced for those of us who can't afford Ridge's iconic "Monte Bello").

- ◆ **Ceritas "Peter Martin Ray Vineyard" Chardonnay ($$$):** From one of the historic vineyards of the Santa Cruz Mountains, first planted in 1943 by the legendary Martin Ray, this nervy, mineral-veined chardonnay from Ceritas's John and Phoebe Raytek renders that grape in its purest, most elemental form—the perfect antidote to all the usual stereotypes about overripe, buttery California chardonnay.

- ◆ **Hirsch Vineyards "San Andreas" Sonoma Coast Pinot Noir ($$):** Perhaps the definitive example of the push toward marginal terroirs, Hirsch's flagship pinot incorporates fruit from across his holdings in the far Sonoma Coast. The liquid embodiment of the chilly, fog-shrouded Pacific Coast, it's California pinot at its most lifted, elegant, and place driven.

- **Arnot-Roberts North Coast Trousseau ($$):** The Arnot-Roberts trousseau is as close to a modern classic as it comes. One of the New California's seminal expressions, it ticked off all of the right boxes (fringe Jura grape, naturalist street cred, chuggable style) at just the right time, but continues to be one of California's most deliciously drinkable wines: all rose hips, raspberry seed, and spiced tea.

- **Edmunds St. John "Bone-Jolly" Gamay Noir ($):** Before anyone had ever heard of the New California, Steve Edmunds was living and breathing its philosophy. Although he's best known for Rhône blends, his classic "Bone-Jolly" gamay—grown three thousand feet above sea level in the granite soils of the Barsotti Ranch vineyard—invokes the bright, crunchy wines of Beaujolais by way of the Sierra Foothills.

- **Sandlands Amador County Chenin Blanc ($$):** Early in his career, Sandlands's Tegan Passalacqua apprenticed in South Africa's Swartland region (the Southern Hemisphere's great chenin blanc stronghold), which possibly explains his knack for coaxing such elegance out of the grape in a warm, dry climate such as Amador County's. It's amazing how much texture and intensity of flavor (pineapple, citrus, honeysuckle) he can condense into such a fresh, low-alcohol package.

- **Broc Cellars Valdiguié ($):** Thanks to a case of mistaken identity, the red valdiguié grape—a native to the Languedoc region in southern France—has a long history in the Golden State, where it was once known as "California gamay." A playful tribute to that obscure chapter of California's past, Chris Brockway's version employs carbonic maceration to highlight the grape's strawberry-scented, easy-drinking side.

- **Forlorn Hope Sémillon "Nacré" ($):** From vines planted before 1941 in Napa's Yount Mill Vineyard, Forlorn Hope's homage to the bracingly dry, long-lived sémillons of Australia's Hunter Valley weighs in at under 11 percent alcohol, but acquires a nutty, waxy depth thanks to winemaker Matthew Rorick's practice of aging the wine for a few years before release.

- **Turley Wine Cellars "Bechthold Vineyard" Cinsault ($):** California's past meets California's future via Turley's translucent, perfumed, peppery carignan from Lodi's centenarian Bechthold Vineyard. A handful of fashionable winemakers now source fruit from the site, but Turley's version always strikes an ideal balance between savory old-vine complexity and "goes down easy" drinkability.

OREGON

· · · · · · · · · · · · · · · · ·

JUST THE HIGHLIGHTS

◆ **Oregon's Willamette Valley has solidified its reputation as one of the great New World terroirs for pinot noir.** Inspired by Burgundy, the region's interpretations of the grape are among North America's most important contributions.

◆ **Oregon's strength lies in thinking small.** The state produces just 1 percent of North America's total output, and—true to its original Burgundian inspiration—has clung fast to an artisanal set of values, producing limited-quantity wines of elegance and restraint.

◆ **There's more to Oregon than just pinot noir.** Lately, certain producers are experimenting with alternative models for the state, often inspired by natural wines from France (and in particular, the Loire Valley).

◆ **The fringe is Oregon's future.** The current trend toward Loire grapes, like cabernet franc and melon de Bourgogne (among others), represents one strategy among many for reimagining Oregon's identity.

For America's fledgling wine regions, imitation of the European classics is not just a sincere form of flattery but also the path to self-discovery. If California initially carved out its identity by comparing itself to Bordeaux, then Oregon, the country's second-most important wine-producing state, originally modeled itself after Burgundy.

Geographically, this choice was only natural. Unlike California, where it was possible to dream up a style of cabernet that could outdo Bordeaux in terms of richness and power, Oregon's temperate, rainy climate would require an alternative reference point. Burgundy—France's notoriously marginal growing region, with its finicky star grape, pinot noir—ticked off all the right boxes.

Over time, however, the basic differences in grape and climate that always existed between California and Oregon would grow into fundamental divisions in attitude and philosophy. In its attempt to rival Bordeaux's elite trophy wines, California adopted a "bigger is better" mentality that favored opulence and exclusivity. Oregon's early pioneers, on the other hand, embraced an opposite set of values, aligning themselves with a Burgundian commitment to the small scale, the heirloom, and the artisanal.

That same modesty still defines Oregon's wine industry, which accounts for just 1 percent of the United States' annual production. Compared to Napa's Michelin-starred restaurants and polished tasting rooms, the Willamette Valley—Oregon's leading zone of production—feels downright folksy.

That doesn't mean, of course, that Oregon's winemakers are any less ambitious, or that their wines haven't acquired a similar prestige. In fact, within the span of just five decades—the blink of an eye in the grand scheme of wine history—the state has established itself as one of the world's premier destinations for pinot noir. And even as it has come to put its own stamp on the grape, an alternative class of winemakers (much like their Golden State counterparts) has started to question the dominant pinot paradigm and rewrite the rules for Oregon's future.

But before we start prophesying about that future, let's look back to the category's origins in the lush hills of the Willamette Valley, where the state's first great pinots came into being.

WILLAMETTE VALLEY PINOT NOIR

In 1965, when David Lett, the late founder of the Willamette Valley's iconic Eyrie Vineyards, planted Oregon's first commercial pinot noir vines, the odds seemed stacked against him. According to conventional wisdom, the future of the US wine industry belonged to California; the prospect of growing grapes north of the state line invited a heavy dose of serious skepticism, if not outright mockery.

But like all visionaries, Lett and the handful of trailblazers who joined him—among them Dick Ponzi, Dick Erath, and David Adelsheim—had an important hunch: that the Pacific Northwest could become the perfect place to make world-class pinot noir (and some pretty solid pinot gris to boot).

We now know that hunch paid off exponentially: Oregon's track record with the grape, which currently accounts for more than 60 percent of the state's plantings, is uncontested. And in contrast to California's own pinot saga, which unfortunately took a decades-long detour into the realm of indulgent ripeness, the style for which Oregon is known today has remained fundamentally faithful to its founders' original vision: one of balance, restraint, and the moderate use of oak.

Even the most thoughtful attempts at approximation, however, never yield exact replicas, and according to Oregon's top producers, that's exactly as it should be. As the Willamette Valley continues to outgrow the need to compare itself to the Côte d'Or, it has defined a distinctly Oregonian style of pinot noir that reflects its own unique sense of place.

Although it's difficult to generalize, and individual styles vary to the same extent as anywhere else, Oregon pinot typically falls somewhere between Burgundy and California on the ripeness scale, displaying fleshier fruit than the former while typically avoiding the saturation that sometimes plagues the latter. This makes Oregon's appeal more immediately accessible or approachable than Burgundy's, but its best wines never sacrifice the sort of savory, soil-driven complexity that rewards deeper contemplation.

Despite some grumblings in the early to mid-aughts that Oregon might be going the way of California (update: it didn't), the pinots coming out of the Willamette Valley are more compelling than ever. That's especially true as winemakers continue to embrace organic and biodynamic farming and—reflecting the greatest lesson the area learned from Burgundy—deepen their understanding of their local terroirs. That means not only working to delineate further the identities of Willamette's seven sub-AVAs—Eola-Amity Hills, Dundee Hills, Ribbon Ridge, Yamhill-Carlton, McMinnville, Chehalem Mountains, and Van Duzer Corridor—but also an explosion of rare single-vineyard bottlings from producers new and old.

As Oregon grows in acclaim, and the cost of land rises in concert with bottle prices—for perspective, in 2015, ex–film producer and wine-industry entrepreneur Mark Tarlov of Chapter 24 Vineyards released a pair of $300 pinot noirs, produced in partnership with star Burgundy winemaker Louis-Michel Liger-Belair—the state is starting to experience growing pains of its own. As a result, the Willamette Valley has emerged as a magnet for big-name investors from Burgundy, including Louis Jadot and Méo-Camuzet, among others, and California, such as Kendall-Jackson.

But there are still plenty of values to be found in the world of Oregon pinot—and for the most part, pricing doesn't come close to the princely sums fetched by Burgundy's rarest gems. For example, under the stewardship of second-generation owner Jason Lett, Eyrie Vineyards' basic estate-grown wine offers a perfect $30-ish introduction to one of the region's legendary names. Along similar lines, look for bottles such as naturalist Kelley Fox's biodynamically farmed "Ahurani" pinot noir, sourced from a site in the McMinnville area, or Montinore Estate's deliciously straightforward Willamette Valley pinot noir, blended from a variety of sites throughout the region and priced less than $20.

For a taste of the best the state has to offer, seek out any of the essential producers below, all of whom turn out archetypal examples of Oregon pinot across a range of different subzones and price points.

Essential Producers: Eyrie Vineyards, Adelsheim, Montinore, Cristom, Bethel Heights, Kelley Fox, Evening Land, Brick House, Cameron, Patricia Green, Hope Well, J. K. Carriere

BEYOND THE PINOT NOIR PARADIGM

There's no denying that times have changed since Willamette's early pioneers arrived in the 1960s and 1970s. Sure, it's still far from approaching peak Napa. But if the area was once a place where small, independent producers could pursue a dream of homespun greatness, the barriers to entry have steepened considerably. That doesn't mean, however, that realizing such a dream is no longer possible. As determined as their peers in California, the state's next generation of talent has responded to these challenges by envisioning an alternate narrative for the future.

What will that future look like? It's still too early to tell. But at this point, one thing appears clear: it will involve deconstructing pinot noir's supremacy and building a fresh—and in many cases, more affordable—paradigm.

It's not like Oregon's new class poses anything close to an existential threat to pinot noir's preeminence. The grape remains central to the state's wine industry, and that's not changing anytime soon (moreover, several of the most prominent "alt-Oregon" producers work with the variety). More than anything, their impact has been to introduce a far more diverse template of influences, not only in terms of grapes they're using, but also in style and sensibility as well.

This transformation is taking hold on multiple levels. Among its more obvious manifestations is the reclamation of gamay. Long treated as an afterthought, the grape has been granted a second life in Oregon, attracting the interest of a growing number of producers. The version from Doug Tunnell's Brick House Vineyards—for decades one of the few prominent examples of the grape—remains a critical benchmark, but it has been joined by a rash of others, including a standout example from Evening Land Vineyards and, on a much smaller scale, the fascinating releases from Bethany Kimmel's The Color Collector project.

In one sense, this new spotlight on gamay couldn't be more fitting. After all, the classic gamay-based wines of Beaujolais have lately been rediscovered as cheaper alternatives to pricy pinot from Burgundy, so why shouldn't the grape fulfill a similar function in Oregon? On the other hand, many of the most relevant renditions of the grape—for instance, the high-toned gamay noir made by Scott and Dana Frank of Bow & Arrow winery in northeast Portland—conjure the gamay's lesser-known French stronghold: the Loire Valley. Along with Leah Jørgensen Cellars and Division Winemaking Company's Kate Norris and Tom Monroe (both also based in Portland), Bow & Arrow belongs to an exciting group of producers who are examining Oregon's identity through the unique prism of Loire grapes—not just gamay but also cabernet franc, chenin blanc, sauvignon blanc, melon de Bourgogne (Muscadet's defining variety), and, last but not least, some pinot noir.

On a practical level, this "Loiregon" movement—as PUNCH senior editor Jon Bonné has called it—makes sense. After all, Burgundy isn't France's only marginal wine region; the damp, chilly Loire Valley represents an equally useful parallel to the Pacific Northwest climate. But a deeper motivation beyond simply highlighting Loire varieties is driving the trend. Let's not forget, the Loire is now the epicenter of France's natural wine movement; the inspiration that Oregon's winemakers are drawing from the French region today owes everything to that philosophy's values and the tradition of honest, affordable table wines it represents.

The recent Loire focus is just one approach to reframing the conversation about Oregon wine. Plenty of others are working toward a similar end using a different set of reference points. Germany, for example, provides the model for Portland's Teutonic Wine Company (its rieslings number among the best produced anywhere in the United States). In its own postmodern way, Smockshop Band—the second label of Hiyu Wine Farm—is conjuring Galicia via skin-fermented albariño from the Columbia Gorge (among several other groundbreaking bottles), and Analemma Wines, based in Mosier, is doing the same with mencía, to cite just a few noteworthy examples.

The goal of these projects isn't to anoint Oregon as the next Loire, or the next Germany, or the next anything at all; it's to help Oregon wine become a truer, more meaningful version of itself—whatever that ultimately comes to resemble.

Essential Producers: Division Winemaking Company, Bow & Arrow, Leah Jørgensen Cellars, Johan Vineyards, Smockshop Band and Hiyu Wine Farm, Minimus Wines, Day Wines, Holden Wine Company, Franchere Wine Company, Analemma, Teutonic Wine Company

THE WINE LIST

♦ **The Eyrie Vineyards Estate Pinot Noir ($$):** With Jason Lett at the helm, Eyrie has only come to more deeply embody the qualities of balance, sustainability, and elegance that have defined its approach from the start. Chock-full of sweet red cherries, damp earth, and a stony precision, this is what Willamette Valley pinot noir was always meant to be.

♦ **Division Winemaking Company Division-Villages "Béton" ($):** A blend of at least 50 percent cabernet franc (depending upon the vintage) with gamay, pinot noir, and côt (the Loire name for malbec), this fragrant red is yet another Loiregon incarnation inspired by the easy-drinking natural reds of Touraine.

◆ **Kelley Fox Wines "Ahurani" Pinot Noir ($$):** Having apprenticed under none other than Eyrie's David Lett, in 2007, Kelley Fox started bottling her own terroir-driven wines that combine the best of Oregon's past and its exciting future. Sourced from the biodynamically certified Momtazi vineyard in the McMinnville AVA, this ruby-hued pinot noir is just one of several highly recommended bottlings.

◆ **Bow & Arrow Willamette Valley "Melon" ($):** Produced in a slightly larger volume than its single-vineyard "Johan" version, Bow & Arrow's entry-level melon de Bourgogne drinks like a denser, riper style of Muscadet, displaying all of the classic citrus and mineral notes but amped up in intensity. Luckily, that logic doesn't apply to the price tag; this costs about what you'd expect to pay for a good bottle of the French stuff (which is to say, it's a steal).

◆ **Teutonic Wine Company David Hill Vineyard Riesling ($$):** Typically clocking in at less than 12 percent alcohol (and displaying the faintest kiss of residual sugar), Teutonic's riesling from the David Hill Vineyard pays respect to the Mosel by way of fifty-year-old vines in the Willamette Valley. Nervy and lean, with plenty of mineral cut, it's all about ripe Granny Smith apple and yellow pears.

NEW YORK

····················

JUST THE HIGHLIGHTS

- **Yes, New York makes wine—and it's actually good.** Though not as well known as their West Coast equivalents, New York's main wine regions—Long Island and the Finger Lakes—are producing better wine than ever before.

- **The state's paradigm is cool-climate freshness.** Both on Long Island and in the Finger Lakes region, grapes struggle for ripeness, resulting in a dominant style that aligns with the current taste for low alcohol and brisk acidity.

- **Cabernet franc is quickly becoming New York's standout red.** Native to the Loire, the grape is showing enormous potential in the Empire State—whether the pale and delicate versions of the Finger Lakes or the earthier expression of Long Island.

Believe it or not, New York is the third-largest wine-producing state in the nation. Clocking in at just 3 percent of the country's output, it's not exactly giving California a run for its money. But even that modest statistic is enough to place New York above Oregon—a far more famous and firmly established zone of production.

If New York doesn't immediately spring to mind as a major player in the domestic wine game, that's partly because its main growing regions— the Finger Lakes and Long Island—came of age so late. Although records of viticulture in the state extend back to the earliest Dutch settlers, New York's modern wine industry continues to lag behind its West Coast counterparts, struggling to establish a clear narrative to offer the public.

On the upside, the wines coming out of both regions today show signs of incredible progress. By now, New York has arrived at a pivotal moment. As it prepares to break out of local markets to become a national contender, the state is emerging as an unlikely source of marginal, cool-climate wines that fully embrace their East Coast origins.

THE FINGER LAKES

Between Long Island and the Finger Lakes, the latter has arguably come the furthest—not just in terms of quality, which has undergone a serious renaissance, but in terms of carving out a clear identity as well. Then again, it also had a bit of a head start.

The Finger Lakes creation myth begins in 1962. At the time, given a long history of failed attempts, it was commonly assumed that European wine grapes (or *Vitis vinifera,* to use the technical term) were ill equipped to survive the harsh New York winters. Winemakers had no choice but to make do with the area's miscellaneous mix of indigenous American varieties and French American hybrids such as vidal blanc, cayuga, and seyval blanc, among others.

Then along came Dr. Konstantin Frank, a Ukrainian-born scientist with a doctorate in viticulture, who solved the problem by grafting European grapevines to cold-resistant American rootstocks. Thanks to his efforts, it became possible to cultivate Old World grapes in the Finger Lakes for the first time, and the region officially entered its modern era.

Now operated by his heirs, the Dr. Konstantin Frank estate remains a benchmark for the area, along with the equally significant Hermann J. Wiemer Vineyard, founded in 1979 by a native of Germany's Mosel region. These pioneers played an instrumental role in positioning the Finger Lakes as North America's answer to the storied wines of Germany, with riesling as its centerpiece.

Today, riesling remains the Finger Lakes' main attraction—a logical choice, considering how the grape's greatness has always been borne out of the struggle for ripeness. In the region's gravelly, limestone-rich soils, the variety displays the same kind of low-alcohol purity and transparency found in its German counterparts, and comes in a similar range of styles, although the emphasis is increasingly on dry (to dryish) expressions.

The best are inspired by the same minimalist approach that defines the latest top rieslings from Germany. Bellwether Wine Cellars' Kris Matthewson, for instance, has become a sommelier favorite for naturally fermented, site-designated wines, such as his "Tuller" and "Seven Sisters" bottlings, sourced from two different vineyards on opposite sides of Seneca Lake. He's joined by fellow Finger Lakes native Nathan Kendall of N. Kendall Wines, who not just is making some of the area's most dynamic riesling but has also started experimenting with local and hybrid grapes, like Delaware and Catawba, via his chëpìka project, in partnership with master sommelier Pascaline Lepeltier.

Although never known for red wine, the Finger Lakes region has proven itself adept at satisfying the newfound thirst for bright, vibrant reds. For one, it has developed a distinctly East Coast cast of pinot noir, more aligned with crunchy, cranberry-scented Jura pinot noir than any California pinot you've ever encountered (Heart & Hands Wine Company makes one of the best). But the red grape that has shown the greatest promise in the Lakes is cabernet franc. Pale in color and distinctly savory, the best versions (look for Keuka Lake Vineyards, Bloomer Creek, and Eminence Road Farm Winery) play up the grape's leafy, herbal qualities with a tart freshness also found in the bistro classics from the Loire.

Essential Producers: Keuka Lake Vineyards, Bellwether Wine Cellars, Red Tail Ridge, Heart & Hands Wine Company, Ravines, Eminence Road Farm Winery, Bloomer Creek, chëpìka

LONG ISLAND

Better known as a playground for New York City's 1 percent, the eastern end of Long Island is among the last places you'd expect to find a serious wine region. But if you follow State Route 25 all the way past the town of Riverhead, the land abruptly divides into two distinct forks—the North Fork and the South Fork—and that's where Long Island wine country officially begins.

Unlike the South Fork, which has all but succumbed to full-blown Hamptons fever, the North Fork has done its best to maintain its original low-key farm-stand vibe, and it's here that you'll find most of the vines.

The biggest challenge facing the area, aside from the outrageous cost of land, is figuring out what it wants to be. After trying on various guises—merlot, for example, is still Long Island's most widely planted variety, a remnant of Bordeaux-influenced aspirations of decades past— the picture still isn't clear.

Even so, certain strong suits are starting to emerge. Cabernet franc shows particular promise, inviting comparisons to the similarly rainy, coastal Loire; as do the area's crisp, invigorating whites, offering one potential window into the region. (To that end, the chenin blanc from the North Fork's Paumanok Vineyards is one of the island's best, as is its cab franc.) Rather than view this identity crisis as a liability, however, Long Island's most promising talents welcome it as an opportunity to experiment.

That attitude definitely applied to the work being done by Regan and Carey Meador of the now-defunct Southold Farm + Cellar. Subsequently closed due to a land dispute with local officials, the winery was responsible for some of Long Island's most forward-thinking wines, produced from unusual grapes such as lagrein and teroldego. Their legacy lives on, however, via projects such as Erik Longabardi's Floral Terranes, a micro-producer that, in addition to making a lineup of ciders, is sourcing fruit from the old Southold vineyards (among other locations) for wines such as his "MX," a spicy blend of teroldego, lagrein, and syrah.

There's also Anthony Nappa, who first turned heads with his signature "White Pinot Noir," fermented off the skins and aged without oak. But as exciting as wines such as these may be, their scale of production is tiny. If Long Island ever hopes to break into the mainstream, it will require a boost from some bigger players.

If anyone is up to the task, it's Christopher Tracy. Over the years, his Channing Daughters Winery, located in the town of Bridgehampton, has emerged as a creative laboratory dedicated to uncovering the great unknown that is Long Island's terroir. Across a vast array of wines (made in multiple styles from twenty-two different grapes), Tracy produces everything from vineyard-designated tocai friulano and skin-contact pinot grigio to lagrein, dornfelder, seven different *pét-nats*, and more. Sure, some experiments might be more successful than others, but how else is a wine region supposed to evolve?

A similar spirit reigns at the North Fork's Macari Vineyards, which, for one of the island's biggest producers, has managed to rack up significant street cred as a leading proponent of organic and biodynamic farming. In addition to a range of Bordeaux blends, Macari dabbles in more experimental fare, such as its "Dos Aguas White," a delicately textured blend of six different grapes (grüner veltliner, viognier, sauvignon blanc, pinot gris, friulano, and gewürztraminer); it also makes a fine *pét-nat* and an elegant, floral pinot meunier.

Essential Producers: Macari Vineyards, Channing Daughters, Anthony Nappa Wines, Paumanok Vineyards, Floral Terranes

THE WINE LIST

- **Bellwether Wine Cellars Dry Riesling "A&D Vineyard" ($):** At the leading edge of Finger Lakes riesling, Bellwether's single-vineyard expressions came as a revelation when they first arrived on the market in 2013. This one, grown on the postglacial subsoils of Keuka Lake, is full of flinty minerality and lime zest.

- **Bloomer Creek "Tanzen Dame" Edelzwicker Blue Cap Trocken ($):** Inspired by Edelzwicker, the traditional Alsatian field blend, this curiosity from naturalist pioneers Kim Engle and Debra Bermingham consists of riesling, gewürztraminer, and cayuga white (a grape native to the region). From fifteen- to twenty-year-old vines, it's fully dry, crisp, and pear scented.

- **Keuka Lake Vineyards Cabernet Franc ($):** Mel Goldman's Keuka Lake Vineyards produces a brilliant range of rieslings from four different parcels, as well as a variety of other highly acclaimed wines. But its garnet-hued, peppery cabernet franc—sourced from the western slope of Seneca Lake—offers the clearest snapshot of the region's own unique stamp on the grape.

- **Channing Daughters "Ramato" ($):** Of all the experiments to have come out of Channing Daughters thus far, its "Ramato" bottling—named after the northeastern Italian tradition of skin-fermented pinot grigio—quickly established itself as one of the winery's benchmarks. With its onion-skin hue and light smack of tannins, it's a savory ode to Long Island's newfound spirit of innovation.

THE ANTIPODES

The first vines were planted in the Australian state of New South Wales at the tail-end of the eighteenth century, when the area was still a British penal colony. New Zealand's wine-making history dates back to the colonial period as well, but it wasn't until the 1990s and early 2000s that anyone started paying attention to either country in any meaningful way. In both cases, the wines that first brought them fame shared a common commercial ambition. (It's no coincidence that large Kiwi brands such as Kim Crawford and Cloudy Bay started invading store shelves around the same time that the American public was introduced to a certain ubiquitous Aussie label stamped with a cartoon kangaroo.) Today, however, as a natural wine insurgency ripples across Australia, and New Zealand mines its extreme southerly latitude to create exciting cool-climate riesling and pinot noir, these Antipodal neighbors have finally found their niche in the zeitgeist.

AUSTRALIA AND NEW ZEALAND

....

JUST THE HIGHLIGHTS

◆ **Both Australia and New Zealand rose to the top of wine's pop charts by inventing their own commercial styles.** For Australia, it was exaggerated, overripe shiraz (aka syrah), whereas New Zealand came to be known for its crowd-pleasing sauvignon blanc.

◆ **The era of overblown Australian shiraz is thankfully waning.** Over the past decade, the country's wine industry has undergone a sea change—not just toward more nuance and balance but also toward greater diversity of grapes, growing areas, and aesthetics.

◆ **The Aussie natural wine scene is booming.** The lo-fi movement has spread to all of Australia's wine regions, but its headquarters can be found in the Adelaide Hills area, ground zero for the country's avant-garde.

◆ **New Zealand is emerging as a Mecca for (extremely) cool-climate pinot noir.** While Kiwi sauvignon blanc remains the local bread and butter, the country's marginal climate has turned it into a promising place for chiseled, mineral pinot.

Although the wines that first put Australia and New Zealand on the map couldn't have been more different in profile or price point, both countries followed a similarly successful playbook for achieving late-1990s success. In short, that consisted of hijacking the global market with a signature hyperbolic style built around a friendly international grape.

In the case of Australia, this mandate manifested in a wave of excessively ripe, inky shiraz (the Aussie name for syrah) from hot, dry places such as Barossa and the McLaren Vale. Pushing oak and alcohol to outrageous extremes, the blockbuster wines of this era drew a defiant line in the sand between the Old World and the New. In New Zealand, the proto-type in question—the grassy, intensely pungent, tropical fruit–driven (think passion fruit, grapefruit, and lime) expression of sauvignon blanc synonymous with the Marlborough region—targeted a less highbrow segment of the market but proved just as unprecedented in its profile.

In both examples, the idea wasn't to impart a sense of place, or even to retain a sense of varietal typicity, but to cater to consumer demand. And for a time, the strategy worked all too well. But as our friends in the Antipodes soon came to discover, relying on a single commercial style is risky. It's fine to be known for just one thing, as long as that thing remains popular. But once it falls out of fashion or simply ceases to be relevant, what happens then?

Each in its own way, Australia and New Zealand are now grappling with the consequences of that question as a growing number of winemakers in both countries work to figure out what else they can offer a world that increasingly craves uniqueness and diversity rather than cookie-cutter sameness.

AUSTRALIA

With every boom comes a bust, and to appreciate fully Australia's cur-rent about-face, it's critical to understand the predicament in which it found itself after its decade-long "binger." By the early-2000s, sales were tanking and the country had become the butt of a running joke, dismissed in traditional circles as making the sort of shiraz you'd sooner run your car on than drink with your dinner.

Little did it matter that Australian wine always encompassed a more complex spectrum than wine snobs gave it credit for. But with over-blown Barossa shiraz casting such a long shadow, what hope could there be for things like such as, age-worthy Hunter Valley sémillon or nervy Clare Valley riesling?

Still, the existence of such wines always pointed to the possibility of a different vision for Australia. And slowly but surely, in the wake of the country's big turn-of-the-century crack-up, this other Australia—or the New Australia, as some have called it—is finally coming into focus. If its contours seem somewhat familiar, that's because the cultural self-reckoning currently reshaping Australia's wine scene parallels the evolution that's playing out right under our noses in California. Like its counterparts in the Golden State—a place with its own cautionary tale to tell about misguided ambitions—today Australia is shedding the excess baggage of its past in favor of nuance and subtlety.

This progress amounts to more than a sort of aesthetic damage control. As in California, the shift ultimately reflects an underlying change in values, driven by the same fundamental question: What would happen if, rather than conform to a preconceived stylistic template, Australia's producers tried to reframe conversation around Old World notions of place and terroir?

It's important to note that these rebels represent a small minority; no one's entertaining any illusions about dismantling the Yellow Tail empire. But the sweeping changes they symbolize are now evident across the country's growing regions, from the Margaret River area in Western Australia, where rising star Sam Vinciullo is defying expec-tations with his delicate, single-vineyard grenache bottlings, to the Victoria region, spread out along Australia's southern coast, where you'll find luminaries such as Jamsheed Wines and Mac Forbes in the Yarra Valley and Patrick Sullivan in nearby Gippsland, to the Hunter Valley region of New South Wales, where Harkham Wines is producing natural, minimally sulfured versions of sémillon (the area's signature grape) and shiraz, among others.

For our purposes, we'll take a closer look at Borosa and Adelaide Hills, the two major outposts of the New Australia. Located in the broader South Australia region, where the contemporary revival has gathered the greatest momentum, they're also the regions that have attracted the largest share of stateside attention and interest from importers (though that's quickly changing).

BAROSSA VALLEY

If the New California provides an analogue to the New Australia, then Barossa—the home of many of the country's most historic estates and the birthplace of Australian wine's "more is more" ethos—is the Down Under equivalent of Napa. But just as Napa has ceased to be a scapegoat for the sins of its past and has even engendered an "alt-Napa" paradigm, Barossa has given birth to a fringe of its own.

Rather than take ripeness and power as the measure of its worth, a small but meaningful sect of Barossa winemakers (and a smattering of peers in the nearby McLaren Vale) are rethinking all the usual notions about Barossa wine.

The bottles redefining the area today (such as naturalist Tom Shobbrook's chuggably fresh "Poolside" shiraz, arguably the New Australia's most direct shot across the stylistic bow) tick off a similar set of aesthetic boxes: lower alcohol (thanks to earlier picking), brighter fruit, and less manipulation in the cellar. But at the same time, their winemakers are reframing Barossa's identity around the area's greatest underutilized asset: a treasure trove of old, knobby shiraz and grenache vines, many of which were planted in the nineteenth and early twentieth centuries.

If the high-octane wines of the past sought to wow drinkers with in-your-face power and intensity, the newfound emphasis upon old-vine elegance and site specificity speaks to a maturing notion of what great wine should be and, more important, where Australia fits inside that definition. So while the current trend toward transparency is admirable in its own right, the impulse ultimately serves a higher purpose: to reclaim Australia in light of some of the Southern Hemisphere's most distinctive terroirs.

This seriousness of intent manifests in various ways. You can sense it in the quiet intensity of the Sami-Odi project's single-parcel syrahs (bottled as such as opposed to "shiraz"—a deliberate stylistic cue). It also comes across in the pinot noir–like delicacy of Carla and Richard Rza Betts's "Sucette" grenache, their tribute to the legendary wines of Châteauneuf-du-Pape's Château Rayas. Sourced from vineyards planted in the late 1800s, these are just two examples of the revolution that has come to Australia's most prestigious and commercially successful region.

Essential Producers: Sami-Odi, Tom Shobbrook Wines, Ruggabellus, An Approach to Relaxation, Brash Higgins

THE ADELAIDE HILLS (BASKET RANGE)

If we imagine the New Australia as several interconnected pockets of influence scattered across the country, the greatest constellation of countercultural energy is centered in one specific place. Virtually unknown a decade ago, the Adelaide Hills—in particular, the teensy town of Basket Range—has quickly established itself as the spiritual epicenter of the New Australia.

It was here, about an hour's drive outside the city of Adelaide, that a small sect of minimal interventionists—notably Jauma's James Erskine, Taras and Amber Ochota of Ochota Barrels, Gentle Folk's Gareth Belton, and Anton van Klopper of Lucy Margaux, among a handful of others—gave birth to the country's natural wine scene. Channeling the area's cooler climate into fresh, energetic wines that would feel right at home in the natural wine bars of Brooklyn and Paris (where they're now turning up in droves), this new cohort quickly gained international notoriety as the poster children of the New Australia.

To American drinkers who had come to look upon Australia with suspicion (and even disdain), the Adelaide Hills provided the earliest clue that something different was afoot Down Under. All of a sudden, wines such as Gentle Folk's aptly titled "Rainbow Juice"—a mind-bending blend of more than twenty different grapes, red and white alike, all fermented on the skins—started popping up on sommelier Instagram feeds alongside the usual natty fare from places such as the Loire Valley, California, Sicily, and others.

The teeming diversity now on display in Adelaide resists easy classification but generally borrows from the wider repertoire of styles associated with the natural wine movement. That includes everything from savory skin-fermented whites and hazy *pét-nats* to co-fermented field blends of odd and unusual grapes, tangy carbonic reds, and more. Skeptics might be tempted to write off such efforts as mere novelty or fad. But the spirit that has taken hold in the Adelaide Hills transcends "weird for the sake of weird." It's all part of a far more expansive story about Australian wine than anyone dared to imagine just a few years back.

Essential Producers: Jauma, Lucy Margaux, Gentle Folk, Commune of Buttons, Ochota Barrels, The Other Right, Domaine Lucci, Murdoch Hill, Borachio

NEW ZEALAND

Unlike the cautionary tale symbolized by the backlash against hedonistic Aussie shiraz, New Zealand's runaway success with sauvignon blanc hasn't relented a bit. Today, the United States is New Zealand's biggest export market—in 2018, we spent more than $456 million on Kiwi wine, a sum exceeded only by Italy and France—and household names such as Kim Crawford and Cloudy Bay have claimed a permanent place on supermarket shelves across the country.

It's not difficult to understand why. At a time when American audiences began to tire of flabby, oaky chardonnay, along came New Zealand with the perfect antidote. Fresh, screw capped, and unabashedly fruity, Marlborough sauvignon blanc tapped into just the right formula.

Now a default summertime staple, identified by its instantly recognizable style, the category has come to define sauvignon blanc for millions of drinkers. To some, however, that's precisely the problem. No matter how popular a style it might be, the country's signature expression is exactly that: a style ready-made for mass consumption. In the wake of its meteoric rise, the question facing New Zealand today is whether it will continue in the same commercial vein or search for a more meaningful version of itself to share with the world.

It's still early, but an increasing number of winemakers are considering the country not as a source of crisp, inexpensive sauvignon blanc, but as a vast repository of untapped cool-climate micro-regions. Home to the southernmost vineyards on the planet, the country's chilly, maritime climate naturally lends itself to the same sort of marginal winemaking—specifically, focused on pinot noir—practiced in places such as Oregon's Willamette Valley and California's far Sonoma Coast.

Much of that activity has centered around the region of Central Otago. Located at the base of the country's South Island, the area, long considered too cold for grape growing, has been reclaimed as one of the New World's most promising pinot strongholds (although it's making some lovely rieslings, too). The best—including those from Quartz Reef and Rippon, among others—combine the succulent yet transparent fruit associated with Oregon with a mineral twinge that, though not exactly Burgundian, lends a Burgundian sort of balance.

This explains what might have attracted a winemaker such as Ted Lemon to the foothills of Central Otago. One of California's great hunters of extreme terroir (via his acclaimed Littorai label), Lemon brings his signature elegance to the biodynamically farmed pinot he's making for Burn Cottage Vineyard, owned by Marquis and Dianne Sauvage. Sourced from three different vineyards, the project's "Cashburn" offers a solid representation of the central Otago style, all wet earth, raspberries, and Earl Grey spice.

While Central Otago remains the focal point for New Zealand pinot noir, it's not the only place where that finicky grape thrives. On the South Island's eastern coast, sandwiched between the Southern Alps and the Pacific, the areas of Canterbury and North Canterbury yield vivid, high-acid wines that exhibit a clawed-from-the-earth quality that is the hallmark of such peripheral climes.

Essential Producers: Quartz Reef, Rippon, Aurum, The Hermit Ram, Prophet's Rock, Arona, Kindeli

THE WINE LIST

◆ **Shobbrook Wines Barossa Valley "Poolside" Syrah ($$)**: Almost rosé-like (or Jura-like) in its ethereal transparency, Tom Shobbrook's "Poolside" is the kind of lively, chillable red designed for sipping, well, by the side of the pool. The anti-Barossa shiraz wears its stylistic independence as a badge of honor as one of the New Australia's defining reds.

◆ **Brash Higgins "GR/M" Blend ($$)**: The *GR* and *M* in question are biodynamically farmed grenache and mourvèdre (or mataro, according to the label) from sandy soils in the McLaren Vale. Under Brad Hickey's masterful hand, they're rendered in a heartbreakingly pretty, pinot-like style but with a spicy feral quality that is pure outback.

- **Lucy Margaux Adelaide Hills "Wildman Blanc" ($$):** Lucy Margaux's 100 percent sauvignon blanc from the town of Totness in the Adelaide Hills advertises its wild side, but it is, if anything, wildly delicious. Low in alcohol and practically dripping with tropical fruit, it's a natural wine with universal appeal.

- **Jauma "Like Raindrops" Grenache ($$):** James Erskine's Jauma wines were among the first emissaries of the New Australia to gain a stateside following. Natural-yeast fermented and bottled under a crown cap, his "Like Raindrops" introduced a whole new paradigm for Australian grenache, using carbonic maceration to transform the grape into a gulpable *vin de soif*.

- **The Hermit Ram "Whole Bunch" Pinot Noir ($):** Based in the windswept, coastal area of North Canterbury, rising star Theo Coles is quietly making some of New Zealand's rawest, purest, and most thoughtful natural wines. The savory depth and freshness on display here—the result of "whole cluster," or, as he calls it, "whole bunch," fermentation (see page 8)—combines with a bracing limestone chalkiness.

SOUTH AFRICA

Of all the wine-producing nations of the Southern Hemisphere, South Africa has probably struggled the hardest to find a narrative that resonates with US drinkers. Part of the reason is political. It wasn't until the 1990s, when international boycotts against the country's apartheid system came to an end, opening export markets for the first time in decades, that South African wines became available to US drinkers in any meaningful sense.

For most of the country's grim twentieth-century history, the majority of its grapes were grown for bulk wine or cheap brandy production. But following a rapid flood of investment and technical innovation, South Africa's quality renaissance soon kicked into full gear, predominantly focused in the more established areas of Stellenbosch and Franschhoek.

But for whatever reason, the country's big breakout moment never quite materialized. It's not that it lacked its share of admirers. For a moment, a modest buzz even developed around its signature chenin blanc (or "steen," as it's called locally). But even as places such as Argentina, Australia, and New Zealand ascended to the heights of international fashion, South Africa struggled to stand out in the crowd. That doesn't mean, however, that its wine industry simply stood still. In fact, after that first wave of international ambitions, the country's wine culture only continued to evolve.

The first signs of change appeared during the early-2000s in the lesser-known Swartland region, north of Capetown, where pioneers such as Eben Sadie of Sadie Family Wines, Chris and Andrea Mullineux of Mullineux & Leeu, and cousins Hein and Adi Badenhorst of A. A. Badenhorst Family Wines began making wines that, like so many of their New World counterparts, tell a deeper story in light of the past: namely, a focus on abandoned old vines, a bounty of lesser-known grapes, and a stripped-down aesthetic designed to allow these raw materials to shine through.

These South African originals have inspired a similar influx of fresh talent. It's still early to make future predictions, but as the contours of this movement come into view, a couple of highlights have emerged.

For one, it's clear that the early attempts to drum up interest in South African chenin blanc had something to them—and now that industry interest in the grape has hit an all-time high, the timing is right for a comeback. If chenin's stylistic identity in South Africa once seemed nebulous, the current crop reveals a far more refined understanding of what the category wants to be: an amazing concentration of fresh fruit flavors without heaviness or high alcohol. For an emblematic example, look for Thistle & Weed's "Duwweltjie" bottling, from a single parcel of vines planted in 1956.

On the red front, cinsault is emerging as South Africa's most exciting grape. Although it has a long history in the country, many of the earliest plantings were uprooted to make way for more varieties such as cabernet and syrah. Inspired by the same frenzy for old vines that has animated places such as California and Australia, South Africa's winemakers are eagerly seeking out the bygone patches that remain,

channeling them into high-toned, berryish wines, such as The Blacksmith's "Barebones" cinsault, fermented using partial carbonic maceration, or Mother Rock's juicy but mineral "Force Celeste," hand harvested from thirty-year-old vines and bottled without fining, filtration, or the slightest hint of oak.

Essential Producers: Storm Point, JH Meyer, Radley & Finch, Mother Rock, The Three Foxes, Silwervis, Beaumont Family Wines, Sadie Family Wines, The Blacksmith, A. A. Badenhorst Family Wines, Lammershoek, Mullineux & Leeu Family Wines

SOUTH AMERICA

At a time when change is the only wine world constant, South America has often seemed like the rare exception. Whatever exciting developments might have been taking hold in other parts of the globe, Chile and Argentina mostly coasted through the past couple decades upholding a predictable status quo. Following the usual late-twentieth-century logic, this boiled down to big corporate brands focusing on commercial versions of familiar French grapes in a bid for world domination. Today, however, as in other exciting New World hotspots, it's the independent and, more often than not, naturally inclined producers who are upending the dominant power structure. While that story is unfolding differently (and with unequal degrees of intensity) in both countries, the progress on display speaks to the desire of younger, progressive winemakers to express something uniquely and innately their own.

CHILE AND ARGENTINA

···························

JUST THE HIGHLIGHTS

◆ **There are reasons to drink South American wine beyond its reputation for inexpensive dependability.** Both Chile and Argentina—but especially Chile, which has lately emerged as the continent's hotbed of innovation—are finally breaking out of the cookie-cutter paradigm that has pigeonholed South America for decades.

◆ **For the first time, the world is discovering what's truly "Chilean" about Chilean wine.** Centered around the revival of *pipeño*—the country's traditional farmer's wine, sourced from centuries-old plantings of the humble país grape—Chile's natural wine explosion has repurposed this time-honored local expression for a global audience.

◆ **There's life to Argentinean wine beyond generic malbec.** The "it" wine of the late 1990s still dominates sales, but a counter-cultural streak has nevertheless managed to emerge, as producers (many belonging to the minimal-interventionist set) branch out via old-vines bonarda (the country's "other" red grape) and salty, skin-fermented torrontés (Argentina's signature white).

For a sense of the trajectory that has defined South American wine through much of its modern history, just consider the continent's greatest mainstream hit: Argentinean malbec. Despite its checkered history in France (historically one of Bordeaux's minor blending grapes, malbec gets little play as a varietal wine beyond its obscure home region of Cahors), it found new life in Argentina's Mendoza region, quickly taking the 1990s by storm. (You can think of it as the red wine equivalent of New Zealand sauvignon blanc; see page 322.)

Despite some promising glimmers of hope, malbec's meteoric rise hasn't exactly ushered in a more progressive era for Argentinean wine. Mass-market incarnations of the grape continue to hold sway, conforming to a predictable mold: the cheap versions soft and jammy, the pricier ones essentially the same, just fuller, heavier, and polished with oak.

Chile, by contrast, never took off in quite the same way. Over the years, it has entertained a handful of different possibilities, including flirtations with pinot noir from cooler areas toward the north of the country (like Casablanca and Leyda), crisp, inexpensive sauvignon blanc (meant to rival New Zealand's), and some perfectly respectable (if not all that compelling) cabernet from the Maipo Valley, near Santiago. There was even a brief moment when it seemed that the inky, herbaceous carménère grape, another reject from southwest France, might come to the rescue as Chile's answer to Argentinean malbec.

Of course, that never happened. But in the meantime, even as Chile's large corporate producers persist in their quest for market share, the nation has slowly but surely given birth to a thriving counterrevolution. Centered in the southern regions of Maule, Bío-Bío, and Itata, this insurgency has upended the accepted narrative about South American wine. In the process, Chile has achieved a newfound relevance of the sort that Argentina has only begun to strive for, anointed as the latest (and most unexpected) natural wine hotspot.

CHILE

The story of how that took place originates in the sixteenth century, when the Spanish conquistadores and a subsequent wave of missionaries first brought viticulture to Chile in the form of an unassuming grape called país (known as *mission* in California and as *listán prieto* in the Canary Islands).

Although largely dismissed during the shift to French varieties and reserved for jug wine production, país historically lent itself to *pipeño*, the traditional wine of Chile's *campesino* (farm laborers). Aged in wooden casks called *pipas* and meant for local production, these pale, rustic reds survived as a cottage industry of sorts in the rural villages of Chile's southern growing areas.

Ironically, it was a Frenchman who first recognized the potential for *pipeño* to be recognized beyond the Chilean countryside. What initially lured Burgundy native Louis-Antoine Luyt to Chile's Maule Valley was the area's bounty of centuries-old vines. Many of Chile's original plantings were uprooted under Pinochet's dictatorship to plant trees for paper production, but the south mustered the staunchest resistance to these reforms and boasts the greatest concentration of old-vine material today.

Having worked five harvests with Marcel Lapierre (see page 66), the late Beaujolais legend, Luyt applied the same naturalist approach to his work in the Maule Valley, where the local production methods—nonchemical farming, preindustrial winemaking practices—mirrored his own minimalist philosophy by default.

In 2007, Luyt released his first país-based wine, "El País de Quenehuao," sourced from grapes purchased from the area's small growers. Rendered in a juicy, gulpable style using carbonic maceration (in the manner of Beaujolais), it became an instant darling of the natural community, officially bringing Chile into the movement's fold. Since relocating to France in 2018, Luyt has focused his efforts upon releasing a series of *pipeño* bottlings made by the independent farmers with whom he collaborated for over a decade.

Today, Chile's *pipeño* revival is in full swing, tapping into the current fashion for minimally processed, low-alcohol reds. In addition to Luyt, the movement's main architects include like-minded producers such as Bío Bío's Roberto Henríquez, a Chilean native who spent time in France working with Anjou's René Mosse, and Itata's Pedro Parra, a consultant to wineries across the globe who now makes a range of nervy, vibrant wines under his own label.

Chile's natural wine scene isn't limited to país and *pipeño*, though. Another central focus is carignan, the country's other old-vine treasure (look for the Viña Maitia project's "Weon," courtesy of French expat David Marcel), plus bright, aromatic cinsault, both of which can appear in *pipeño* blends but increasingly stand on their own. There's also a smidgen of salty, floral white wine to be found, made from grapes such as muscat and sémillon and occasionally macerated on their skins in traditional clay vessels called *tinajas*.

The movement's heartbeat, however, continues to be *pipeño*. Beyond generating a new-found interest in Chile, the renaissance the category is enjoying represents an act of cultural preservation that is all the more meaningful in light of the country's past.

If Chile's previous efforts with grapes such as pinot noir and sauvignon blanc never seemed to stick, that's because they failed to carve out an identity of their own—something distinctly Chilean, as opposed to being seen as affordable alternatives to whatever else. But with its hundreds of years of history, the *pipeño* tradition signals something the world hasn't seen until now: the rare example of an indigenous South American wine.

Essential Producers: Louis-Antoine Luyt, Roberto Henríquez, Pedro Parra y Familia, Clos des Fous, Viña Maitia, Cacique Maravilla, Rogue Vine, A Los Viñateros Bravos

ARGENTINA

Although "big malbec" maintains its monopoly over Argentina's wine industry, stacking the odds against an alternative narrative such as Chile's, it doesn't mean the country has nothing to offer drinkers of a more curious bent, or that malbec is inherently devoid of interest.

When sustainably grown and crafted on a smaller scale—critically, with a minimum of oak—the grape can yield vibrant, brambly, dark-fruited values such as Jimena Lopez's Bodini Malbec, harvested by hand from vineyards in the Luján de Cuyo subregion of Mendoza, or RJ Viñedos estate's "MDZ," an unoaked expression designed for easy drinking.

We're also starting to see at least a few tiny cracks in the otherwise impregnable armor of malbec. Although it is definitely premature to start speculating about the rise of a New Argentina, one of the most encouraging developments is the mini-renaissance taking place around bonarda (sometimes spelled bornarda), a grape that, until the modern malbec boom colonized the country, claimed the title of Argentina's most widely planted variety. (If you're wondering, no, it's not the same as the bonarda found in northern Italy, but rather Savoie's douce noir, also known as charbono in California.) A traditional workhorse grape historically used in cheap blends, it's now being rediscovered for its ability to produce precisely the sort of fruity, light-bodied reds that have currency with drinkers today. In addition to standard bearers such as the Altos Las Hormigas project's "Colonia Las Liebres," which high-lights the grape's herbal, strawberry side, seek out the "Tinto" bottling from the Cara Sur collaborative, one of Argentina's most promising new producers.

The country contains other pockets of intrigue as well. Notably, in the region of Patagonia, the acclaimed Bodega Chacra winery is mak-ing high-altitude, cool-climate pinot noir and, in collaboration with Meursault's legendary Jean-Marc Roulot, a couple of steely chardonnays.

And repping the naturalist fringe, winemaker Matías Michelini is responsible for some of Argentina's noteworthiest wines under his aptly named Vía Revolucionaria brand, including a skin-contact wine from old-vine torrontés and his punchy, carbonic "Bonarda Pura," both fermented with natural yeasts and bottled unsulfured.

Essential Producers: Bodega Chacra, Bodini, Cara Sur, Vía Revolucionaria, Altos Las Hormigas, Familia Cecchin, RJ Viñedos

THE WINE LIST

- **A Los Viñateros Bravos "Granítico" Itata Blanco ($):** This is what you get when you take Leonardo Erazo's hands-off approach to winemaking, add muscatel's flowery aromatics and sémillon's savory depth, and then multiply to the power of Itata's centuries-old vines. Something like a white wine counterpoint to *pipeño*, it's fresh, raw, and one of the continent's most compelling whites.

- **Louis-Antoine Luyt Pipeño "Portezuelo" ($):** True to the category's original spirit as a thirst-quenching farmer's wine, Luyt bottles all of his *pipeños* in a chug-friendly liter-size format. With its mouth-watering acidity and flavors of hibiscus and wild strawberry, his "Portezuelo" (from 250-year-old vines!) recasts time-honored tradition in a new postmodern package.

- **Pedro Parra y Familia Cinsault "Imaginador" ($):** Technically labeled as cinsault, the wine's predominant grape, Parra's "Imaginador" is, in reality, a wild field blend of varieties (including muscat, país sémillon, and carignan), all harvested and fermented together. Savory, with an edge of smoky minerality, it's full of vivacious red fruit and bright acids (the product of Itata's granitic soils).

- **Vía Revolucionaria "Torrontés Brutal" ($):** The white torrontés grape usually lends itself to fruity, aromatic (in other words, perfectly inoffensive) wines that you drink as a slightly more interesting alternative to South American sauvignon blanc. This isn't that kind of torrontés. Winemaker Matías Michelini subjects his grapes to extended fermentation on the skins, resulting in a cloudy, copper-hued "orange wine" with flavors of dried apricot and sage.

◆ **Cara Sur Bonarda "Tinto" Valle de Calingasta ($):** Harvested from a single organically farmed vineyard planted in 1950, Cara Sur's "Calingasta" shows just how complex and satisfying bonarda can be when farmed for low yields and produced with respect for place. Juicy and brambly, with a savory edge, this is naturally fermented for eight months in concrete eggs to preserve its rose-petal freshness and pristine cherry fruit.

APPENDIX I: ESSENTIAL WINE SHOPS

Arlequin Wine Merchant, San Francisco, CA

Bacchanal Wine, New Orleans, LA

Chambers Street Wines, New York, NY

Crush Wine & Spirits, New York, NY

Diversey Wine, Chicago, IL

Division Wines, Portland, OR

Domaine LA, Los Angeles, CA

Domestique, Washington, DC

Flatiron Wine & Spirits, San Francisco, CA, and New York, NY

Henry & Son, Minneapolis, MN

Kermit Lynch Wine Merchant, Berkeley, CA

K & L Wine Merchant, Redwood City, San Francisco, and Hollywood, CA

Leon and Son, Brooklyn, NY, and Grand Rapids, MI

Lou Wine Shop, Los Angeles, CA

Ordinaire Wine Shop & Wine Bar, Oakland, CA

Perman Wine Selections, Chicago, IL

The Austin Wine Merchant, Austin, TX

The Wine Bottega, Boston, MA

The Wine House, Los Angeles, CA

Tiny's Bottle Shop, Philadelphia, PA

Vine Wine, Brooklyn, NY

APPENDIX II: ESSENTIAL READING

Bonné, Jon. *The New California Wine*, Ten Speed Press, 2013.

Feiring, Alice. *Natural Wine for the People*, Ten Speed Press, 2019.

Feiring, Alice and Pascaline Lepeltier. *The Dirty Guide to Wine*, Countryman Press, 2017.

Goode, Jamie and Sam Harrop. *Authentic Wine*, University of California Press, 2013.

Johnson, Hugh and Jancis Robinson. *The World Atlas of Wine*, Mitchell Beasley, 2019.

Lynch, Kermit. *Adventures on the Wine Route*, Farrar, Straus and Giroux, 1988.

MacNeil, Karen. *The Wine Bible*, Workman Publishing Company, 2015.

Nossiter, Jonathan. *Liquid Memory*, Farrar, Straus and Giroux, 2010.

Parr, Rajat and Jordan Mackay. *The Sommelier's Atlas of Taste*, Ten Speed Press, 2018.

Robinson, Jancis and Julia Harding. *Oxford Companion to Wine*, Oxford University Press, 1994.

Robinson, Jancis, Julia Harding, and José Vouillamoz. *Wine Grapes*, Penguin Group, 2012.

Rosenthal, Neal. *Reflections of a Wine Merchant*, Farrar, Straus and Giroux, 2008.

APPENDIX III: ESSENTIAL IMPORTERS

Becky Wasserman Selections

Blue Danube Wine

Brazos Wine Imports

Camille Riviere Selections

Circo Vino

COEUR Wine Company

David Bowler

De Maison Selections

Domaine Select

Grand Cru Selections

Jenny & Francois Selections

Jose Pastor Selections

Kermit Lynch Wine Merchant

Louis/Dressner Selections

Martine's Wines

M.F.W. Wine Co.

Polaner Selections

Rare Wine Co.

Rosenthal Wine Merchant

Schatzi Wines

Selection Massale

Skurnik Wines

T. Edward Wines and Spirits

Vias Imports

Vine Street Imports

Vom Boden

Weygandt-Metzler Importing

Zev Rovine Selections

ACKNOWLEDGMENTS

First and foremost, thank you to the team at Ten Speed Press. Thank you to my brilliant editors, Julie Bennett and Ashley Pierce, for bringing this book to life and for all your patience and insight along the way. Thanks also to Annie Marino, Jane Chinn, and Chloe Aryeh for your invaluable work behind the scenes.

To Talia Baiocchi, my editor at PUNCH and biggest professional advocate, who gave me my first wine writing gig more than a decade ago and ushered this manuscript through each stage of its existence. This book is as much your vision as it is mine.

To my dear friends and favorite drinking partners, Jane Shlimovich and Jonathan Lipsmeyer, for all the emptied bottles and late-night dinner conversations. You've been with me on this journey from the start.

To Carmen Arteche and Antoine Schelling for never flinching when your daughter informed you she was planning to marry a wine writer, and for sponsoring my summer residency in your backyard in Geneva. I promise I'll cover more Swiss wine in the next one.

To Mark Friedman, the original wine hipster and bon vivant, for teaching me the true meaning of value and instilling a passion that turned into this. For all your guidance, both oenophilic and otherwise, I owe you more than you'll ever know.

To my parents, Rich and Jackie, for your unconditional love and support, and for always believing in me and my writing. This book is dedicated to you.

Finally, and above all, to my wife, Adèle. You, more than anyone, helped make this possible. Thank you for being my partner, my ally, and my best friend. There's no one on Earth with whom I'd rather share a bottle of wine.

INDEX

················

A

acidity, 18
Adelaide Hills, 320–21
aging, 20–21
aglianico, 172, 173–74
albariño, 188, 189–90
alcohol, 18
Alsace, 101–7
altesse, 96, 98, 99
Alto Piemonte, 131
Amarone della Valpolicella, 139,
    141–42
amontillado, 214, 216
ancestral method, 12–13
appassimento, 15, 139, 141–42, 156
Argentina, 276, 329–31, 334–36
assyrtiko, 268, 269, 270
Aube, 61
Australia, 276, 315–21, 323–24
Austria, 247–55
Auxey-Duresses, 46–47
Avellino, 175–76

B

baga, 228–29
Bairrada, 228–29
balance, 16–18
Barbaresco, 120, 121–27, 130
barbera, 128, 130
Barolo, 120, 121–27, 130
Barossa Valley, 319–20
Basilicata, 172–77
Basket Range, 320–21

Basque Country, 195–97
Beaujolais, 64–71
blaufränkisch, 250, 251–52
bonarda, 334
Bordeaux, 50–55
botrytis, 14
Bourgogne Passetoutgrains, 49
Bourgogne Rouge, 48, 49
Brunello di Montalcino, 132, 136–
    37, 138
brut nature Champagne, 61–62
bual, 234
Burgenland, 251–52, 254
Burgundy, 40–49, 300, 301

C

cabernet franc, 84, 85–87, 308, 311
cabernet sauvignon, 50, 276, 280,
    281–82
California, 276, 277, 279, 280–99
Campania, 172–77
Canary Islands, 206–8
carbonic maceration, 9, 32–33, 71
carménère, 276
Catalonia, 198–204
Cava, 198, 199–202, 204
Chablis, 43–44, 47
Champagne, 56–63
chardonnay, 40, 46
Charmat method, 12
chenin blanc, 84–85, 276, 325, 327
Chianti, 132, 134–35, 138
Chile, 276, 329–33, 335–36

Published in the United States by Ten Speed Press, an imprint of
Random House, a division of Penguin Random House LLC, New York.
www.tenspeed.com

Ten Speed Press and the Ten Speed Press colophon are registered
trademarks of Penguin Random House LLC.

Library of Congress Cataloging-in-Publication Data
Names: Sussman, Zachary, 1983- author.
Title: The essential wine book : a modern guide to the changing world of
    wine / Zachary Sussman.
Description: First edition. | California : Ten Speed Press, [2020] | Includes
    index.
Identifiers: LCCN 2020011709 (print) | LCCN 2020011710 (ebook) | ISBN
    9781984856777 (hardcover) | ISBN 9781984856784 (ebook)
Subjects: LCSH: Wine tasting. | Wine and wine making.
Classification: LCC TP548.5.A5 S87 2020 (print) | LCC TP548.5.A5 (ebook)|
    DDC 641.2/2--dc23
LC record available at https://lccn.loc.gov/2020011709
LC ebook record available at https://lccn.loc.gov/2020011710

Hardcover ISBN: 978-1-9848-5677-7
eBook ISBN: 978-1-9848-5678-4

Printed in China

Design by Annie Marino

10 9 8 7 6 5 4 3 2

First Edition